W9-DAN-055

STUDIES IN MEDIEVAL JEWISH PHILOSOPHY

BY THE SAME AUTHOR

Ancient Jewish Philosophy (Wayne State University Press, 1964)

Maimonides' Treatise on Logic (American Academy for Jewish Research, 1938)

Philosophical Terms in the Moreh Nebukim (Columbia University Press, 1924; AMS Press, 1966; Dvir, 1969)

The Problem of Space in Jewish Medieval Philosophy (Columbia University Press, 1917; AMS Press, 1966)

ISRAEL EFROS

Studies in MEDIEVAL JEWISH PHILOSOPHY

Columbia University Press
New York and London 1974

Publication of this work has been made possible by generous gifts from Jacob and Hilda Blaustein and from the American Academy for Jewish Research.

LIBRARY OF CONGRESS CATALOGING IN PUBLICATION DATA

Efros, Israel Isaac, 1890–
Studies in medieval Jewish philosophy.

Substantially the same material as originally published in the author's ha-Filosofyah ha-yehudit bi-yeme ha-benayim.
Includes bibliographies.
CONTENTS: The philosophy of Saadia gaon. — Three essays.
1. Philosophy, Jewish. 2. Philosophy, Medieval. 3. Saadiah ben Joseph, gaon, 892?–942. al-Amānāt wa-al-iʿtiqādāt. 4. Judah, ha-Levi, 12th cent. Kitāb al-Hujjah. 5. Moses ben Maimon, 1135–1204. Dalālat al-ha'irīn. 6. Abraham bar Hiyya, ha-Nasi, 12th cent.
I. Title.
B755.E33 181'.3 73–12512
ISBN 0–231–03194–7

Printed in the United States of America

TO MY DEAR MILDRED

PREFACE

THIS WORK comprises two different fields: ideas and terms, and therefore supplements my previous two books, both published by the Columbia University Press: *The Problem of Space in Jewish Medieval Philosophy* (1917) and *Philosophical Terms in the Moreh Nebukim* (1924).

The first part presents the philosophy of Saadia Gaon, who, though standing at the very threshold of medieval thought, dealt in a lively polemic fashion with all its major problems inherited from a syncretism of Platonic, Aristotelian, and Neoplatonic speculation, and with tendencies toward Arabic and Christian theology. It views therefore the whole of medieval thought through the spectrum of one man, while my *Problem of Space in Jewish Medieval Philosophy* pierces it with one problem: space and infinity. The other view was vertical; this is horizontal.

The third essay of the second part belongs to the philosophy of ideas, but all the rest of this work is devoted to terminology, like my *Philosophical Terms in the Moreh Nebukim.* It was the Tibbon-family out of which came the Hebrew translation of the *Moreh Nebukim* (Maimonides' *Guide of the Perplexed*), that elaborated a vocabulary, endowing the Hebrew tongue with that plastic power to express abstract notions without which its revival would have been difficult. But that family did not work *ex nihilo.* A half century before it, Abraham bar Ḥiyya, the Prince (1065–1136), who held a high position at a Moslem court, worked out a philosophical and, particularly, a comprehensive mathematical terminology which is the substance of the latter part. But here, too, the interest is not only philological, for it includes conceptual analysis and confrontations of attitudes.

My heartiest thanks are due to Professor Salo Baron and Professor Shalom Spiegel for their encouraging interest in this work. I am also grateful to the American Academy for Jewish Research, which, under the presidency of Professor Saul Lieberman, made this publication possible, and also to Jacob and Hilda Blaustein for their kindness.

ISRAEL EFROS

CONTENTS

Part I

THE PHILOSOPHY OF SAADIA GAON

Chapter One

THE GENERAL INTELLECTUAL UNREST

DURING the lifetime of Saadia Gaon (882–942), *gaon* (or chief) of the Babylonian academy at Sura and influential pioneer in medieval Jewish thinking, the Arab controversies between rationalism and orthodoxy reached a climax when in 912 al-Ashʿari mounted the pulpit of the mosque in al-Basra and publicly repented being a liberal or a Muʿtazilite, calling upon the faithful to realign their forces around the Sunnite banner of anthropomorphism, determinism, and the pre-existence of the Koran. We feel the reverberations of these battles in Saadia's philosophical book, *Emunot we-Deʿot* (Beliefs and Convictions), which is the theme of our following discussion. But Saadia's ways were not those of al-Ashʿari, for Jewish orthodoxy as taught by the Geonim in Sura and Pumbedita coincided to a great extent with Arab liberalism.[1]

That Saadia, an eager polemicist, was not fighting abstract external doctrines but rather those current around and in the Jewish fold, one can infer from his general career, filled with combat against threats to Judaism, and from many explicit passages in his book where he mentions opposing doctrines with which he had personal contact, referring even to those members of his own city who advocated such doctrines.[2]

[1] Jacob Guttmann in his *Die Religionsphilosophie des Saadia* (1882) p. 31, says that Saadia's views follow mainly those of al-Jubbai, the Muʿtazilite. Concerning the influence of the Muʿtazilah on the last Geonim and their period, see M. Schreiner in *Monatsschrift,* XXX 5, pp. 314–19, I. Goldziher in *Revue des Études Juives,* XLVII, p. 179, and I. Efros, "R. Hai Gaon," in *Hashiloah,* XXX, pp. 431–38. For a study of the life of Saadia, see the standard work on this subject by Henry Malter, *Life and Works of Saadia Gaon* (Philadelphia, 1921) and the bibliographical supplement by Isaac Werfel in *Rav Saadya Gaon* (Heb.), ed. J. L. Fishman (Jerusalem, 1943), pp. 644–57.

[2] References to Saadia's *Emunot we-Deʿot* are made to part and page, or part, chapter, and page, in the Yosefov edition. The English quotations mainly follow Samuel Rosenblatt's translation, entitled *The Book of Beliefs and Opinions* (Yale

Let us mention several such references: "It is said about the ignorant in our own town that they believe..." (introd., 6, 48). "Just as some monotheists refuse to admit that God is unable to bring back yesterday..." (introd., 5, 47). "It has come to my attention that one of the heretics in a dispute with a monotheist argued against this proof, saying that it is possible to traverse an infinite number of parts by walking..." (I, 1, 59). "It has come to my attention that some of our own people thought the passage of Pr. 8, 22 referred to these incorporeals..." (I, 3, 65). "And someone I know of our own people who maintained the eternity of some elements..." (I, 3, sixth theory). "I have seen that some of our people bring proof to refute the theory of the abrogation of the Torah from general considerations..." (III, 7, 115). "I must say that I have found certain people who call themselves Jews professing the doctrine of metempsychosis..." (VI, 8, 160). And let us note particularly the programmatic statement in introd., 2, 38:

When I considered these evils, both in their own nature and in their particular manifestations, my heart was grieved for my race, the race of mankind, and my soul was moved on account of our own people Israel, as I saw in my time many of the believers clinging to unsound doctrines and mistaken beliefs, while many of those who deny the faith boast of their unbelief and despise the men of truth, although they are themselves in error.

From these references and also from his *Refutations of Hayawaihi of Balkh*,[3] we see that heresy of skepticism invaded Judaism because of

University Press, 1948). See my "Saadia's Book of Beliefs and Opinions in English" in *The Jewish Quarterly Review*, XL, pp. 413–16. Sometimes I quoted from Alexander Altmann's English abrigment entitled *Saadya Gaon, The Book of Doctrines and Beliefs* (Oxford, 1946). The Hebrew book is occasionally cited and is designated by the abbreviation *Em.* or *Emunot*. The Arabic original *Kitāb al-Amānāt wa'l-I'tiqādāt*, ed. S. Landauer (Leiden, 1880) is designated by the abbreviation *Am.* or *Amānāt*. The citation in the text from *Emunot*, VI, 8, 160: "people who call themselves Jews" refers to the sect. יודגנים or יודענים for which see David Kaufmann, *Attributenlehre* (Gotha, 1877), 84, note 144, and Jacob Guttmann, *Die Religionsphilosophie des Saadia*, 214, note 1. Concerning the spread of Greek thought among Jews, also, see Guttman, p. 19.

[3] For a discussion of Hayawaihi ha-Balkhi, see Malter, *The Life and Works of Saadia Gaon*, pp. 384–87. Hayawaiki leaned toward Zoroastrian dualism, believing that moral evil came from birth and that all creation was stained. See Israel Davidson, *Saadia's Polemic against Hiwi al-Balkhi* (New York, 1915) (Vol. V of "Texts and Studies of the Jewish Theological Seminary of America"). For Saadia's criticism of

people's inability to accept biblical anthropomorphism or to find traces of a moral administration of the universe.[4] There were some who studied the concept of the origin of the world and arrived at the conclusion that there was never a beginning or that there was a primordial matter, while others arrived at a dualism or at some other non-Jewish cosmogonic faith.[5] And there were some who discussed the question of whether God could abrogate His law — and they had Christianity in mind[6] — or who, because of their confidence in reason, saw no need for revelation and prophecy.[7] And there were also some who, despairing of an objective criterion in morals, took a hedonistic stand and identified the good with the sweet and pleasant,[8] or who were in quest of a rational support for eschatological beliefs and found none.[9]

On the other hand, in Judaism as in Islam, some looked upon this expansion of reason with fear and trepidation, seeing in speculation a corridor to heresy,[10] and some took the anthropomorphic passages literally and accepted the divine attributes.[11] True, Saadia did not identify anthropomorphism, as Maimonides did, with sheer heresy,[12] but he saw the danger that the intelligent might abandon anthropomorphism and faith together.

Thus Saadia did not write his book[13] as a philosophical spectator but as a man in direct touch with extreme views that were wrestling with one another for dominance. And although his fight was directed against both sides, against those who thought they were rationalists and those who discarded any rational criterion, his weapon was still reason, and its ways of operation interested him greatly. Hence, as early as the introduction, he criticized sharply all who questioned or abused this tool — the sophists who had no objective truth, the skeptics who doubted all,

---

dualism, see *Emunot*, I, 50; I, 3, 67–68; II, 2, 88; VI, 1, 149; VII, 1, 163. See now also Moses Zucker, על תרגום רס״ב לתורה, particularly the section of the first chapter dealing with the spread of heresy, pp. 12–142.

4 Introd. 4, 43; 7, 53. 5 I, 3, the sixth cosmogonic theory.

6 III, 7–8; VIII, 9, 185. 7 III, 3, 109.

8 III, 2, 107. See also introd. 5, 47.

9 VII, 1, 162–63; VII, 6, 170. 10 Introd., 6, 48.

11 II, 8, 95. See also III, 10, 121.

12 *Mishneh Torah*, I, 5, chs. 3, 7; *Moreh Nebukim*, I, 36.

13 Saadia wrote his *Emunot we-De*ʿ*ot* in the year 933. See I, 4, 81: כי אין לעולם כי אם ד׳ אלפים ושש מאות ותשעים ושלש שנה. See also VII, 8, 172: שמעת שיצאה אומתינו לבני העולם אלפים ומאתים שנה.

and the "ignorant" who denied even perception. We shall follow Saadia and examine this tool before approaching the other philosophical problems. We shall discuss the sources of the mind, their relative validity, and the ways of reason, and thus arrive at an understanding of the two terms in the title of Saadia's book, the *Emunot* and the *Deʿot*, which also indicate the book's purpose.

Chapter Two

SAADIA'S THEORY OF KNOWLEDGE

THE PROBLEM of knowledge occupies a prominent place in Saadia's work. It is woven into the discussion of his *Emunot we-Deʿot*, the introduction of which is devoted to a systematic presentation of this subject. There are also many important epistemological statements in his commentaries on the Bible and the *Sefer Yeṣirah*. He did not accept the idea maintained by his Arab contemporary, al-Farabi, that there is a spheral spirit called the Active Intellect, who moves our sense-experience to conceptual knowledge; so that, according to al-Farabi, the mind had to be its own agent in the process of percepts becoming concepts. How is this agency to be conceived? What is the role of experience in the process of thought, and what, if any, is originally mental? What, furthermore, is the role of the mind with reference to faith or, as he calls it, tradition? These questions we shall seek to answer in this chapter.

There are, according to Saadia, three sources of knowledge: sensation, *nous* (intuitions), and necessity (necessary inference). "And we, the congregation of monotheists, believe in these three sources and add a fourth which we have derived from the other sources, namely reliable tradition."[1]

[1] *Emunot we-Deʿot* (Warsaw, 1913), introd., 43–44: שלשה משכים הראשון ידיעת הנראה והשני מדע השכל והשלישי ידיעת מה שההכרח מביא אליו... אבל אנחנו קהל המיח־דים מאמינים באלה השלשה משכים אשר למדעים ונחבר אליהם משך רביעי הוצאנו אותו בשלש ראיות ושב לנו שרש והוא ההגדה הנאמנת כי היא בנויה על מדע החוש ומדע השכל ומה שחייבו. In the Arabic original, *Al-Amânât wa'l-Iʿtiqâdât*, ed. S. Landauer (Leyden, 1880), 12, the four מואד are called: עלם אלשאהד, עלם אלעקל, עלם מא דפעת אלצ̇רור אליה אלעלם אלצחיח יכון עלי ,49 :In *Tafsīr Iyob* .(עלם אלצ̇רוריאת also) אלצאדק אלכ̇בר צ̇רבין אמא במשאהדה̈... ואמא בכ̇בר צאדק, where sensation includes intuition and inference, which, according to the author, are based on it. In *Em.*, II, 96: שכל כתוב ומקובל. In *Em.*, IX, 185, 189: מושכל כתוב ומקובל. In *Em.*, VII, 171: כתוב שכל קבלה. In *Em.*, IV, 128: מוחש שכל כתוב וקבלה. In *Em.*, VII, 163: מוצא הטבע והשכל והכתוב והקבלה where nature stands for perception and tradition is divided into Scriptures and oral tradition, even as the Mutakallimūn designated both the Koran and tradition by خبر (see Schmoelders, *Essai sur les écoles philosophiques chez les Arabes*, 140, note 1; Kaufmann, *Attributenlehre*, 2, note 2. In all these examples, except that of *Em.*, introd., 43–44, שכל means not only the second but also the third source. For

Guttmann has shown that in this doctrine of four sources, Saadia was indebted to the Mutakallimūn;[2] but more of this later. Our discussion will follow the order of these four varieties of cognition.

I. SENSATION

1. The nature of sensation, as presented by Saadia, shows traces of two Greek influences. In the introduction to his *Emunot we-Deʿot*, p. 45, he speaks of a conjunction (Ar. وصلة, Heb. דבוק) between the eye and the object. In *Em.*, I, 74, he says: "It is known that our eyes perceive only that which is composed of four elements, for their natures combine [Ar. تتصل, Heb. מתחברים] with the natures of our eyes. If there were a fifth element, it would have nothing kindred in our eyes with which to combine so as to be perceived." And in *Em.*, II, 102, he says: "Things are seen only by means of colors appearing on their surfaces which are related to the four elements, and they combine [Ar. فتتصل, Heb. ומתחברים] with the forces of their kind in the seeing eye by means of the air." We have here the Aristotelian emphasis on color, as well as on air as a medium. This medium, Saadia emphasizes also in *Em.*, I, 70 for the auditory, olfactory, and visual sensations. But Aristotle did not assume any direct contact between the eye and the object, but only a color-stimulus, an excitation, carried by the medium from the object to the eye. It was Empedocles, followed with some modification by the Stoics, who maintained that vision is due to an emanation from the object, an efflux of tiny particles of the four elements which combine with their kindred elements in the eye; and exactly the same view is stated in the aforegoing passages of Saadia.[3]

---

the five sources of wisdom in *Tafsīr Mishlei*, 126, *vide infra*, note 77. Joseph ibn Ṣaddiq, *ʿOlam Qaṭan*, 5, uses the term מדע ההכרח, which in Saadia's terminology (צ̇רוריאת = ἀπόδειξις) stands for demonstration, for the first and second source, that is, for self-evident propositions, which should not surprise us for the term ضروريات is used in Arabic to indicate also the first principles of thought (see Horten, *Theologie des Islam*, 196). Saadia himself uses that Arabic term in this sense in *Tafsīr Iyob*, 40: פחכמה הי בהדה אלחאל מן אלצחה כצחה עלם אלחואס ואלצ̇רוריאת. Derenbourg mistranslated the term by וצרכיהם, which makes no sense in this passage. For other terms for tradition, see *Am.*, 52, אלכ̇בר *Em.*, I, 70 ההגדה; *Tafsīr Mishlei*, 7, 124: אלאת̇אר; Commentary on *Sefer Yeṣirah*, 6: מחדת̇את; *Am.*, 6, תקליד *Em.*, introd., 39 קבלה; *Tafsīr Mishlei*, 126–27: נקל and מנקול.

2 J. Guttmann, *Die Religionsphilosophie des Saadia*, 22, note 5.

3 Concerning Empedocles, see Ludwig Stein, *Erkenntnistheorie der Stoa*, 18, 19.

2. In agreement with Aristotle and the Stoics, Saadia affirms the utter reliability of sensation. Whatever we perceive by means of a contact between the object and our sense-organ is undoubtedly true as perceived. Any idea that is contrary to our perception is false.[4] On the verse in *Sefer Yeṣirah*: "Establish the thing on its evidence and erect the Creator on His foundation," he comments:

The meaning of this is that the only way to prove the existence of the wise Creator is to prove the realities. For we, the congregation of believers, acknowledge in the first place that our senses give us only the truth. This light is really a light and that shadow is really a shadow; this hot object is truly hot, and that cold object is truly cold; there is no doubt about this substance, nor about that accident.[5]

The opening of this passage reveals the motive of Saadia's realism; namely, to have a solid foundation of reality in order to build on it a cosmological proof of God. This procedure, from the world to God, characterizes the opening of his *Emunot we-Deʿot*, as it did also the system of the Mutakallimūn; but while their cosmological basis is, as shown by Maimonides in his *Moreh nebukim*, I, chs. 73–74, a distrust of the senses and an atomism of space and time requiring a constant creator, Saadia differs radically in basing his proof on a complete trust of the senses and in maintaining a permanence of substances that comes up again, as we shall see, in his theory of miracles. His realism seems to go beyond the Stoics who distinguished between the sensation, for example, of heat, and the statement "this is hot," regarding the latter as not strictly a sensation but as a mind-picture, a φαντασία, which may

---

Concerning Aristotle, see William Alexander Hammond, *Aristotle's Psychology* (New York, 1902) introd., XXXVIII–XLII; Aristotle, *De anima*, 404b 10, 419a 10, 427a 2; De sensu, 438a 2; E. Zeller, *The Stoics, Epicureans and Sceptics* (London, 1892), 78, 457. S. Horovitz, *Die Psychologie Saadias* (Breslau, 1898), 54, note 101, seeks to connect Saadia's view at least indirectly with some utterances of Aristotle, but he fails to note Saadia's emphasis on contact and combination of elements, which is Empedoclean.

[4] *Em.*, introd., 44, 45: כל מה שמביא לדחות מאומה מן המוחש... שהוא שקר... כי מדע החוש כל אשר יפול חושינו האמתי בדבוק אשר בינינו וביניו ראוי שנדע שהוא הוא באמת כאשר השגנוהו אין בו ספק. See also Aristotle, *De anima*, 427b 2; Zeller, *The Stoics*, 79, 80; E. Vernon Arnold, *Roman Stoicism* (New York, 1958), 131.

[5] *Tafsīr Kitāb al-mubādī* (to be designated herein as *Sefer Yeṣirah*), ed. M. Lambert, p. 38: לאנא ג̇מאעה̈ אלמומין אנמא נקר אולא באן הד̇ה אלחואס לא תודי אלינא אלא תקא פהד̇א אלנור נור עלי אלחקיק וכד̇לך אלט̇לאם והד̇א אלחאר חאר עלי אלצחה̈ וכד̇לך והד̇א אלג̇והר לא שך פיה וכד̇לך אלערץ̇ אלבארד.

be an error.[6] But Saadia took cognizance of the possibility of error in sensation. We must beware of illusion, lest we take a reflection for a reality. And we must furthermore beware of two causes of error: insufficient knowledge of our object and carelessness in our search of the object, else we are likely to miss a person even though he stands before us. Adequate knowledge of our object and carefulness in our search—these two conditions Saadia together with the Stoics stipulated for a right assent to a sensation.[7] We shall return to these Stoic conditions in connection with the third source of knowledge; but we must note here the implication that sensation is not autonomous, that it needs reason's aid and restraint to be completely reliable.

3. Sensation admits no difference in the degree of validity, for all men are equal in perceptual knowledge; and no man has any superiority over another in this respect, not even over animals.[8] It is also the foundation of all our concepts, the basis of all our knowledge. Reason extracts its cognition from perception even as we extract gold from minerals. Our mental knowledge then is derivative (*iktisāb*), and to reject sensation is to eliminate also the second and third sources of knowledge. Hence where perceptual evidence is available, no further proof is necessary; and all knowledge, progressing only by means of perception of matter, comes to an end when we transcend the apex of the material universe.[9] And hence, Saadia regards the *mutajāhilūn*, among whom he includes the Sophists, who deny the truth of both sensation and reason, as

[6] See Arnold, *Roman Stoicism*, 131. For Aristotle's view, see Theodore Gomperz, *Greek Thinkers* (London, 1955), IV, 187.

[7] *Em.*, introd., 37, 45; Arnold, *Roman Stoicism*, 133.

[8] *Em.*, introd., 51: כי כל בני אדם שוים במדעים החושיים. This is contrary to the Epicurean view, for which see Zeller, *The Stoics*, pp. 426–27. See also *Em.*, II, 83: וכל דבר שיפול עליו החוש הוא הדבר הכולל אשר אין בו יתרון לקצת בני אדם על קצתם שיהיה אחד מהם יותר יודע מן האחר בו אבל אין להם בו יתרון על הבהמות. This is in agreement with Aristotle, *De anima*, 427b5. Maimonides maintains this view of "no superiority" in his treatise on Logic (see my edition of the *Sināʿat al-manṭik*, introd., p. 14); but comp. his *Moreh*, I, 31.

[9] *Em.*, introd., 37: המושכלות מפני שהיו יסודותם מושמים על המוחשים. *Ibid.*, 44: שכל המדעים בנויים על מה שהשגנו בחושינו. *Tafsīr Iyyob*, 109: ת̇ם תכלם פי אלמערפה̈ אנהא אכתסאב יסתכ̇רג̇ה אלעאקל מן עלם אלחואס כמא יסתכ̇רג̇ אלד̇הב מן אלמעאדן. *Em.*, introd., 43: ובכפירתו בראשון כופר בשני ובשלישי מפני שהם בנויים עליו. *Em.*, I, 55: כי אלו היה זה אפשר לא היה צריך לראיה ולא לעיון ולא להוציא דבר מתוך דבר. *Em.*, II, 86: שכל הידיעות אינם נודעות כי אם במצוע הגשם... וכאשר יצא הידוע מהיותו גשם או בתוך גשם כבר נמנע שהיה אחריו ידוע כלל.

exceeding in folly all the other classes of sceptics: sensationists, relativists, and agnostics. He sees no hope for them in any appeal to sense or reason, but in suffering; for in their cry of hunger, thirst, or other bodily pain, there is an admission of perception and the basis for a reclamation of Truth.[10]

Does the derivative nature of all knowledge mean that the mind has nought to contribute and plays only a passive role? An answer to this question is to be found in our next section.

II. NOUS

4. This source, which gives us our immediate knowledge, is called by Saadia *'aḳl* (Heb. *sekel*) — which we translate by the term Nous, used by Aristotle to indicate the faculty of immediate cognition in distiction from Logos[11] — and also *tebunah*, or understanding. It is also designated by other expressions meaning *principia* of knowledge and discernment.[12] The knowledge attained through this source is described

[10] *Em.*, I, 80 and see S. Horovitz, *Dər Mikrokosmos des Josef ibn Ṣaddiḳ* (Breslau, 1903), introd. V, note 16, Similarly in *Tafsīr Mishlei*, 166t קולה הדׄא פי אלגׄאהל אלמתנאהי והו אלדׄי לא יצדק באן [פי] אלדניא עלמא כאלסופסטאייה... ולדׄלך נהי אלכׄואץ אן ינאטׄרו אלמתגׄאהלין ואנמא יצׄרבון ליתאדב גירהם בהם. Similarly, for the attitude of the Sophists to sensation, in Maimonides, *Moreh Nebukim*, I, 73 end. In *Em.*, III, 114, concerning those who deny tradition, Saadia says: עד שלא יאמינו כ״א במה שיפול חושם עליו בעת נפילתו בלבד וזה הדעת קרוב מדעת המתעלמים (אלמתגׄאהלין). The reason that the anti-traditionists approximate the *mutajāhilun,* although they affirm perception, is because, as Saadia continues: כבר אמרו בספרים כי ההגדה הנאמנת הדבר המושג בראות (Ar. כצחה̈, hence כאמתת) אמת נאמנת. In *Tafsīr Mishlei*, 52, he mentions the *mutajāhilun* together with *dahariyun* as engaging in investigation only to trap the heedless with petty difficulties. Saadia mentions the view of *dahar* as accepting sensation only, in *Em.*, I, 76, See also *Tafsīr Isaiah*, 115.

[11] See Zeller, *Aristotle*, (New York and Bombay, 1897), I, 201; II, 181.

[12] For the term *'aql*, see note 1. In *Tafsīr Mishlei*, 126, it is synonymous with תמייז and means therefore reason in general (*vide infra* note 78). In *Tafsīr Mishlei*, 13: *haskel.* The ideas obtained by the Nous, Saadia calls מעקולאת in *Em.*, introd., 45, though in many other places that term means concepts or knowledge in general. For *Tebunah*, see *Tafsīr Mishlei*, 29, though on p. 101 (*ibid.*) that term is applied to traditional laws, and *ḥokmah* to rational laws. For *principia*, see *Em.*, IV, 107: ומן החכמה אך מראשיתה דבר צדק ועזוב הכזב. The term for מראשיתה is in Arabic מן אואילהא, which means the first principles of thought (see Horten, *Die Theologie des Islam*, 131), and Tibbon's rendering is inadequate. The example is also given in *Em.*, introd., 43, under מדע השכל. Comp. *Em.*, II, 102: (i.e., במחשבתנו) כאשר יתקיים בה הטבת הטוב וגנות הכזב and *Em.*, III, 117: מה שיש בשכלנו מטוב הצדק וגנות הכזב.

as being in our Nous (cf. the Stoic ἔννοιαι from ἐν νῷ),[13] as that which springs only in the human mind, as the concepts formed in the mind in a state of health, and as that which is grounded in its own self, that is, self-evident.[14] There are ideas, Saadia says, that rise to meet their seeker and others that lead their seeker to themselves.[15] By the first kind, Saadia means noetic knowledge. The example given in the introduction to the *Emunot* is the proposition that truth is good and falsehood is despicable; but the scope is much wider. It includes such conceptual matters as spring of themselves and become apparent by themselves, like fractions, equations, and square roots, like the idea that a hundred equals a hundred or a half of two hundred; it includes the principle of contradiction that being and non-being cannot be attributed to the same thing at the same time; and it includes the idea of the existence of God.[16] In *Em.*, III, 106, Saadia states several principles, which he calls "universal necessities of thought" (Ar. واجبات العقل الكليات, Heb. חיובי השכל), and which he regards as the sum and substance of all the "rational laws" of the Bible. First, we must meet our benefactor with reward if he needs it, or with gratitude if he needs no reward; and hence divine worship

---

One of these *principia* is the idea of God and is therefore called ראשית דעת. See *Tafsīr Mishlei*, 14: ואמא קולה יראת ה׳ [ראשית דעת]... אן אלמערפה̈ אול מא תוג̇בה ואג̇לתה ואשרפתה תקוי אללה ג̇ל ג̇לאלה פכמא תקע ללאנסאן אלמערפה̈ פקד וקע לה ת̇ם עלם אלתמייז אלד̇י ראסה and *ibid.*, 127: וג̇וב אלטאעה̈ תלאותהא ועקיבתהא סוא ומקדמה ואשרפה אלמערפה̈ באללה אד̇ ליס ימכן אן יחס בחאסה̈. *Vide infra*, note 78.

13 See Arnold, *Roman Stoicism*, 135.

14 See *Em.*, introd., 43, 45 and quotation from *Tafsīr Mishlei*, 13, *infra*, note 16.

15 *Sefer Yesirah*, 14: אלחאצלאת עלי צ̇רבין אמא אן תנהץ̇ הי אלי טאלבהא או אן תנקל אליהא טאלבהא.

16 *Tafsīr Mishlei*, 13: פאמא השכל פהו מא יתעלמה אלמתעלם מן אלחכים מן אלאמור אלמעקולה̈ אלתי תקום בנפסה כקסמה̈ אלעדד ואלמקאבלה̈ ואלג̇דר פאנהא תערץ̇ באנפסהא אן אלמאיה̈ תקאבל אלמאיה̈ ואן אלמאיה̈ נצף אלמאיתין. For the principle of contradiction, see *Em.*, II, 102: איך יתקיים במחשבתנו הענין הזה ר״ל הבורא ית׳ וחוש מחושינו לא נפל עליו ואומר כאשר נתקיים בה הטבת הטוב וגנות הכזב וחושינו לא נפלו עליו וכאשר נעלה בשכלנו המנע מקבץ נמצא ונעדר ושאר המתרחקים והחושים לא ראו את זה. The grouping of this principle with the other two intuitions shows that its origin is meant to be the Nous. Indeed in *Em.*, III, 107, it is stated as implied in the self-evident idea that truth is good and falsehood is despicable: ומן החכמה אך מראשיתה דבר צדק ועזוב הכזב... והכזב הוא האמירה על הדבר לא כאשר הוא... ותליץ עליו הנפש בהפך בתכונת זולתה מקבילות שני התכונות בנפש ומתהפכות ותשער מהמנעם בדבר נכרי. Aristotle also maintained that this principle is an "ultimate belief" and "the starting point for all other axioms" (*Metaph.*, 1005b30). For the idea of God, see quotations from *Tafsīr Mishlei*, 14, 127, *supra*, note 12.

and gratitude. Second, the wise man does not permit himself to be reviled and cursed; and hence no blasphemy of God. Third, God forbids his creatures to sin against each other; and hence all laws prohibiting social wrongdoing. These were meant by Saadia as knowledge of the second class, as is shown by the following consideration. (1) The first principle is sometimes given by Arab and Jwish thinkers as an illustration of self-evident propositions.[17] (2) The principles are given without proof but, as "universal necessities of thought," which reflects the Stoic term κοιναὶ ἔννοιαι. (3) Saadia states concerning them that God implanted in our mind—a phrase to which we shall revert later—a sense of rightness of the acts that they dictate and a sense of wrongness of the doings they forbid. (4) At the end of that section, Saadia states that reflection (Ar. تأمل, Heb. הסתכלות) would disclose the reasons of the rational laws, and he then proceeds to the disclosure in the next section, implying that theretofore these laws and the principles under which they were subsumed were discussed only as knowledge of the second class, that is, as intuitions or preconceptions. This is indeed in keeping with his promise in *Em.*, introd., 44, that he would prove tradition by means of all the three sources: sensation, intuition, and inference (the proof from sensation is contained in the opening of that section). There is also one other body of knowledge that the mind accepts without call for proof, namely, a people's oral traditions governing its religious, political, occupational, and domestic life; but more of this later.

In Arabic and Hebrew medieval philosophy, the propositions requiring no proof are usually divided into four groups: perceptions, axioms, moral conventions adopted by all or most peoples, and traditions.[18] These can be traced back to different origins. The origin of the first two groups is Aristotelian;[19] that of the third is to be found in the Stoic doctrine of κοιναὶ ἔννοιαι and *consensus gentium*, the Arabic and Hebrew names for this group (Ar. *mašhūrāt*, Heb. *meforsamot*) meaning κοιναὶ; and that of the fourth is, as we shall see, Peripatetic. Saadia is in complete agreement with the ultimate character of these groups. Perceptions, no

17 See my edition of Maimonides' *Ṣinā'at al-manṭiḳ* (American Academy for Jewish Research, 1938), introd., 19 and ch. 8; Maimonides' *Shemonah Perakim,* 6. See also Joseph ibn Ṣaddiḳ, *'Olam Ḳaṭan,* ed. Horovitz (Breslau, 1903), 60 and Schreiner, *Der Kalam in der jüdischer Literatur,* (Berlin, 1895), 28.

18 *Ibid.,* and *Ruaḥ Ḥen,* ch. 6.

19 Arnold, *Roman Stoicism,* 138.

doubt because of their distinct channels of approach to the mind, he regards as a class by themselves. The arithmetical axioms and the Law of Contradiction are illustrative of the second group; the ethical laws, of the third; and "reliable tradition," of the fourth. The question is: where would Saadia place the idea of God, not as "necessity" but as immediate knowledge? The Stoics regarded it as a *consensus gentium*, one of the κοιναὶ ἔννοιαι, and it would therefore be placed in the third group. But Saadia's idea of our immediate knowledge of God is not Stoic. Nor is it entirely in accord with the view of *Ruaḥ Ḥen*, ch. 6, which places it, for those who have not attained it by means of reason, in the fourth group. Saadia regards it as the beginning of knowledge and its first affirmation, and hence would place it in the second group, together with mathematical and logical axioms.[20] The appeal of the idea of God is not to its universality but to its inherent self-evidence.

5. The causes of error in this type of knowledge are dreams and faulty investigation.[21] Dreams are the product neither of the external senses nor of inference and hence belong only to immediate knowledge. Perhaps the relation is also to be found in a common psychic origin; for, according to Aristotle, the same imaginative faculty that gives rise to dreams is also employed in the field of conduct,[22] which is, as we have seen, a large part of the realm of immediate knowledge. Similarly, the author of *Ruaḥ Ḥen*, ch. 6, states: "those laws which have been accepted by all peoples, like those prohibiting theft and murder and commanding filial honor, are called rational laws, because practical reason *which is of the imaginative faculty* accepts them." And also for the "first ideas," the *muskalot rishonot*, we have the authority of Avicenna, who states that these are formed by the constructive imagination, which he calls *mufakkirah*.[23] If so, we gain also a special locus in the brains for the Nous or the source of immediate knowledge, namely, that of constructive imagina-

[20] Comp. however Horovitz, *Die Psychologie Saadias*, 51, note 94.

[21] *Em.*, introd., 45: המושכלות כל אשר יצטייר בשכלנו הנצל מכל פגע והוא מדע אמת אין בו ספק אחר שנדע איך נעיין ואחר כן נשלים העיון ונשמר מן הדמיונים והחלומות. The word التخيلات (= הדמיונים) is in brackets in the Arabic text. It certainly implies nothing distinct from dreams which alone are discussed by Saadia in the sequel. It corresponds to the term "phantasms" (φάντασματα) applied to dreams both by Aristotle and the Stoics. See Zeller, *Aristotle*, II, 72; Arnold, *Roman Stoicism*, 132. The same word التخيلات is used by Saadia on the same page for false perceptions.

[22] Hammond, *Aristotle's Psychology*, introd., LXI, note 1.

[23] See A. M. Goichon, *Lexique de la langue philosophique d'ibn Sīnā*, s.v., مفكرة.

tion, or the anterior area, as different from discursive reason located in the middle area. Saadia too uses the term *fikr*, perhaps both as constructive imagination and as the Nous, in *Tafsīr Mishlei*, 96: "the power of *fikr* and memory and discernment in the brains" (אלפכר ואלדכר ואלתמייז אלתי פי אלדמאג. Similarly, *Em.*, X, 202: ונצרה ופכרה ודכרה), which classification thus conforms to Galen's classification of internal senses into imagination, thought and memory.[24] Hence it is because of a common psychic origin that dreams may be said to be the errors of the Nous. According to Saadia, dreams are mostly erroneous, arising from the thoughts and the food of the past day and from the chyme dominating the temperament. Yet they contain "a slight hint from on high" (*Em.*, introd., 45). Aristotle also, though opposing in his systematic works the idea of God-sent dreams, was inclined in his earlier popular writings to give them credence.[25] At any rate, the sphere of the second class of knowledge becomes now further enlarged by the inclusion of the prophetic element of dreams.

As to the other source of error, Saadia says: "we must know how to think and complete our thinking" (*ibid.*). This statement seems strange as applied to self-evident knowledge requiring no proof. Let us also point to another difficulty. In *Em.*, introd., 43, he says that the second and third sources of knowledge are built on the first so that to deny sensation is to deny also immediate and mediate knowledge. The difficulty is that the second source becomes inferential and therefore no different from the third source. How then are we to understand the preconceptions as dependent on sensation and thinking and at the same time as self-evident? The answer is that just as we saw in the case of perceptions that error may arise in the search of a percept through insufficient knowledge and lack of thoroughness, so because of the same factors errors may arise when we seek the general preconceptions in individual situations. Thus, Epictetus in his *Discourses*, I, 22, emphasizes: "Preconceptions are common to all men.... When then does contradiction arise? It arises in the application of our preconceptions to the particular cases.... Education means learning how to apply the natural preconceptions to the particular cases." Similarly in the realm of arithmetical operations, the self-evidence of the number of which 100 is a half, applies also to the number of which

24 For Galen's classification and the term פכר, see Wolfson, "The Internal Senses" in *Harvard Theological Review* (1935), 72, 91. See also *infra*, note 36.

25 Zeller, *Aristotle*, II, 77; Gomperz, *Greek Thinkers*, IV, 186, 215.

178 or 1897 is a half, the finding of which may require some patience and technique. The self-evidence of an idea does not necessarily imply the self-evidence of the road leading to it. The thought as it springs in the mind may at once command our assent, but it is not always recognizable in the heavy garments of reality; and we need Saadia's caution "to know how to think and complete the thinking," which according to Saadia is always based on sensation. Lying is ugly, but before we condemn a person we must carefully study the given case until the moral truth of the situation reveals itself in its self-evidence.

6. What precisely is the meaning of the a priori nature of this second class of knowledge? Kaufmann thought that the name as well as the illustrations leave no doubt that Saadia meant innate ideas.[26] Horovitz, on the other hand, pointed to Saadia's statement that "all knowledge is based on what we perceive by our senses" as proving that Saadia's position was pronounced empiricism (*ausgesprochener* "Empiricismus") and concluded therefore that the passages in *Tafsīr Mishlei*, 13, 29 must be interpreted in accord with strict empiricism. In the same manner, the Stoics too speak of ἔμφυτοι προλήψεις even though, as Zeller maintained, no innateness was intended.[27] Now as for the last point, more recent scholars do not seem to agree with Zeller;[28] and Saadia, at any rate, might have taken those expressions literally. Even Aristotle, who "contests the possibility of any innate knowledge" (Zeller, *Aristotle*, I, 200) was nevertheless understood by al-Parabi as maintaining that the mind accepts the first principles by endowment and nature from childhood on.[29] But let us examine Saadia's utterances on this subject, and we shall find that he goes even beyond this view attributed by al-Farabi to Aristotle. We saw that he emphasized in several places that all our knowledge is based on our sensations, that it is derivative or *iktisāb*. But against these there are several utterances pointing to the contrary.

26 David Kaufmann, *Attributenlehre*, 2, note 3.

27 Horovitz, *Die Psychologie Saadias*, 50, note 94.

28 Ludwig Stein, *Die Erkenntnistheorie der Stoa* (Berlin, 1886–1888), 271; R. D. Hicks, *Stoic and Epicurean* (New York, 1910), 67; Arnold, *Roman Stoicism*, 138.

29 Alfarabi's *Philosophische Abhandlungen*, ed. F. Dieterici, pp. 40, 41: واما العقل الذى يذكره ارسطوطاليس فى كتاب البرهان فانه انما يعنى به قوة النفس التى بها يحصل للانسان اليقين بالقدمات الكلية الصادقة الضرورية لا عن قياس اصلا ولا عن فكر بل بالفطرة والطبع او من صباه ومن حيث لا يشعر من اين حصلت فان هذه القوة جزؤما من النفس يحصل العرفة الاولى لا بفكر ولا بيامل اصلا.

There are the two passages mentioned by Horovitz. The first reads: "The meaning of *mishpaṭ* is what the learner grasps of those religious matters in which reason holds sway, commanding all that God *implanted* in the mind as worthy and renouncing all that God impressed upon the understainding as ugly." The second states: "Since there are two ways of obtaining wisdom, one being in the nature and substance (of the mind) and the other by acquisition, the sage divided his utterance, and said concerning the acquisitional kind, 'Happy is the man who findeth wisdom,' for he searched and found; and concerning the 'substantial' kind, he said 'and the man that getteth understanding' for it comes by the grace of God."[30] Now as for the first passage, Horovitz does not mention that the same idea with similar phrasing is found also in the *Emunot* where these "implantations" are called, after the manner of the Stoics, "universal necessities of thought" so that there too and also in his commentary on Proverbs, 179, we would have to interpret the text in harmony with strict empiricism.[31] But how can such an interpretation be applied to the second passage mentioned by Horovitz, where *tebunah* is sharply differentiated from *ḥokmah* in not being acquired but in being of the nature and substance of the mind, a grace of God? But there is another very interesting passage that not only disproves empiricism but also shows us how to reconcile the contradictory statements and indicates the relative functions of thought and experience.

The audible things [says Saadia] are discovered by the organ of hearing, and man testifies: this is what I have heard and none other. The same is true of the other organs of sensation. Similarly there is in the mind a knowing force

30 *Tafsīr Mishlei*, 13: ומעני משפט מא יתלקנה אלמתעלם מן אלאמור אלדיאניה אלתי יקצ֗י בהא אלעקל פיאמרה בכל מא קד גרסה אלבארי פי עקלה מסתחסנא וינהאה עין כל מא רכבה אלפאטר פי תמייזה מסתקבחא. *Ibid.*, 29: למא כאנת אלפנון אלתי בהא תנאל אלחכמה מנהא מא הו פי אלבניה ואלענצר ומנהא מא הו אכתסאב קסם אלחכים אלקול פקאל פי אלאנואע אלאכתסאביה אשרי אדם מצא חכמה לאנה טלב פוגד וקאל פי אלפנון אלענצריה ואדם יפיק תבונה לאנהא תופיק מן אלמכ֗תרע.

31 *Em.*, III, 106: וכאשר היה זה מחיובי השכל (ואגבאת אלעקל אלכליאת)... וכל ענין מאלה שמצוה בו נטע (גרס) בשכלנו טובתו וכל ענין מהם שהזכיר ממנו נטע (גרס) בשכלנו גנותו. *Tafsīr Mishlei*, 187: או אנה כלמא גרס אללה פי עקול אלנאס חסנהא או קבחהא פהו מעלום יקף עליהא כל צחיח אלעקל. The reference is here to the rational laws, which, as we have seen, incorporate self-evident propositions. *Tafsīr Mishlei*, 179: ליס כל אלמצאלח מגרוסה פי עקול אלנאס פלדלך יחתאגון אלי מעלמין ומבצרין יפהמון ען רבהם אלשראיע אלסמעיה. Similarly *ibid.*, 180. Comp. also *Em.*, X, 199: לא היה נוטע (לם יגרס) הבורא במדות האדם אהבת שאר דברים.

which, when confronted by intellectual matters, verifies them, so that the person becomes convinced that they are undoubtedly the concepts. According to this example all knowledge lies concealed in the mind; and the purpose of learning and inference is only to discover it after its awakening, so that when it stands before the mind, the mind testifies concerning it that it is the truth.[32]

Now it is true that Aristotle in *De anima*, III, 4, 429a25, favors the Platonic dictum that the soul is the place of ideas—καὶ εὖ δὴ οἱ λέγοντης τὴν ψυχήν εἶναι τοπον εἰδῶν — but he emphasizes that, before knowing, the mind has a mere potentiality of knowing, so that the dictum is reduced to mean that a potential mind is the place of potential ideas. This distinction between potentiality and actuality, so basic to Aristotle's dynamic philosophy, was not a part of Saadia's metaphysics, which is based not on the notion of matter and form but on that of substance and accident. Saadia's statement therefore is not in accord with the Aristotelian view but rather with the Platonic theory of innate knowledge; except for the fact that Plato, who believed in the pre-existence of the soul, spoke of *Anamnesis*, or recollection, and Saadia, who denied that belief, spoke of awakening. Knowledge, then, lies concealed in the mind, and reflection only discovers it, even as the ear discovers sound. One more statement may be cited to disprove the complete dependence of the mind upon sensation.

It has become clear to me that the soul is wise through its own essence, because of various reasons. (1) It cannot acquire its knowledge from the body, for the latter has no wisdom. (2) It has been verified that the blind person dreams that he sees; so that if he had no visual experience through his body, he must have obtained it through his soul. Hence he who believed the soul to be a juncture and combination and contact of senses was mistaken, because since it is the soul which gives the organs the power of sensation, how could they give it substance?[33]

32 *Tafsīr Mishlei*, 9: אלמסמועאת אטהרתהא פט̇הר פשהד אלאנסאן עלי ד̇לך אלשי אנה הו אלמסמוע לא גירה ועלי הדא באקי אלחואס. כד̇לך פי אלעקל קוה̈ עאלמה̈ פאד̇א טאלעתהא אלאמור אלמעקולה̈ איקנת בהא וצח ענד אלאנסאן אנהא הי לא מחאלה̈ אלמעקולה̈. פעלי הד̇א אלמת̇אל כל עלם פהו מכנון פי אלעקל ואנמא אלמראד באלתעלם ואלאכתסאב ג̇מיעא ליט̇הרא ד̇לך בעד אלאת̇ארה̈ פאד̇א הו אנתצב ללעקל שהד עליה אנה אלחק. פלד̇לך ג̇על הד̇א אלכתאב ונט̇ראה לינבהו עמא פי אלעקל. Baḥya in his *Al-Hidāja 'ilā farā'id al-qulūb*, ed. Yahuda (Leiden, 1921), 14, stated the same idea with almost the same phrases: ...אל אלעלם מרכוז ומכנון פי גריזה̈ כל אנסאן ואלפהם אלעאקל ירום אלבחת̇ עמא פי קותה ופי באטנה מן אלעלם חתי יכשף ענה ויט̇הרה.

33 *Em.*, VI, 153: התבאר לי כי הנפש הזאת חכמה לעצמה (עאלמה̈ לד̇אתהא) מכמה פנים אחד מהם כי לא יתכן שקנתה החכמה מן הגוף כי אין זה מענינו. ועוד בעבור מה

From all this we learn that to Saadia the mind plays by no means a passive role in the process of learning, that it is not a blank tablet, but that quite to the contrary it comes endowed with all knowledge; that this knowledge requires awakening through experience and through reason working on the material of experience; and that in so far as our innate knowledge has to be discovered and made articulate, it is at the same time all based on our sensation. Saadia's view then is radically different from thoroughgoing empiricism. It is both empiricism and rationalism; it is empirical rationalism. He even goes beyond the Stoics, who limited innateness to our common notions. The difference between Saadia's second and third source is only that in the first case the mind, through experience, discovers ideas as self-evident, as illuminated from within, whereas in the second case the reflective mind discovers ideas as illuminated by inference. In both, cases there is only a discovery, even as the ear discovers music. Learning does not produce, but only awakens and recognizes concepts.

III. NECESSITY

7. The third source of knowledge Saadia calls "that to which necessity leads," "knowledge of necessities," "necessary knowledge," and also metaphorically "righteousness."[34] For the meaning of the term, let us quote from Aristotle, *Metaph.*, 1064b35 (see also 1015b5): "necessity (ἀνάγκη) not in the sense of violence, but that which we appeal to in demonstration" (ἀποδείξις). Saadia offers various examples of necessity: from the indication of fire in the presence of smoke to the construction of astronomical theories on the basis of observations of lunar movements. But he seems to include also analogy[35] under necessity.

שהתאמת כי הסומא רואה בחלומו כאלו הוא רואה וכיון שלא השיג זה מחמת גופו לא השיגו כי אם מחמת נפשו. ובזה טעה עוד מי שחשבה התקשר החושים והסתבכם והפגשם והוא שהיא היא הנותנת לכלים החוש ואיך יתנו לה הם העצם. Comp. however Arist., *Post Anal.*, I, 18, 81a40: "It is also clear that the loss of any one of the senses entails the loss of a corresponding portion of knowledge, and that, since we learn either by induction or demonstration, this knowledge cannot be acquired.

[34] *Vide supra*, note 1 and *Em.*, introd., 51 במדע ובהכרח, Ar. באלעלם ואלצ̇רוראת. For "righteousness," probably under the influence of the Ar. word صدق meaning "truth," see *Tafsīr Mishlei*, 13: ומעני צדק הו מא יקבלה אלמתעלם בחג̈ה עאדלה̈ אעני במסתכ̇רג̇ מן מחמול ומוצ̇וע כאלאשכאל אלהנדסיה̈ אלתי מנהא מא יעלם בחג̈ה ומנהא באת̇נתין ומנהא בת̇לאת̇ ומא פוק ד̇לך.

[35] See *Em.*, introd., 47 where הקשה על המוחש is included in the third source. Comp. הקשה על in *Em.*, I, 68; III, 116.

To Aristotle, there are only two kinds of scientific thought: induction and deduction. While Saadia, as we have seen, acknowledged these two processes (analogy is but an imperfect induction), his description of correct thinking presents a somewhat different picture. There are two elements, he says, in the attainment of knowledge: *instruction* (i.e., learning the principles and roots of science from previous scholars), and *discovery* or *acquisition* (i.e., unfolding the implications and corollaries). These involve four powers; *reception*, *retention*, *exploration*, and *discernment*. Reception is called *hearing* while in the process of obtaining ideas from an outside source; when completed, it is called *learning*. Retention is the power to store up ideas so that they can be recalled. Exploration is the mental wandering about. If the subject of investigation is a reported action, it will divide it into its parts; and if the meaning of a test is examined it will gather all the possibilities—leaving out none—that may help to explain it. And discernment, which should always come after exploration, is the power to discriminate among all these possibilities; so that in the case of an action, it will approve what is worthy and reject what is unworthy, and in the case of an idea, it will accept what it can regard as true and repudiate the false, without taking into consideration the opinion of people, be they few or many.[36] Similarly, in his commentary on the *Sefer Yeṣirah*, Saadia says:

Man must first know, then reflect and discern, and then believe.... I shall

[36] *Tafsīr Mishlei*, 7–9: וכמאל אלעלם בפנון ארבעה אלאול אלקבול ת̇ם אלחפט̇ ת̇ם אלכ̇אטר ת̇ם אלתמייז וקסמי אלמערפה̈ אללדין המא אלתלקין ואלאסתנבאט... פאמא אלתלקין... פאמא אלאכתסאב... והד̇אן אלקסמאן אעני אלעלם אלמתעלם ואלאסתנבאט מחתאג̇אן אלי הד̇ה אלארבע קוי אלמקדם ד̇כרהא אעני קוה̈ אלקבול ואלחפט̇ ואלכ̇אטר ואלתמייז... וקוה̈ אלתמייז הי אבדא עקיבה̈ אלכ̇אטר לאנהא אנמא תמייז תלך אלפנון ואלצ̇רוב אלתי אחצ̇רהא אלכ̇אטר... In this passage *iktisāb=istinbāṭ*, or inference, whereas on p. 21 (*ibid.*) in the statement אואיל אלעלום אכתסאב ותמאמהא בכ̇אטר ותמייז ולד̇לך צדר אולא בני אם תקח אמרי וגו׳ ת̇ם קאל אם תבקשנה ככסף וגו׳ ת̇ם קאל אד̇א פעלת יא טאלב אלחכמה̈ הדין אלאמרין אז תבין יראת ה׳ וגו׳ אז תבין צדק ומשפט וגו׳ ואמא בלא תעלם מן עאלם פליס ינפע אלתפכר שיא וכד̇לך תעלם בלא פכר ותמייז לא ינפע שיא *iktisāb=talkīn*, or learning from others. Furthermore, in the first passage *istinbāṭ=iktisūb* or inference, whereas on p. 126–27 (*ibid.*) *istinbāṭ=taḥrīr* (*vide infra*, note 80), i.e., proving ideas rather than the discovery thereof. In passage B and in the sequel of passage A, *Tafakkur* stands for both *ḥāṭir* and *tamyīz*, and *fikr=ḥāṭir*, but in S.Y. (see quotation in next note), *fikr* stands for both *tamyīz* and *ḥāṭir* which is called there *ḥāshir*. In *Tafsīr Mishlei*, 96 קוה אלפכר ואלד̇כר ואלתמייז פי אלדמאג, the term *fikr* may mean constructive imagination, for which see Wolfson, *The Internal Senses*, 91 ff.

explain here an important part of discernment. There is no way to discern anything until we embrace all the points which characterize it. These must be embraced by the power of synthesis. When all these points are before you, and you have omitted none, the faculty of analysis begins to operate, rejecting all that is false and accepting only that which is true, or approving that which is good and disapproving that which is wrong. When the work of the analytic faculty is done, the faculty of *belief* accepts that which was discerned and judged, adopts it and guards it. It is for this reason that the author says: "Know, think, and believe."[37]

This process of elimination, beginning with the widest possible base of possibilities, is illustrated by a rather extreme and artificial example that Saadia gives for the time-taking character of thought. We can conceive, he says,[38] of ten steps in a quest of proof. (1) Proof is speech, speech is sound, and sound is of many kinds. (2) We eliminate sounds of inanimate things, then (3) sounds of irrational animals, (4) natural human sounds, (5) sounds of single letters, (6) single words, (7) combinations of words that are not complete sentences, (8) necessary and impossible propositions that require no proof, leaving only the possible proposition, which (9) we prove, and then (10) drawing the conclusion. Thus, Saadia says, the thinker begins with a tangle of things, upon which he applies the process of elimination, obtaining nine possibilities from ten, then eight from nine, and seven from eight, until all the alloy is removed and the tested and purified remains.

Another feature of the process of thought is stated by Saadia in the form of six propositions. First, the beginnings of knowledge are coarse and their ends are fine. It starts with sensation, which belongs to both man and beast, and proceeds, through a process of abstraction, from matter to its qualities, then to quantity, and thence to space and time, until it reaches its goal, which is finer than all the stages that preceeded it. Second, man reaches a state of knowledge after which there is no knowledge; that is, knowledge is finite. Three reasons are given for this

[37] S. Y., 37: אלאנסאן אולא ינבגי אן יעלם ת̇ם יפתכר וימייז ת̇ם יעתקד מא צח לה באלפכר אלצחיח אנה חק והוד̇א אשרח האהנא באבא עט̇ימא מן אלתמייז ואקול לא סביל אלי תמייז שי חתי תג̇מע ג̇מיע אלוג̇וה אלתי יכ̇אץ פיהא וסבילהא אן תג̇מע באלקוה̈ אלחאשרה̈ פאד̇א אחצ̇רתהא כלהא ולם תכ̇לף̇ מנהא שי דברתהא חיניד̇ אלקוה̈ אלממיזה̈ פאבטלת מא כאן באטלא וחקקת מא כאן חקא או אסתחסנת מא כאן חסנא ואסתקבחת מא כאן קביחא פאד̇א תם פעל אלקוה̈ אלממיזה̈ אקבלת אלקוה̈ אלמעתקדה̈ ד̇לך אלשי אלממיז אלחכם פאעתקדתה וחפט̇תה פלד̇לך קאל ודע וחשב וצור.

[38] *Em.*, introd., 40–41.

proposition: (1) man, being limited in his body, must also be limited in his powers, one of which is knowledge; (2) knowledge can be encompassed by man only because it is finite, for otherwise it could not be encompassed and therefore it could not be known;[39] (3) the root of all knowledge, the percept, being undoubtedly finite, the branch cannot be infinite. Third, knowledge is an ascent from stage to stage, because it has roots from which it springs and is therefore different from ignorance, which is only an absence of knowledge. Saadia emphasizes at some length this idea that ignorance, being only negative and rootless, cannot serve as stages for ascent to the top where the idea of God resides. It is a call for rationalism in faith. Fourth, the last stage furnishes the subtlest notion of all. Fifth, we must not conceive our last notion in as coarse a form as our first, for thereby we distort the process of knowledge. Sixth, in fact, we destroy all the fruits of our labor and return to ignorance. Thus thought is pyramidal. We begin with a broad and concrete basis; and as we climb, the material thins until we have nothing to hold on to. But, says Saadia, the finest is also the strongest, even as the soul controls the body and wisdom governs the soul, and the degree of potency among the elements is in an inverse ratio to their solidity.[40]

8. No less than Yehudah Halevi, Saadia is aware of the limitation of mind and of its inability to solve certain problems. There is the problem of the nature of God, whose attributes, except that He is loving, wise, and omnipotent, cannot be known.[41] There is the problem of how the four elements came into being out of nought, and why fire rises and the wind is elusive and water flows and earth sinks. Coming to the world of combined elements, we face many unanswerable questions; what is the nature of the stars and their respective distances and motions; what is the nature of mountains, seas, and rocks; what is the nature of animals and why their respective organs and passions; and why does one number have a square root while another number does not have it.[42] But Saadia

39 *Em.*, II, 84. כי המדע איננו נתפש (אנמא ינחצר) לאדם אלא מפני שיש לו תכלית ואם יחשב שאין לו תכלית אז יבטל להתפש לו (אנחצארה) וכאשר יבטל זה יבטל שידעהו אדם. Similarly, *Moreh Nebukim*, III, 16: והידיעה היא ענין מקיף וכולל הדבר ומה שאין לו תכלית לא יקיפהו מדע ולא יכילהו.

40 *Em.*, II, 86, 94, 95.

41 *Em.*, II, 91, 92; *Tafsīr Iyob*, 109; *Tafsīr Mishlei*, 142; S.Y., 6.

42 *Tafsīr Mishlei*, 11, 185–88; *Tafsīr Iyob*, 80, 85; S. Y. 14. See also regarding the understandability of reward and punishment in *Tafsīr Iyob*, 97 and comp. *Kuzari*, V, 21

stresses these limitations of reason not, as Halevi does, in order to aggrandize the faculty of faith, but to direct the mind to its proper sphere where alone it can be productive and fertile. "It is only after agreement is reached on the insolubility of these problems that true investigation and research become possible."[43] More about this in §11.

But even in its own sphere, the mind must be wary of pitfalls, for here, even to a greater degree than in the previous classes, is error possible; and it is here that differences of opinion prevail.[44] As in sensation and preconception, error in inference is due to ignorance, that is, of the art of inference and especially of the object of one's search, and to haste and superficiality.[45] Thought, like all human action, and as distinguished from divine thought, is subject to time and is therefore a procession from part to part,[46] and hence impatience or haste will produce error. Saadia therefore offers a number of rules of inference and summarizes them under five headings. First, an inference is invalid when based on a sensation that can be explained with the aid of another theory. Second, it is invalid when based on an idea that can be explained with the aid of another theory. Third, it is invalid when it contradicts another truth. Fourth, it is invalid when it contradicts itself. Saadia's explanation must be added here. When one infers from his own experience of an action that the good is pleasant, one must realize that someone else may find the same action distinctly unpleasant, so that there will be two contradictory evaluations of the same act.[47] Fifth, the rejection of a view is invalid when it is as repugnant, or even more so, from the standpoint of the basic principle, as the acceptance of that view. An example of this is the antithesis of the idea that God cannot bring back the yesterday because it would limit God's power—an antithesis that is worse than the thesis, because it ascribes absurdities to God. In this summary, Saadia does not state the rule he gave in his general discussion before the fifth, namely that a thesis cannot be inferred from a cause that also leads to the antithesis; for example, we cannot maintain eternity on the ground that we have never seen creation, for neither have we observed

43 *Tafsīr Mishlei,* 187.

44 *Em.,* introd., 44.

45 *Ibid.,* 37.

46 See Arist., *De mem.,* 450a6, and my "Some Aspects of Yehudah Halevi's Mysticism," note 3, in Part two of this volume.

47 Similarly, *Tafsīr Mishlei,* 15.

eternity. It seems that he includes it in the fifth rule of the summary, for both have parallel phrasing and are basically the same: not to infer an idea from a principle when the opposite is equally acceptable, or when it is equally repugnant as its opposite, from the standpoint of the same principle.[48]

To these rules Saadia adds his two cautions: to guard our sensations and intuitions against illusions and dreams, and to be patient and avoid haste and carelessness in our investigation; so that altogether we have seven rules of thought.[49] This last caution is of Stoic origin. According to the Stoics, error is due either to a hasty movement of the will or to a feebleness of the will;[50] similarly, according to Saadia, error results from "seeking knowledge too lightly," "hastening to judge before the completion of the logical process," "becoming quickly annoyed or impatient to the extent of being unable to complete an investigation," and also from "feebleness of heart."[51] The Stoics spoke of wrong assent as sin (ἁμαρτία, peccatum); Saadia calls it ذنب (Heb. חטא).[52] The Stoics urged careful attention or application (ἐπιβολή); Saadia insists upon صبر and مهل, perseverence and deliberateness.[53]

9. There are therefore two kinds of belief: true and false. A belief is defined by Saadia as "a notion springing in the soul concerning a certain thing in a certain condition. And when the butter of thought is churned, the mind encompasses it and grasps it and takes in into the soul and fuses with it; and the man believes the notion which came to him and stores it away in his soul for another time."[54] Then Saadia proceeds to state that belief (*iʿtiqād*) may be true or false. It is *true* when the person knows the thing as it really is: small or large, white or black, existent or non-existent. It is *false* when he thinks the reverse of what

48 Comp. however *Shebil ha-emunah* on *Em.*, introd., 48.

49 *Em.*, introd., 45–48.

50 Arnold, *Roman Stoicism,* 68, 133.

51 *Em.*, introd., 37, 51; Arnold, *Roman Stoicism.*

52 *Em.*, introd., 41; Arnold, *Roman Stoicism.*

53 *Em.*, introd., 41, 49; Arnold, *Roman Stoicism.*

54 *Am.*, 11: פינבגי אן נבין מא אלאעתקאד ונקול אנה מעני יקום פי אלנפס לכל שי מעלום באלחאל אלתי הו עליהא פאדֿא כֿרגֿת זבדהֿ אלנטֿר אכתנפתהא אלעקול פאנטות עליהא וחצלתהא פי אלנפס פמאזגֿתהא פצאר אלאנסאן מעתקדא לדֿלך אלמעני אלדֿי חצל לה ודפעה פי נפסה לוקת אכֿר או לאוקאת. For the idea of encompassing, see *supra,* note 39. For the idea of fusion, see *Em.*, II, 103: תאמינהו נפשו ותמזג ברוחו. See also the expression חמאת המיץ (Ar. זבד מכֿיץֿ) in *Em.*, X, 212.

the object really is. This is the correspondence theory of truth, and we find it in Aristotle, *Metaph.*, 1027a20; 1051–35. Hence, Saadia insists, the wise man is he who regards the facts as fundamental and lets his thought be governed by them, whereas the fool thinks that the facts follow his opinions.[55] Maimonides in *Moreh*, I, 71, quotes this idea from Themistius, and Narboni remarks that he should have quoted it from Arist., *Metaph.*, IV, 5: "If the thoughts and opinions of men were all true, then everything would at the same time be true and false; because frequently one man believes the opposite of another, and thinks that those who have not the same opinion as he himself are wrong." The connection between this passage and the Themistius-Saadia dictum is somewhat remote, as was pointed out by M. Friedlander in his translation of the *Moreh* (a.l.) and Neumark in his *Toledot ha-pilosofia be-Israel*, II, 373. A much clearer statement, probably the source for Themistius and Saadia, is Aristotle's *Metaph.*, IX, 10: Οὐ γὰρ διὰ τὸ ἡμᾶς οἴεσθαι ἀληθῶς σε λευκὸν εἶναι εἶ συ λευκός ἀλλὰ διὰ τὸ σὲ λευκόν εἶναι ἡμεῖς οἱ φάντες τοῦτο ἀληθεύμεν. "It is not because we are right in thinking that you are white that you are white; it is because you are white that we are right in saying so."

We have to explain two difficulties in the quotation from Saadia: first the rather verbose and unclear description of the act of belief; second, whether belief can be false when carried through the entire description or only in a part thereof. From the fact that just before this cited passage Saadia ascribes "the churning of butter of thought" to the good and patient thinkers, and from the above cited passage where Saadia says: "Man must first know, then reflect and discern, and then believe" implying confidence in a belief that follows the synthetic and analytic process of thought, and furthermore from a comparison with the views of other thinkers, it must be evident that falsehood can apply only to that kind of belief that is described in the first sentence of the quotation, namely, "a notion springing in the soul" without investigation or proof. This is also the Maimonides defines it in *Moreh*, I, 50 (i.e., as "a notion conceived in the soul"), except that he stipulates what is implied by Saadia, namely, "when it is accompanied by belief that it is (in reality) as conceived." It is what the Stoics called συγκατάθεσις, or assent, which is an act of the will and may be true or false. It is what Plato called

[55] *Em.*, introd., 42; I, 78, 79; VI, 156.

δόξα, opinion, as different from ἐπιστήμη, knowledge (*Theaet.* 187A). It is what Isaac Israeli called אלראי in his *Book of Definitions*—see Arabic fragments, published by H. Hirschfeld in *The Jewish Quarterly Review*, 15 (1903), p. 690: חד אלראי אעתקאד שי אמא חד אלפכר קוה̈ עקליה תחל פי אלאשיא. But when we patiently allow the butter of thought to be churned, the mind, says Saadia, "encompasses it, grasps it, and takes it into the soul and fuses with it." Here a grasping and a seizure is described, corresponding to the second step, called by the Stoics κατάλεψις, which Cicero translates by *comprehensio*, and which is a ratification of the assent, a grasping as with the hand. Thus Cicero in his *Academica*, I, 41 reports about Zeno: *sed cum acceptum iam et approbatum esse comprehensionem appellabat, similem iis rebus quae manu propenderentur.* This act of encompassing is so essential to the act of cognition that Saadia inferred that knowledge must be finite, for in order to be known it must be encompassed; and Maimonides inferred that the infinite, since it cannot be encompassed, cannot be known.[56] Saadia's idea of fusion goes back to Aristotle's doctrine in his *Metaph.*, XII, 7: "for it [i.e., thought] becomes an object of thought in coming into contact with and thinking its objects, so that thought and object of thought are the same;" but it is also the next step in Zeno's theory, namely the integration of the comprehension with the mind in which it becomes firmly rooted so that no arguments can remove it. Thus Cicero further reports in his *Academica*: *et si ita erat comprensum ut convelli ratione non posset, scientiam, sin aliter inscientiam, nonminabat, ex qua consisteret etiam opinio quae esset imbecilla et cuma falso incognitoque communis.* It is what Zeno meant by his last gesture when after he had opened his palm and called it "picture," and then partially closed his fingers and called it "assent," and then made a closed fist and called it "comprehension," he closed in the left hand over the right, and, pressing his fist tight, he said "this is science." It is this science that Saadia calls *iʿtiqād*, belief, or really, conviction. Similarly, Maimonides concludes his discussion of belief: "If in addition to this we are convinced that the thing cannot be different in any way from what we believe it to be and the mind can find no argument for the rejection of that belief... then the belief is true."

Thus, as we interpret Saadia, he posits two kinds of belief: the assentive

[56] See *supra*, note 39.

belief, which is an act of will and may be true or false, and the cataleptic or comprehensive belief, which is an act of thought and is true. Both apply to subjects of religion as well as of general science. The criterion of truth is the mind: Saadia trusted in careful and patient thinking for the attainment of truth.[57]

The problem of the meaning of belief recurred in Jewish thought. Maimonides, accompanied by Narboni, entirely followed Saadia. Crescas, who in his *Or Adonai* (Vienna, 1868), 49 opposed the idea that the will plays a role in belief and that belief can be true or false, really denied assentive belief. Albo in his *ʿIqqarim*, I, 19, and Abrabanel in his commentary on *Moreh Nebukim*, I, 50, both of them insisting that belief is an acceptance of a transmitted religious doctrine on the basis of its prophetic or miraculous origin, discarded completely the rationalistic view of Saadia and Maimonides. If we may anticipate a distinction, which we shall make later, between *'amānāt* and *ʿiʿtiqādāt*, they affirmed the former and denied the latter.

IV. TRADITION

10. Saadia took over the idea of tradition as a source of knowledge, from the Mutakallimūn. But the latter did not originate it. It came to them from the Syrians; for Paula Persa in his *Logica* says: "Knowledge, either a man seeks and finds, or it is acquired by instruction. Instruction is partly transmitted directly from man to man, and partly by men who came with a message, that is, from the angels." The Syrians in turn took it over from the Aristotelian commentators; for, as J. P. N. Land shows, from the opening words of Aristotle's *Posterior Analytics*: "all doctrine and all intellectual discipline arise from pre-existent knowledge,"[a] Alexander of Aphrodisias inferred the authority of tradition.[58]

11. This source is necessary in addition to sensation and reason. "I have heard," says Saadia in *Em.*, III, 109, "that there are men who say

[57] See also *Em.*, introd., 41: כי התלמידים כשהם משלימים הלימוד לא תהיה ביניהם מחלוקת ולא ערבוב and *Tafsīr Iyob*, 40: אן ללעקל פעלא צחיחא כפעל אלנטׄר ואלסמע ואלשם וסאיר אלחואס. *Em.*, introd., 49: והודיענו כי כאשר נעיין ונחקור יצא לנו הברור השלם בכל שער כאשר הודיענו על יד נביאו.

[58] J. P. N. Land, *Anecdota Syriaca*, IV (Leyden, 1862–1875), 104. Paula Persa's *Logica*, in Land's edition, p. 2. See also the Syriac passage.

According to Pyrrho, all rational knowledge is only a matter of tradition and habit (see Zeller, *Stoics*, 523); but this is hardly a link in the history of tradition as an additional source of knowledge.

there is no need of prophets and apostles and our minds themselves can guide us to a knowledge of right and wrong." He does not specify here who these men are, but elsewhere he refers to the Brahmans as maintaining that view.[59] Saadia however argues that not all that is necessary for man's salvation is implanted in the human mind, that unaided reason cannot determine the precise way of observing even the rational laws. The mind decrees gratitude to God and the "messengers" teach us the formula and its seasons. The mind abhors adultery and the prophets define it. The mind rejects stealing, but when does acquisition end and stealing begin? The prophets standardize it. If we were left to ourselves, there would be confusion and disagreement.[60] Tradition is needed not only in the realm of action but also in that of knowledge. Philosophy, though capable of unfolding the truth, takes time. Some cannot attain results in their thinking because of some defect, some may become wearied in the process, and some may be confused by doubts. Hence the need *in the interim* for prophets and apostles, without our relinquishing the slow process of thought.[61] Saadia does not state like Halevi that religion goes further in its discovery of divine truth than philosophy. According to him, wherever religion asserts, reason can prove.[62] This does not contradict his admission of the limitation of philosophy, noted in §8, for to prove the existence of a thing does not necessarily mean to understand its essence or causes. Logically then, though not ontologically nor etiologically, there is no superrational margin in religion, and Halevi's conflict between faith and reason does not exist for Saadia. See also §§13, 14.

12. The validity of tradition is sanctioned by the three other sources. Sensation authorized the beginning of tradition, which was accompanied by overwhelming miracles. These were of two kinds: violation of natural laws and transformation of substances. The transformation was always pre-announced to avoid loss of confidence in things.[63] Intuition dictates,

59 *Em.*, III, 109: ושמעתי כי יש אנשים שאומרים כי אין לב״א צורך לנביאים ושכליהם מספיקים להם להישירם במה שיש בהם מן הטוב ומן הרע. *Tafsīr Mishlei*, 179: ליס כמא יקול בעץ̇ אלתארכין אנה לא חאגה̈ ללכ̇לק אלי רסול והם אלבראהמה̈ ומן יקול אלד̇לך. *Em.*, III, 121: אם יאמרו לכם הברהמיים אנחנו קבלנו מאדם הראשון... ואין לכם לקבל דברי נביא.

60 *Em.*, III, 109–10, and references in note 59, *supra*.

61 *Em.*, introd., 51.

62 *Vide supra*, note 57.

63 *Em.*, introd., 44, 51; III, 110, 113.

as we have seen, the three principles, the "universal necessities of thought," which underlie the rational laws, and also a fourth principle, the admissibility that God imposes duties upon man in order to reward him, which accounts for the non-rational laws.[64] And "necessity" finds causes and benefits for these laws.[65] Reason approves not only the particular contents of tradition, but also tradition per se, in sacred as well as secular realms; for without it, man would lose much guidance in commerce, crafts, and conduct, the king's laws would be disobeyed except by those who hear their proclamation, ancestral inheritance would be questioned, and parenthood itself—a matter of doubt.[66] Saadia's statement: "God made room in the minds for the reception of faithful tradition and a place in the souls where it may rest, in order that His books and traditions may be known to later generations," and the nature of the illustrations, seem to show that the assent to tradition is meant to belong to the second class of knowledge, to be intuitive rather than reasoned, though discursive reason too approves the contents of tradition. This is in keeping with the general Jewish and Arabic view, which, as we have seen, goes back to Alexander of Aphrodisias, that the *mexubalot* or traditions require no proof. To be sure, Saadia recognized the possibility of error in tradition, as he did in the other three sources of knowledge. By mistake or intention a false tradition may come into being. But this is impossible when a tradition originates in a mass of people in which mistake and fraud cannot escape detection.[67]

13. We have seen that the three sources of knowledge affirm the fourth; is it also true that the fourth affirms the first three? Does religion reciprocate the assent given by reason? Saadia's answer is on the affirmative side. The Bible posits the authority of sensation, intuition, and inferential reason, so that whatever contradicts them is false.[68] It com-

64 *Em.*, III, 106.

65 *Em.*, III, 107–08.

66 *Em.*, III, 114.

67 *Ibid.* See also *Em.*, introd., 50, 51. In *Em.*, introd., 52; III, 117, Saadia maintains that we must believe also in a pre-Mosaic revelation, and that the Torah of Moses is fuller than that of Abraham. Similarly Shahrastani, *Kitab al-Milal wal-hiḥal,* ed. Cureton, 163: وهم امة موسى وكتابهم التورية وهو اول كتاب نزل من السماء اعنى ان ما كان نزل على ابراهيم وغيره من الانبياء ما كان يسمى كتاباً بل صحفاً. See Neumark, *Toledot ha-Pilosofiah be-Israel,* I (Warsaw, 1921), 121.

68 *Em.*, introd., 44; IX, 189.

mands us to engage in philosophy and investigation within the sphere where solutions of problems are possible.[69] Within these limits, the sages never meant to discourage thought. They only cautioned against putting aside the prophetic teachings and relying upon the mind to attain the truth; for we may never attain it and, at any rate, in the meantime, we will live in error.[70] Hence, whenever a Biblical passage seems in its literal sense to run counter to reason or tradition, it must be interpreted and harmonized therewith. "I will lay down a rule that wherever a statement occurs in the Scriptures, describing God and His deeds, which... contradicts what true reason affirms, there is no doubt that it is a figure of speech." "Whatever is in the Scriptures must be taken literally except where it contradicts sensation, reason, other passages of the Bible, or tradition; in such cases there is reward for a harmonizing interpretation." Hence all passages that are anthropomorphic or deterministic must be interpreted. But there are limits to this privilege and duty to interpret. To explain away commandments is to be a false prophet; to abandon the literal meaning where the doctrine of creation is involved is to be a heretic; to regard resurrection as symbolic is ultimately to take the story of creation and miracles and the traditional commandments as symbolic and thus to leave the Jewish fold.[71] These are beyond the limits of *ta'wīl* (Heb. *sebara*) and, to Saadia, they are not contradictory to reason.

14. The title of Saadia's main philosophical work, *Al-'Amānāt w'al-'I'tiḳādāt*, has been usually rendered by "Faith and Reason," implying a conflict between them which the book is to reconcile. Malter, in his *Life and Works of Saadia Gaon*, 193, renders it by the "Book of Philosophic Doctrines and Religious Beliefs," which does not differ from the usual translation, except for unaccountably making faith and reason change places. Neumark, in the *Hebrew Union College Annual*, I, 523, rightly disapproves of this rendering, because **אעתקאד** "is used for the designation of religious beliefs, dogmas [so Halevi, Maimuni and

69 *Em.*, introd., 49, 51. *Tafsīr Mishlei*, 9: ואלת̇אלת̇ אקאמה̈ שי ט̇הר ללעקל מקאם שי ט̇הר ללטבע. *Ibid.*, 11: פלמא עזל אלחכים הד̇ה נאהיה̈ אלתפת חינד̇ אלי טאלב אלחכמה̈ פקאל לה ולכן סל עמא בעד הד̇ה אלחכמה̈ ממא אמרך רבך.

70 S. Y., 6: והד̇א קול צחיח לכן עבארתה ליס כמא יט̇ן אלמתוהם אנהם מנעוא מן אלנט̇ר פי אלמחדת̇את איהא בדי בה לכני אקול אנהם מנעוא מן ד̇לך לילא יתכטא אלי אמור אלבארי תבארך ותע׳. See also S. Y., 1; *Em.*, introd., 49.

71 *Em.*, II, 90, 96; V, 147; VII, 165, 170; IX, 189; and *Tafsīr Mishlei*, 7.

others]."[72] His own view is that אעתקאד designates preferably the faith of the speaker and that the title means therefore the philosophic and religious views of Israel and the philosophic and religious views of other peoples with whom Israel, or Saadia, is in conflict. But Neumark, too, overlooked the important passage in the introduction from which the title was taken.

What brought me to this [i.e., the writing of the book] is that I have observed many men in their *'amānāt* and *'iʿtiḳādāt*, some of them have arrived at the truth and know it and rejoice with it... and some arrived at the truth but do not verify it nor uphold it... and some have verified the absurd which they think is the truth and uphold the false and abandon the straight... and some occupy themselves with a certain opinion for some time and then reject it... then they betake themselves to another opinion and again despise it.... My heart pained for my own kind, and my soul was stirred for our people, the children of Israel, because I have observed in my time many believers whose *'imān* is not pure and whose *'iʿtiḳād* [i.e., their assent] is incorrect.

Here we see that both *'amānāt* and *'iʿtiḳādāt* refer to the same people, men in general, and Israel in particular, and also that no distinction is to be made on the basis of true and false, for Saadia complains that he has found them both incorrect or unsubstantiated, requiring correction or a firm rational basis. It is for these people that he wrote his book, giving the right dogmas (*'amānāt* means primarily faith and trust, and hence the acceptance of an idea on faith or divine authority) with such rational substantiation that they may become cataleptic beliefs or convictions.[73] "Dogmas and Convictions" —this is how we should render *'Al-'Amānāt w'al-'Iʿtiḳādāt*. That this is the correct meaning of the terms is further proven by the following expression in Saadia's chapter on Resurrection, as published by Bacher in the Steinschneider-*Festschrift*

72 For אעתקאד in non-religious matters, see *Em.*, 19: ודאך כאלדין אעתקדוא מן אלמג̈רה̈ למא ישאהדון מן ביאצ̇הא כאן עליה מדאר פלך אלשמס קדימא and all through that passage. See also *Em.*, introd., 45: כל אשר יפול חושנו האמתי... ראו שנדע (נעתקד) שהוא הוא באמת כאשר השגנוהו.

73 *Em.*, introd., 39: וישוב המאמין בקבלה להאמין בעיון ובהבנה. *Am.*, 6: וצאר אלמומן תקלידא יומן נט̇רא ופהמא. Similarly Baḥya in *Hobot ha-Lebabot* introd. (Vienna, 1856), 13: ותהיה כנשים וקטנים אשר הוא בידיהם דרך קבלה. אבל אם אתה איש דעת ותבונה שתוכל לעמוד בהם על ברור מה שקבלת מן החכמים בשם הנביאים... אתה מצווה להשתמש בהם עד שתעמוד על הענין ויתברר לך מדרך הקבלה והשכל יחד. See also *ibid.*, pp. 12, 15, and *Ruaḥ Ḥen*, ch. 6: ועם כל זה אין ראוי לאדם להתעצל מלחקור כל זה בשכלו עד הגיעו אל אמתתם עם האמינו ג״כ בקבלה האמתית עד שיהיו נודעות אצלו מצד המופת ומצד הקבלה.

(Heb. p. 101), where after refuting objections from natural laws to the doctrine of resurrection, he says: וקר אעתקאדי הדה אלאמאנה̈, which is meaningless on the basis of Neumark's differentiation and can only mean "and my *conviction* of this dogma has become established." It is in this sense that Maimonides, also, used the term אעתקאד in the introduction to the *Moreh* וחצל פי אעתקאדה צחה̈ שריעתנא.... ובאטנהא חכמה̈ ועלתה מפידה̈ פי אעתקאדאת אלחק עלי חקיקתה (ed. Munk-Joel, pp. 2, 8). Heb. בהאמנתי אמתת תורתנו.... ותוכה חכמה מועלת בהאמנת האמת על אמתתו.

Interesting as a support for the distinction between the terms *ʿamānāt* and *iʿtiqādāt* is the way Yehudah Halevi uses these two terms in his *Kuzari*. When the king of the Khazars speaks to the philosopher and when the philosopher himself speaks about religion they use the term *iʿtiqād*, that is, rational faith. However, when the king despairs of receiving spiritual satisfaction from the philosopher and from Christian and Arab sages, he turns to the Rabbi with the question: What is your *iʿtiqād*? But the Rabbi speaks about *īmān*. Furthermore, when Halevi speaks about rational religion or the thinking of the Mutakallimūn, he returns to the term *iʿtiqād*. See *Kuzari*, ed. Hirschfeld (Leipzig, 1887), I, 13, p. 17; II, 81, 139; V, 1, 296; V, 19, 337; V, 20, 337.

The passage from Saadia's introduction also clearly reveals the purpose of Saadia to be different from that of the author of the *Guide*. Maimonides' aim was definitely a reconciliation between faith and philosophy. Saadia, who had not yet felt the full impact of Aristotelianism on religion, saw in philosophy a support and stabilizer for religion, which the people for whom he wrote the book, who either had unclear religious doctrines or were vacillating because of a *lack* of verification and rational firmness, needed. There was no conflict then between knowledge and religion; they were both, Saadia said, man's ornament in both worlds.[74]

15. The question however arises: Is there any difference in priority between tradition and reason? We have seen that where the Bible conflicts with reason it must be interpreted; but this does not answer our question, for in those cases, Saadia would say, the interpretation gives us the only intended meaning. But contrary to Malter's idea that Saadia regarded reason as secondary and religion primary—an idea that Neumark op-

[74] *Tafsīr Mishlei*, 16: אלעלם ואלדין ג̇מיעא המה זין אלאנסאן פי אלדארין ג̇מיעא כמא יתזון באללוא ואלעקוד.

posed without giving full evidence[75]—it can be shown that the reverse is true.

Among the kinds of priority discussed by Aristotle in *Categories*, 12; *Metaph.*, IV, 11, and by Maimonides in *Millot Higgayon*, 12, there are three that pertain to our discussion: time, nature and substance, and rank. The first and the last kinds are clear. As to nature and substance, Aristotle defines it as the quality of "those which can be without other things, while the others cannot be without them." Now it can be shown that Saadia regarded reason as prior in all these three senses. He maintains that there is no value in the observation of the traditional laws unless they have been preceeded by the observation of the rational laws, namely justice and fairness, which constitute the entrance of the *isagoge* of religion.[76] This is perhaps only temporal priority, though Yehudah Halevi, in *Kuzari*, II, 48, who took this view over from Saadia, called it a priority both of nature and time. Nothing but temporal priority is meant also in *Em.*, III, 122, and *Tafsīr Bereshit*, 3, where Saadia states that the Torah is not the only source for our laws and beliefs but that there are two other sources: reason before it and tradition after it. But Saadia also explicitly gave reason priority in the sense of substance. In *Em.*, VII, 163, he states that he examined four sources of knowledge: nature (i.e., sense-perception), reason, Scriptures, and tradition, to see whether there is any refutation to the dogma of resurrection, and that he "began with nature because its priority is that of substance." Thus, in an arrangement according to substance, that is, epistemological indispensability, reason is prior to the Bible. Similarly in *Em.*, IV, 128, he states that he has proofs for the doctrine of the freedom of will from perception, reason, Scriptures, and tradition, and he proceeds to discuss them in that order. In *Em.*, V, 147, and again in *Em.*, VII, 165, he gives the same order; whereas the order in *Em.*, VII, 171: "Scriptures, reason and tradition," can only be accidental. Of particular significance is the

75 Malter, *Life and Works of Saadia Gaon*, 175, and Neumark, *Toledot ha-Pilosofiah be-Israel*, I, 524.

76 *Tafsīr Mishlei*, 140: ואלאנאמה̈ תסמי אלמדכ̇ל אלי כל עלם מן מנטק ונג̇ום והנדסה̈ וטב איסאגוגי. פאן סבק אלמתעלם באלכתאב בעינה קבל אלמדכ̇ל אליה לם יפהמה. וכד̇־ לך ללטאעאת מבאדי הי מפאתיח להא לא ינתפע אלעבד בבעצ̇הא דון בעץ̇ ושרח ד̇לך אן אלשראיע אלסמעיה̈... לא ינפע אלתמסך בהא דון אן יקדם קבלהא אלשראיע אלעקל אלחק ואלעדל ואלאנצאף. Similarly *ibid.*, 180: פקד וג̇ב אן תתקדם אלשראיע אלכ̇בריה̈ אלשראיע אלמנטקיה̈ אלעדל אלחק ואלאנצאף.

statement in *Tafsīr Mishlei* where he gives the order of the sources of knowledge as **כ̇מסה̈ אצול אלחכמה̈ והי אלשאהד ואלעקל ואלמכתוב ואלמנקול ואלאסתנבאט** and adds that the author of the book of Proverbs should have followed this order, but he began instead with tradition "in order to make it dear to us and because it embraces the other four sources."[77] Here we see Saadia explicitly stating what should be the order of the sources of knowledge, no doubt, as we have seen, according to priority of nature and substance. Now what are these sources? Horovitz, in his *Psychologie Saadias*, 48, note 90; 51, note 94, identifies them with the four sources of the introduction of the *Emunot* except for the division of tradition into the Bible and oral tradition. This is incorrect for the following reasons. First, if *'istinbāṭ* means here necessary inference or deduction, its place after the Bible and tradition does not conform to the order established in the previous quotations. Second, *'aql* here cannot mean here the Nous or immediate knowledge, for Saadia designates it also as **עלם אלתמייז** which is, as we have seen, the faculty of discernment.[78] It must therefore mean here, as in all the previous statements of the order of the sources of knowledge, thought in general, immediate and mediate. This is another reason why *'istinbāṭ*, the fifth source, cannot mean here inference without duplicating the second source. What then does *'istinbāṭ* mean here? Elsewhere[79] Saadia does use this term in the

77 *Tafsīr Mishlei*, 126–27: כ̇מסה̈ אצול אלחכמה̈ והי אלשאהד ואלעקל ואלמכתוב ואלמנקול ואלאסתנבאט... אבתדי מן אלכ̇מס מעארף בעלם אלנקל אלד̇י ינקלה אלעלמא טבקה̈ בעד טבקה̈ גיר מכתוב ולא אלעקל ידל עליה ולא ימנעה... ת̇ם עלם אלחואס... ת̇ם עלם אלתמייז אלד̇י ראסה ומקדמה ואשרפה אלמערפה̈ באללה אד̇ ליס ימכן אן יחס בחאסה̈ קאל פיה להיות בה׳ מבטחך... ת̇ם עלם אלמכתוב... ת̇ם עלם אלתחריר אלד̇י הו מולף מן תלך אלארבע מעארף קאל פיה להודיעך קשט לאן אלחגה̈ פיה תט̇הר ופיה יקע אלאסתנבאט יכ̇תאר אלמחתג̇ אצלח אלטרק ללכלאם לילא יאכ̇ד̇ טריקא תכ̇רגה אלי אלטען ליס אנה יבדע מד̇הבא בל אנמא יבדע מא יחוט בה אלמד̇הב אלחק. ועלי מא נקדרה קד כאן אלאולי אן ירתב הד̇ה אלכ̇מסה̈ פנון עלי מא צדרנא אן יכון אלשאהד אולא ת̇ם אלמעקול ת̇ם אלמכתוב ת̇ם אלמנקול ת̇ם אלחגה̈ לכן ליעט̇ם ענדנא מא נקלה אלצאדקון רתבה אולא ואיצ̇א לאן אלארבעה̈ יג̇מעהא אלנקל אלצחיח.

78 *Vide supra*, notes 36, 37, and *Tafsīr Mishlei*, 96, 160; *Em.*, X, 199: התאוה והכעס וההכרה (ואלתמייז). Horovitz's inference that Saadia regarded the idea of God as immediate knowledge is correct but not because it is subsumed, in the passage quoted in note 77, under עקל which, as it is identified with תמייז, can only mean reason in general, but because it is the beginning of תמייז, one of the *principia* of knowledge. See also quotation from *Tafsīr Mishlei*, 14 in note 12, above.

79 See note 36, above, and *Tafsīr Mishlei*, 141: ואקסאם אלעלום אלאסתנבאט ואלתחפט̇ ואלתעלם.

sense of inference, but here he designates it himself as *taḥrīr* (he also calls the Talmud *taḥrīr* in distinction from the Mishnah, which is *fiqh*), that is, an accurate study of a text,[80] leading, as he himself states, not to new ideas but to new ways of grasping the true idea. Perhaps he had in mind *qiyās*, maintaining like the Zahirites that the conclusion is not an innovation but is included (*mafhum*) in the text.[81] The term *'istinbāṭ* too is used by Arabs as an elucidation of a particular Koranic text by the "verbal resources" obtained from the reading of the whole text.[82] The place therefore of *'istinbāṭ* or *taḥrīr* is therefore logically after the Bible and tradition which it uses as its text. Thus we see that in this passage, also, where the author emphasizes what he thinks is the order of the sources of knowledge, sensation and reason come prior to the Scriptures.

But reason is prior also in the third sense, that of rank and excellence. Hence in *Em*,, introd., 51, Saadia asks why faith if philosophy leads to the truth, and answers, as we have seen, that faith is necessary in the interim. This is also the position of Baḥya in his *Al-Hidāja ʿila Forā'id al-Qulub*, ed. Yahuda, p. 15, and of the author of *Ruaḥ Ḥen*, ch. 6. Bahya, though stating that "tradition is prior by nature because learners need it at first"—**אן אלנקל ואן כאן אקדם באלטבע מן טריק צ̇רורה̈ אלמתעלמי̇ן וחאג̇תהם אליה אולא**—essentially agrees to the "interim-theory" of Saadia. Hence, as we have seen, his purpose in writing the *Emunot we-Deʿot* is to show that he who believes by tradition may begin to believe by reason. Furthermore, with all his emphasis on miracles, Saadia maintains that if a prophet proclaims laws that are repugnant to the mind, even if he attests his utterances by miracles, he must not be obeyed.[83]

80 The term תחריר usually means exact investigation. Thus *Am.*, 281, note 4: עלי אלתחריר (Tibbon: על דרך הדקדוק), *Tafsīr Mishlei*, 51: פחררו מא כאן פיה ממא תוגבה אלעקול, *Kuzari*, I, 62: (T. והדקדוק) אלפלאספה̈ והם מן אלבחת̇ ואלתחריר, *Moreh*, II, 9: פי זמאן ארסטו (T. דוקדק) עדד אלאפלאך לא יתחרר. But Saadia employs the term also in the sense of an accurate study of the words of a text, sometimes for the purpose of substantiating certain views or doctrines. See Saadia's chapter on Resurrection, pub. by Bacher in Steinschneider's *Festschrift*, 110: ובעד מא חררת הד̇ה אלתחריראת (*Em.*, VII, 171: ואחר שדקדקתי אלו הדקדוקים); *Tafsīr Mishlei*, 52: בחוטה̈ אלכתאב ותחרירה וזואידה ונואקצה. Hence it came to mean Talmud in *Tafsīr Mishlei*, 124: מן כמס סמן אלי עשר יראע̇ פי אלקראן ואלי כ̇מס עשרה̈ פי אלפקה ואלי ת̇מאני עשרה̈ פי אלתחריר.

81 See C. Snouck Hurgronje, in *Literatur-Blatt für Oriental. Philologie* (1884), 423.

82 See A. M. Goichon, *Introduction à Avicenne* (Paris, 1933), 37.

83 *Em.*, III, 117.

CONCLUSION

Saadia starts with four sources; but sensation is basic to all, even to axiomatic knowledge which sense-experience helps to bring out in life's complex. As for reason, it is prior to tradition the basic ideas of which we should strive to grasp philosophically, so that our *'amānāt* may become *'iʿtiqādāt*. Unlike Maimonides, he saw no conflict between faith and philosophy; and unlike Yehudah Halevi, he refrained from tearing them asunder and giving to each its own domain.

Fundamentally, then, there are two sources: sense and reason. Between them there is a mutual need. Sense requires mind for its subtilization into concepts; and mind, though it comes equipped with ideas, needs sense-experience for their discovery, that is, for its own self-consciousness. Thus Saadia's theory of knowledge differs from Platonism in its realistic attitude to objects of sensation, and from both Aristotelianism and Stoicism in its thoroughgoing rationalism.

Chapter Three

CREATION

THE ARAB thinkers called Mutakallimūn began their theological systems with proofs that the universe was not without a beginning but was created, and having proved this they naturally inferred the existence of a Creator or God. Maimonides, in his *Moreh Nebukim*, I, 71, opposed this method, "the method of all the Arabian Mutakallimun... and also of those of our own faith who imitated them and walked in their ways," because they allowed such a basic doctrine as the existence of God to depend on a belief in creation that lacks demonstrative proof and is of the nature of an antinomy. He therefore took the road of philosophers and tried to prove the divine existence even on the basis of a world without a beginning. Saadia was one of those "who walked in their ways," and the first treatise in his *Emunot we-Deʿot* is devoted to the thesis of creation.

In conformity with his tendency, in the case of any problem, to muster all views opposed to his own and fell them one by one until his view alone remains, he assembles here thirteen theories concerning the genesis of the universe, a sort of cosmogonic compendium, all of which he strikes down—except the first, which he regards as true. The theories are as follows: (1) *creatio ex nihilo*, (2) pre-existent spirituals, (3) emanations, (4) emanation plus eternals, (5) dualism, (6) four elements, (7) four elements plus a primordial matter, (8) Aristotelianism, (9) chance, (10) eternalism, (11) sophism, (12) denial of knowledge, (13) denial of perception. Saadia also cites cosmogonic views in his commentary on *Sefer Yeṣirah*, but there they are nine and stated in a different order.

Now, it is the second view, namely, that all things were created from eternal spiritual substances, that requires our particular attention. It is generally presented as a composite of atomism and Timaean Platonism, and hence corresponding, in its atomic aspect, to the second cosmogonic theory in Saadia's *Tafsīr* on *Sefer Yeṣirah*.[1] But here, as Malter

[1] See J. Guttmann, *Die Religionsphilosophie des Saadia*, 45, note 2; M. Lambert, *Commentaire sur le Sefer Yesira par le Gaon Saadya de Fayyoum*, 17, note 3; H. Malter,

notes, a difficulty arises. For in the *Tafsīr*, the views are listed in the order of increasing acceptability, whereas here the order is that of decreasing acceptability;[2] so that the view that is here next to the most reasonable ranks there as next to the most repugnant. Malter offers a solution, but there are other difficulties. First, atomism constitutes the ninth view in the *ʿAmānāt*. Second, here a Creator is assumed, whereas in the ninth view atomism dispenses with a deity. Third, it cannot be a presentation of Greek atomism, which maintains that atoms have forms and sizes, nor of the Arabic type according to which atoms are indeed spaceless but continuously created. Fourth, Saadia was too sharply discerning and too fond of piling up arguments and views, for the sake of the mere weight of numbers, to group together two such discrepant views as atomism and Platonism, a combination that is somewhat ironic since Plato was so opposed to Democritus that he refrained from mentioning him and is even said to have wished to burn up the latter's writings.[3]

Neumark,[4] without going into the details of the text, states that the view follows the *Timaeus*, where, he says, Plato describes the genesis of the world as moving from the point to the line, from the line to the plane, and from the plane to the various polyhedrons from which God created all spheres. This theory Saadia, or his sources, fitted into Plato's theory of Ideas, which resulted in a combination of atomism and Platonism, the Ideas being the spiritual atoms, the mathematical points, from which corporeal existence developed. But where did Neumark find in the *Timaeus* that the world came from points? Quite the contrary is true, as we shall soon see. His reference to "mathematical points" is correct; but evidently he uses this as a general phrase for atoms, or perhaps, together with Guttmann with whom he agrees as to source,[5] for the ὕλη. Had he felt the technical implication of that phrase he might have been led to a different source for the second view.

We shall try to show that this second cosmogonic view is basically Pythagorean with some Platonic modifications, to offer in this light some

---

Life and Works of Saadia Gaon, 203; M. Ventura, *La Philosophie de Saadia Gaon*, 114, 117, note 100.

2 Malter, *Life and Works of Saadia Gaon*. Comp. D. Neumark, *Toledot ha-Pilosofiah be-Israel*, II, 181–91.

3 Thomas L. Heath, *The Thirteen Books of Euclid's Elements*, (Chicago, 1952), I, 38.

4 *Toledot ha-Pilosofiah be-Israel*, II, 120, 154.

5 *Ibid.*, 503.

exegetical comments on the text, and hence to identify this view with the eighth in the *Tafsīr*.

1. In *Metaph.*, 986a1, Aristotle states that, according to the Pythagoreans, the elements of numbers are the elements of all things; and in *Metaph.*, 987a19, that number is the substance of all things (see also 1080b18). The basis for this arithmetical conception of the world' is the correspondence of the geometrical point to number *one*, as is shown by the Pythagorean definition of a point μονὰς θέσιν ἔχουσα, a unit having position.[6] The implication that the point has minimum volume was combated by Parmenides and Zeno, so that Plato, came to regard the geometrical point as a "geometrical fiction", and to speak of "indivisible lines"[7] which, according to A. E. Taylor,[8] means infinitely divisible lines; for a line is a continuum and will always break up into lines, never into points. He defined the point merely as the "beginning of a line," that is, zero, and assigned the role of indivisible magnitude and the primary real of all things to the plane.[9] Aristotle, like Plato, and like Euclid in his second definition of a line, takes the point as "the boundary of a line,"[10] and regards the line as essentially linear and hence does not consist of points but always of lines.[11] The Arab neo-Pythagoreans, the *Ikhwān al-Ṣafā*, blended these two distinct views, defining the point together with Plato as the beginning of a line, that is, as non-magnitudinal, and at the same time, together with Pythagoras, as equivalent to the arithmetical *one*.[12] Among Jewish thinkers, we find the Platonic-Aristo-

6 See Arist., *Metaph.*, 1080b20, 32. See also John Burnet, *Early Greek Philosophy* (London, 1920), 290; A. E. Taylor, *Plato* (New York, 1936), 505. Similarly Shahrastani, *Kitab al-Milal wal-Niḥal*, ed. Cureton (London, 1846, reprint, Leipzig, 1923), 270: ואוקע אלנקטה̈ פי מקאבלה̈ אלואחד ואלכ̇ט פי מקאבלה אלאת̇נין ואלסטח פי מקאבלה̈ אלת̇לת̇ה̈ ואלג̇סם פי מקאבלה̈ אלארבעה̈. In *Fons Vitae*, II, 22, the equation is: point = 1, plane = 4, solid = 8, thus following the *Ikhwān al-Ṣafā*. See Dieterici, "Zahl und Maass nach den Arabischen Philosophen," *Zeitschrift der morgenlandischen Gesellschaft*, 18 (1864), 694.

7 Arist., *Metaph.*, 992a20.

8 *Plato*, 506.

9 Arist., *De Gen. et Corr.*, 316a30; *De Coelo*, 298b35. See also Heath, *The Thirteen Books of Euclid's Elements*, 156.

10 *Topics*, 141b20, 21.

11 *Physics*, 231a24–26, 231b15–16; *Metaph.*, 1016b26.

12 Dieterici, *Ikhwan Es-Safâ* (Leipzig, 1803–1886), 292: אלנקטה̈ אלתי הי ראס אלכ̇ט̈ ואנהא פי צנאעה̈ אלהנדסה̈ מת̇ל אלואחד אלד̇י קבל אלאת̇נין פי צנאעה̈ אלעדד. But entirely in a Platonic manner on p. 591: פראס אלכ̇ט̈ יסמ̈י נקטה̈ וליס הו בג̇ז מן אלכ̇ט̈.

telian view dominant, but Gabirol, Abraham ibn Ezra, and Albo follow Pythagoras.[13]

There was another controversy, as to whether number is immanent or transcendent. According to Aristotle, the Pythagoreans "supposed real things to be numbers—not separable numbers, however, but numbers of which real things consist"; whereas the Platonists, "who make number separable assume that it both exists and is separable... and similarly with the spatial magnitudes of mathematics."[14] Here too the Platonic contention was grafted upon its opponent. Shahrastani presents Pythagoreanism as maintaining that number, the principle of all things, is the first-created;[15] Averroes is presented as maintaining that the objects of mathematics are bodiless substances and that points are substances like *universalia*;[16] and according to Isaac b. Shem-Tob,[17] both the Pythagoreans and the Platonists regarded number and magnitude as separable.

One other issue. To the Pythagoreans, the reality of number is the reality of the points residing in, and constituting the essence of, things. Plato however introduced a hierarchy in Being, and distinguished the "mathematicals" (τὰ μαθηματικά) from number or Forms, giving them "an intermediate grade, differing from sensible things in being eternal

[13] The following references show the Platonic-Aristotelian view והנקודה היא קצת הקו (ספר היסודות לר׳ יצחק הישראלי 45), ותהיה הנקודה בגדר הזה תכלית הקו או המחיצה אשר בין שני קוים נדבקים זה אל זה (המשיחה והתשבורת לר׳ אברהם בר׳ חייא, א, ג), והמתדבק הוא אשר אפשר שיונח בו חלק יחלקהו ויהיה משותף לשני המתחלקים (אמונה רמה לר׳ אברהם אבן דאוד 5), הפילוסופים לא יאמינו שהקו מורכב מנקודות (עץ חיים לאהרן בן אליה, פרק ד), דע כי הנקודה... היא תכלית הקו וקצהו ואינה חלק ממנו כמו שחשבו הטפשים באמרם שהקו הוא מחובר מנקודות (יסוד עולם לר׳ יצחק ישראלי 4, 3) שא״א בנקודה שתשאר הקו ושיתחדש ממנה על צד ההתדבקות חלק אחר חלק... שהנקודה כל מה שתכפול לא תצא מגדר הנקודה כי לא יתחדש ממנה כ״א דבר בלתי מתחלק (מלחמות השם הוצ׳ לייפציג, 345, והשוה ספר היסודות 48, 47, 45), והקו לו שני תכליות גודרות מהם וכל אחת מהם היא נקודה (ראשית חכמה לרש״ט פלקירא 43). For the Pythagorean view, see Gabirol, *Fons Vitae* II, 22: *Numerus resoluitur in unitates, et quantitas quae subsistet in substantia resolvitur in puncta, et puncta sunt unitates quae scilicet sustinentur in materia quae est substantia*; Abraham ibn Ezra on Ex. 26, 6. כי כל גוף אינו דבר אחד רק הוא מחובר מאחדים וככה השם הנכבד שהוא אחד כולל הכל ונקרא אחד and Albo, *I'qqarim* ch. 10 והיותר אמתי ממנו בשם האחד הנקודה שלא תחלק לא בפועל ולא במחשבה... אלא שהיא בעלת מצב.

[14] *Metaph.*, 1090a20–35; 1090b5. See also 987b25–28. Comp. however Gomperz, *Greek Thinkers*, I, 104.

[15] Shahrastani, *Kitab al-Milal wal-Nihal*, 267.

[16] Horten, *Die Metaphysik des Averroes*, 44, 45, 49, 121.

[17] Quoted by Wolfson, *Crescas*, 395.

and unchangeable, from Forms in being many alike while the Form itself is in each case unique" (Arist. *Metaph.* 987b12). These mathematicals are taken by Taylor[18] to be geometrical notions, that is, not points, which are a "geometrical fiction" to Plato, but lines, planes, and solids. And again a fusion took place, and this separation of number from geometrical notions as two distinct transcendent beings, or even in some hierarchical form, was ascribed to the Pythagoreans. Thus Shahrastani,[19] in his exposition of Pythagoreanism, counts geometrical relations together with numbers and letters as elements of things; and Alexander Polyhistor epitomizes the Pythagorean view as a causal hierarchy: From numbers—points, from points—lines, from lines—planes, from planes,—solids and then the four elements.[20]

Thus two distinct and opposing trends were blended under the name of Pythagoreanism, assuming points as non-magnitudinal, transcendent, and corresponding to, yet apart from, numbers. According to Plato, numbers and the "mathematicals"—except the fictitious points—are eternal, whereas in the Pythagorean view, presented by Shahrastani and Alexander Polyhistor, both numbers and points are created. We are now ready for the exegesis.

2. "The second view," Saadia says, "is that the Creator of bodies has with Him eternal spiritual things from which He created these composite bodies." From the sequel we learn that among these eternal spirituals are points: consequently the others must be numbers and letters, which Pythagoras, according to Shahrastani, included among the elements.[21] All these are spiritual in the sense of incorporeal. The assumption of points is un-Platonic, that of transcendence and, as in Saadia's polemic, of unspatiality is un-Pythagorean; yet it all passed, as we have seen, under the name of Pythagoreanism. One might take the spirituals as signifying mind, soul, and *hyle*, all of which the *Ikhwān al-Ṣafā* call

18 *Plato,* 514. Cf. J. Burnet, *Greek Philosophy,* I, 314–18.

19 *Kitab al-Milal wal-Nihal,* 269.

20 Diogenes Laertius, VIII, 25: Ἀρχὴν μὲν ἁπάντων μονάδα. ἐκ δὲ τῆς μονάδος ἀόριστον δυάδα ὡς ἂν ὕλην τῇ μονάδι αἰτίῳ ὄντι ὑποστῆναι. ἐκ δὲ τῆς μονάδος καὶ τῆς ἀορίστου δυάδος τοὺς ἀριθμούς. ἐκ δὲ τῶν ἀριθμῶν τὰ σημεῖα. ἐκ δὲ τούτων τὰς γραμμάς, ἐξ ὧν τὰ ἐπίπεδα σχήματα. ἐκ δὲ τῶν ἐπιπέδων τὰ στερεὰ σχήματα. ἐκ δὲ τούτων τὰ αἰσθητὰ σώματα, ὧν καὶ τὰ στοιχεῖα εἶναι τέτταρα. Comp. Arist., *Metaph.,* 1080b20.

21 *Kitab al-Milal wal-Nihal,* 269.

spiritual,[22] or the *substantiae spirituales* of Gabirol in *Fons Vitae*, II, 24, *quae sunt natura et tres animae et intelligentia.* Such an interpretation would not differ essentially, for Pythagoras, according to Shahrastani, accepted mind, soul, nature, and *hyle*, corresponding, though not number but only numbered (מעדוד > עדד), to the first four elemental numbers.[23] Still, numbers and letters are more analogous to points; and we shall see that, like Shahrastani, Saadia himself in the *Tafsīr* and also Gabirol in *Fons Vitae* group together these three elements. The *Ikhwān al-Ṣafā* speak of points, as well as of lines and planes, as עקלי̈ and והמי̈,[24] which terms are epistemological equivalents of the metaphysical "spiritual."

"The adherents of this view," Saadia continues, "imagine that the Creator assembled from amongst them [i.e., from amongst the spirituals] tiny points which are the indivisible parts." These are not atoms for reasons given above, but geometrical points that Euclid and Aristotle defined as indivisible.[25] Gabirol, in *Fons Vitae*, II, 16, cautions against confusing the point with the atom, the former being a part of the body only *accidentaliter*, *nec naturaliter*, *nec essentialiter*, whereas the latter is part of the body's essence. Isaac Israeli too, in *Sefer Yesodot*, 43, differentiates between them; although, at first blush, the opposite seems to be true. He states that an opponent of his Empedoclean theory of elements might cite "the sage Democritus" who said that "body is

[22] Dieterici, *Ikhwān*, 3: אלעקל הו גוהר רוחני... ואלנפס גוהר רוחאניה̈ פאצ̇ת מן אלעקל... ואלהיולי אלאול גוהר רוחאניה̈ פאצ̇ת מן אלנפס. See also Palqera's *Ha-mebakkesh*, 107: כדי שיהיו הדברים הטבעיים נאותים לדברים הרוחניים כי הדברים שאינם גופיים הם של ארבע מדרגות השם יתברך ותחתיו השכל הכללי הפועל ותחתיו הנפש הכללית הגלגלית ותחתיה החומר הראשון ואלו אינם גופים. Shahrastani, *Kitab al-Milal wal-Nihal*, 268–69, in his presentation of Pythagoreanism speaks of mind, soul, and nature as elements embodying numbers 2, 3, 4, respectively, and also of the *hyle* as אלואחד אלמסתפאד. The *Ikhwān* however (see Dieterici in *Zeitschrift der morgenländischen Gesellschaft*, XVIII, 693, cited *supra* note 6) make the *hyle* correspond to 4, and are followed by Palqera, *Ha-mebaqqesh*, 105.

[23] See *supra*, note 22.

[24] Dieterici, *Ikhwān*, 293–94. הנדסה̈ עקליה̈ וחסיה̈... ולסנא נקול אן הד̇ה אלנקטה̈ הי שי לא גזء לה לכן אלנקטה̈ אלעקליה̈ הי אלתי לא גזء להא. See also *Kitāb Ikhwān al-Ṣafa*, redacted by Ahmad ibn ʿAbd Allah (Bombay, 1887), I, 53–54, where mention is made of הנדסה̈ עקליה̈, כט̇ עקלי̈, כ̇טח עקלי̈, נקטה̈ עקליה̈, כט̇ והמי̈, סטח והמי̈, גסם והמי̈. For the meaning of והם see Goichon, *Lexique de la langue philosophique d'ibn Sīnā*, 442. See also Dieterici in *Zeitschrift der morgenländischen Gesellschaft*, cited *supra*, note 6.

[25] Arist., *Metaph.*, 1016b26.

composed of planes, planes are composed of lines, and lines of points," and he might also mention the Muʿtazilite view that "body is composed of atoms, that is, points." It would seem then that Israeli identifies points with atoms; in fact he ascribes the point-theory to the atomist Democritus. But this ascription is erroneous, for Democritus maintained that bodies cannot be composed of points, which are only extremities of lines.[26] That it is the Pythagorean points that Israeli has in mind, and that, far from identifying them with atoms, he really separates them from atoms, is shown by the fact that he first combats the point-theory, and only on p. 49 does he turn to the Muʿtazilite doctrine, and there he raises the question of whether the atoms are spatial—a question that does not occur in his argument against "Democritus." The expression "atoms that is, points" is, therefore, his opponents' contention, not his own. Thus a distinction was made between points and atoms, and we should not confuse them in the interpretation of our text.

"And He made out of them," Saadia continues, "a straight line and then He cut that line into two halves." Here, where scholars note a change of source and the beginning of the parallel to Plato's *Timaeus*, we really discern the unity of design and a coherence with the first part. In *Timaeus*, 36b5, there is no mention of a line but of a fabric woven out of the soul-stuff of the Same and the Other. Why does Saadia speak of a line? Because the nature of this creative act is different from that of the *Timaeus*. The Timaean band of soul-stuff is regarded as cosmic matter; whereas Saadia, unlike Plato, begins with the point that can yield only a line, that is, length. The same reason accounts for the next divergence: the Timaean band is split lengthwise; Saadia does not say "lengthwise," for such a division is impossible in a mathematical line.

Then the two halves were fastened, one across the other like the Ar. Lam-Alif or the letter K.[27] This also is found in the *Timaeus*, as well as in the second part of Parmenides' poem, the part that is Pythagorean.[28] But here it has for its additional purpose to generate a plane by the intersection of the lines.

"Then He cut [Ar. קטעהמא Tibbon גזר] them from their point of fastening and He made out of one of them the all-surrounding sphere,

26 See Ingeborg Hammer Jensen, "Demokrit und Platon," *Archiv f. Gesch. der Philosophie,* XXIII (Berlin, 1910), 105.

27 See Guttmann, *Die Religionsphilosophie des Saadia,* 46, note 2.

28 See Burnet, *Early Greek Philosophy,* 187.

and out of the other—the smaller spheres." In the *Timaeus*, the Demiurgus *bent* each band around into a circle. The word "cut," in Saadia text, seems pointless. Tibbon mistook the meaning of the Ar. קטעהמא, which means here "he made them cross" (read perhaps: אקטעהמא). The same expression in a similar context is used in the *Tafsīr*,[29] where it undoubtedly has this meaning.

The *Timaeus* now proceeds to discuss the genesis of diverse subjects until 47E where the discovery of "necessity" in the paradise of reason compels the author to begin his account anew. The notion of space is introduced, and then we are told how God formed the four elements "by giving them a distinct configuration, by mean of shapes and numbers" (53B). Here the number-theory makes its appearance. From half-square triangles there was formed the cube, which is the appropriate form of the earth-corpuscle, and from "half-triangles" there came into being the tetrahedron (fire), the octahedron (air), and the icasohedron (water). The dodecahedron was reserved "for the whole, adorning it with constellations." This is Pythagorean,[30] but it does not begin back enough, not, of course, with the point, which Plato regards as a "geometrical fiction," not even with the line, which he does posit in *Laws*, 894a as an ἀρχή, but with the plane, which is his cosmic unit, thus ignoring the first three cosmogonic steps in the Pythagorean account, summarized, as stated, by Alexander Polyhistor. Saadia's statement about the geometrical construction of the four elements does not constitute a revision or a second account, but flows entirely along Pythagorean lines from his previous statements. According to him, God formed "out of those spiritual parts" (i.e., the points) a conic form, an octahedron, a dodecahedron, an icasohedron and created from these forms fire, earth, air, and water, respectively. The geometrical forms of these elements do not agree entirely with those of *Timaeus*, but the *Ikhwān al-Ṣafā* also had a different arrangement.[31]

29 Lambert, *Commentaire sur le Sefer Yesira par le Gaon Saadyahde Fayyoum*, 83: ודלך אדֿא כֿטּ פי אלהוא׳ כֿטוטא מסתקימהֿ פי דואיר ומתֿלתֿאת ומרבּעאת ורסם כֿטוטא מנערגהֿ פי דואיר ומתֿלתֿאת ומרבעאת גֿא׳ מן אנעטאף בעצֿהא עלי בעץֿ ומקאטעהֿ בעצֿהא בעצֿא אשכאל בסאיט ומגֿסמאת. See also note 33.

30 Taylor, *Plato*, 458 note 1; Burnet, *Early Greek Philosophy*, 292 ff.

31 Dieterici, *Ikhwan*, 439: ואלכֿמסהֿ אלאשכאל אלפאצֿלהֿ אלמדֿכורהֿ פי כתאב אקלידס והי אלשכל אלנארי̈ דֿו אלארבע אלסטוח אלמתֿלּתֿהֿ ואלשכל אלארצֿי̈ דֿו אלסתֿהּ אלסטוח אלמתֿלּתֿהֿ ואלשכל אלמאי̈ דֿו אלתֿמאניהֿ אלסטוח אלמתֿלּתֿהֿ ואלשכל אלהואי̈ דֿו אלעשרין קאעדהֿ מתֿלּתֿהֿ ואלשכל אלפלכי̈ דֿו אתֿני עשר קאעדהֿ מכֿמּסהֿ. This does not

3. Thus the second view is not a composite of atomism and Timaeanism, but Pythagoreanism as it was understood about the time of Saadia. Now what relation does this view bear to any of the views in the *Tafsīr*? Hitherto scholars thought that the doctrine of the *Sefer Yeṣirah* or the eighth view of the *Tafsīr* was disregarded in the *Amānāt*-enumeration of the cosmogonic theories, either because Saadia did not take the *Sefer Yeṣirah*-view seriously (Guttmann), or because he deals here with views that are either positively true or positively wrong but not with those that are just tolerable (Malter), or because he did not reject this view as he did the others (Neumark).[32] But if our interpretation of the second *Amānāt*-view is correct, it becomes identical with the eighth view of the *Tafsīr*, that is, the stand point of the *Sefer Yeṣirah*. They are both Pythagorean. True, in the *Amānāt* the spiritual substances are viewed as eternal, whereas in the *Tafsīr* they are created, but, as Saadia himself states in the seventh view of the *Tafsīr*, the anteriority of numbers and geometrical figures is acceptable if regarded only in a potential sense, objectionable if taken in an actual sense. Hence, in the *Amānāt*, in the list of objectionable cosmogonies, he gives the view with its objectionable Platonic feature, which includes actual anteriority and eternity, whereas in the *Tafsīr*, presenting it as the Abrahamitic view, he carefully specifies that numbers and letters are not to be taken as abstract and separable, but, that is, in the originally Pythagorean conception. The various cosmogonic steps of the *Amānāt* are reproduced in the *Tafsīr* as follows: "He [the adherent of this view] does not posit them [the 10 numbers and the 22 letters] as pure and separated. He maintains that He created the air and deposited there these 32 things. According to him, the air consists of distinct particles which number traverses [so Lambert, Barzillai however: יתחכהו למספר]. And when it moved forward according to straight and oblique lines, it generated figures." In this account, the "air" is a monotheistic adaptation of the Pythagorean-Platonic receptable or χώρα. The distinct particles are the points. Number traverses (or cuts) them, because each point is a numerical *one*. The straight and oblique lines, like the Lam-Alif of the *Amānāt*, make the planes. In another

---

agree, as Dieterici notes, with Euclid's *Elements*, XIII, XIV, XV. See Dieterici, *Die Lehre vom Weltseele*, 3; *Propadeutik*, 30, 129. Palqera, *Reshit Hokmah*, 43, speaks of Euclid as a Pythagorean. אקלידס הפיתיגורי.

[32] Guttmann, *Die Religionsphilosophie des Saadia*, 26; Malter, *Saadia Gaon*, 204; Neumark, *Toledot ha-Pilosofiah be-Israel*, II, 191.

passage in the *Tafsīr*, Saadia says: "Thus when He drew in the air straight lines in circles, triangles, and squares, and also traced oblique lines in circles, triangles, and squares, there came into being, out of the bending and crossing of one line over the other, plane and solid figures."[33] The "bending and crossing" is reminiscent of the bending and crossing of lines to form spheres, which we have noted in the *Amānāt*.

Gabirol also identified the point-theory, or the second view of the *Amānāt*, with the eighth of the *Tafsīr*, which is the theory of the *Sefer Yeṣirah*; for in *Fons Vitae*, II, 21, after stating the gist of his teaching that quantity subsisting in substance is a conjunction of unities, which he explains in the sequel as being points, he remarks with unmistakable reference to the eighth view of the *Tafsīr*: *ac per noc dictum est illud, quod compositio mundi non evenit nisi ex lineamento numeri et litterarum in aere*.

4. Saadia does not accept the view of the *Sefer Yeṣirah*, even if we do not regard numbers and letters as eternal. He is opposed to every system that affirms a process and a gradation in creation. All came into being at once, "like the flesh and the bones and the veins in the embryo, like the kernel and the flesh and the skin in the fruit, like the redness and the glow in the fire." Only in the movement from potentiality to actuality were there six days of creation. And for this opinion, which is that of the Torah, he adduces four proofs that we will consider in our next chapter.

[33] Lambert, *Commentaire sur le Sefer Yeṣira par le Gaon Saadya de Fayyoum,* 10: והו פליס ידעיה מחצׄה מפרדהׄ ואנמא יקול אנה כׄלק אלהוא• ואודעה הדׄה אללׄבׄ שי ואנדה אן אלהוא• אגׄזא• מנׄזאהׄ יקטעהא אלעדד ואדׄא סאר פיהא עלי כטוט מסתקימהׄ ומנערגׄהׄ אחדתׄת אשכאלא. See *supra* note 29. The Heb. version in Barzillai's commentary on the *Sefer Yeṣirah,* 272: כי האויר יחלקהו לחלקים ויחתכהו למספר.

Chapter Four

GOD

1. HIS EXISTENCE

THE VARIOUS cosmological proofs generally adduced for the existence of God may be divided, I think, into three categories: (1) proofs from creation (already in Plato), (2) proofs from the weakness of the world, for example, its dependence upon a mover, even if eternal (Aristotle), and (3) proofs from the world's greatness, that is, its orderliness, its wisdom, its harmony (Plato, Aristotle, Stoics).[1] It seems that the third, esthetic, viewpoint is the most generous category, admitting a wider range of philosophical schools.

In *Emunot we-Deʿot*, Saadia chooses the first category. "There is no means of proving the existence of a Creator other than that of creation."[2] This seems to show that he knew other proofs but did not think them convincing. What are the others that he rejected?

The proofs he adduced for creation are four. First, the proof from finitude. The world with all its spheres is finite in space. And since there cannot be an infinite force in a finite body, and since duration is due to a force, "a force that maintains," it follows that the world must have had a beginning and must have an end.[3] It should be observed that this idea, that duration cannot be due to inertia but must an active maintaining force, is involved in the Kalam's atomism of time and constant creation. Saadia then, agrees with the presupposition but not with the conclusion. We will meet this concept of "a force that maintains" again

[1] See the various proofs and references in E. Zeller, *Die Philosophie der Griechen* (Leipzig, 1919–1923), 2[1] p. 717, note 6; p. 927; 2[2] pp. 358–62. See also R. D. Hicks, *Stoic and Epicurean,* 41.

[2] *Emunot,* II, 1, 88: אין דרך לראיה שאינו מדרך החידוש בשום פנים. There are traces of the proof from the world's greatness also in the *Em.*, for example, II, 4, 91; 6, 93. Nevertheless, these expressions only characterize God's actions, and seem to offer no sufficient proof for God's existence. Maimonides statement in *Moreh,* III, 13, 17: ודע מן הגדולה שבראיות על חדוש העולם למי שמודה על האמת הוא... כי לכל דבר מהם תכלית אחר ושזה מפני זה והיא ראיה על כונת מכוין seems to indicate a preference for the third kind.

[3] כח השומר *Em.*, I, 1, 56.

at the end of Chapter 8, in connection with Saadia's concept of man's predetermined duration of life. Second, the proof from composition. All things are composite and therefore require a composer. Third, the proof from accidents. Nothing is free from "accidents," for example, growth and decay, motions, and all kinds of qualities that come and go, so that each accident is finite in time, and therefore the world must be finite. One might argue: True, every accident is finite, but they may be infinite in succession. But Saadia, as will be seen, rejects the notion of an infinite series. Fourth, the proof from time. If time were without a beginning, it would have passed over an infinite number of days and years until it arrived at this moment; but since the infinite cannot be traversed, how can we explain this moment of our existence?[4] And here Saadia makes an Aristotelian distinction between the ability to divide a thing infinitely, an ability that is only mental (in Aristotelian terminology: potential), and the idea of an infinite extent, which is supposed to be actual, and therefore absurd. These are the four proofs of treatise I, ch. 1, in the *Emunot*, and the conclusion is: since the world was created, there must be a Creator.

But in his commentary on *Sefer Yeṣirah*,[5] the approach is somewhat different. There is no proof from time, although he uses the concept of time in his polemic against the eternalists in his introduction to the book. And if we compare the three other arguments as advanced there with their formulations in the *Emunot*, which he composed two years later, we find interesting differences. The first proof in the commentary parallels the second proof here, except for the fact that there the proof is not from the *composition* of parts, but from the parts themselves, their scatteredness.[6] It describes the stars in their various movements and degrees of brightness, but it does not aim to prove first their creation and then a Creator. It moves from the orderliness of the stars directly to God. In other words, it is the argument from design, which Maimonides regarded as the strongest proof of a Creator. The second proof in the commentary corresponds to the first proof here, but it lacks the

4 *Em.*, I, 1, 59.

5 Commentary on *Sefer Yeṣirah*, ch. 1 (end).

6 The superimposition, in the second proof of the *Emunot*, of a second formulation over the formulation in the commentary is easily discerned. It begins with the expression מקבוץ החלקים והרכבת הפרקים and ends with the words ומצאתי הכתוב אומר כי פירוד חלקי החיים וחיבורם יורה על חידושם.

intermediate link regarding the impossibility of an infinite force residing in a finite body and infers from the limitation of the world the existence of a limiter and an encompasser. The third proof there, the one from accidents, is the third one here, but with this important difference: the conclusion is not that the world must have been created but that there must be One who always provides the passing accidents of things. Thus, at least the first and the third proofs are *not* through creation. The first is from the greatness of the world, and the third from its weakness. And it is these, and to some extent also the second proof, that Saadia afterward found frail; and when he started his work on the *Emunot we-De'ot* he changed them, adapting them to the method of proof through creation (*derek ha-ḥiddush*), because "there is no means of proving the existence of a Creator other than of creation." And the question arises, what has caused these changes?

The answer is to be found in the difference in character and aim of the two books. At the center of the *Emunot* stands the concept of God. And should there be any other way to a knowledge of His existence, it might lead to pluralism, for as Saadia says: "To demonstrate the existence of more than one God, would require a second proof, outside of that first proof. There is however no means of proving the existence of a Creator other than that of creation." And the whole anti-attributistic conception of God prefers the proof from the bare concept of creation, because all we know of God is that He created. This is the viewpoint in the *Emunot*, whereas in Saadia's commentary of *Sefer Yeṣirah*, creation is the central concept. There his approach is theosophic,[7] trying to describe how God resides in the cosmos and fills it, so that Saadia was not content with a proof that would confirm a one-time contact between God and the world. He sought a constant contact, and more, a divine outpouring throughout the world. He sought divinity in the universe in the present. Therefore, in the commentary he followed the road of the second and third proofs in our threefold division of the cosmogonic arguments, namely the frailty of the world on the one hand, requiring constant creativeness of limits and accidents, and, on the other hand, the greatness of the world, the great variety of stars in movement and brightness. But we must add that even in the *Emunot*, where Saadia crystallizes a rationalistic transcendentalism, he did not forget entirely

7 See Lambert's introduction to Saadia's commentary, p. VIII.

his former viewpoint. We shall find more of this struggle between viewpoints later on.

2. HIS ESSENCE

The essence of God is the theme of the second treatise. In the exordium of this treatise, Saadia shows how the human thought reaches God through a process of subtilization.[8] It starts with sensation, progressively abstracting and subtilizing its data, until it reaches the "subtlest of all." The steps on this road, from the percept to the infinite, are: the dwelling of thought on the accidents (i.e., qualities) of an object, then on quantity, on place, on time, step after step, until thought reaches the last "known," beyond which there is no known, because the mind has reached a "known" beyond matter or anything residing in matter, and the perceptual ground has slipped from under the scaling mind.

Let us observe in passing that although the ascent is gradual, from the subtle to the subtler, it is still strange that the apex of the pyramid, that is, the end of all abstractions and subtilizations, should be identified as God, for then we have pantheism. And at the end of the ascent the mind is still dependent upon an unexplained leap to the last known whose subtlety is different from the previous "knowns," not only in degree but also in kind, because it is the absolute that is "beyond matter or resident in matter." It is also noteworthy that Saadia considers quantity to be a subtler category than quality, even though in other passages[9] he places it before quality in the order of categories, in keeping with the Aristotelian order. Solomon ibn Gabirol too, in *Meqor Ḥayyim*, II, 8–9, regards quantity a subtler category.

After this preface to the second treatise, the main intention of which is that on the threshold of the last known we must be ready to abandon all elements of corporealism, as otherwise we slip back to lower stages, Saadia presents us with five divine attributes (Ar. *maʿāni*, Heb. *inyanim*), namely, one, living, omnipotent, omniscient, and with no resemblance to anything else—all aiming against the anthropomorphists who interpret some Biblical expressions about God in terms of their "material" meaning rather than their figurative implication. It is in the light of this

[8] דקק, דקדק, דקות Ar. תדקיק, תלטיף. See *Amānāt*, 74.

[9] See *Em.*, II, 9 and 11, and commentary on *Sefer Yeṣirah* (Ar.), p. 20, and comp. Palqera's *Liqqutim min Sefer Meqor Hayyim*, II, 8–9. Concerning the Aristotelian order, see I. Madkour, *L'Organon d'Aristotle dans le monde arabe* (Paris, 1934), p. 89.

anti-anthropomorphism that we must seek the sense of these attributes. Saadia's further discussion in Chapters 4 and 5 concentrates on the three middle characteristics and unfolds the problem, so central throughout the Middle Ages, of divine attributes. David Kaufmann feels that Saadia rejected all divine attributes. David Neumark finds that Saadia admitted the three middle ideas. And Isaac Julius Guttmann, without entering into the essence of the discussion, states that "we must accept his stand as it is, together with all the contradictions it contains."[10] But there are no contradictions, and we must not assume any in such close proximity and in the discussion of a problem so important by a personality so sharp and firm as Saadia.

To clarify, we must begin with the fact that Saadia himself in many places explicitly asserts that one must not ascribe any attribute, be it of substance or accident, to God; and that if such attributes are mentioned in the Bible, or he himself occasionally writes as if affirming attributes, it is only by "the extension of language" and "transference of meanings." For

> if language were to restrict itself to univocals, its employment would be very much curtailed, and it would be impossible to express by its means any more than a small portion of what we aim to convey.... Were we, in our effort to give an account of God, to make use of expressions that are literally true, it would be necessary to desist from speaking of Him as one that hears, sees, pities, and wills, so that there would be nothing left for us to affirm except the fact of His existence.[11]

These attributes are not therefore univocal terms and must not be taken in their material sense. Saadia calls this, at the end of III, 3, a "principle" (*shoresh*) for the interpretation of his system.

Let us return therefore to *Emunot*, II, 4, to the discussion of the three attributes: living, omnipotent, and omniscient. "According to what our reason discloses to us, it is clear that only he that has the power can create, and that only one that is alive has the power, and that whatever is created and well made can emanate only from one who knew, before he made it, how the thing to be created was to come into being." But the knowledge of these three characteristics does not mean, according to Saadia, three steps in a mental process. We arrive at them at once

[10] See Isaac Julius Guttmann, הפילוסופיה של היהדות p. 374, note 144.

[11] *Em.*, II, 10. See also I, 3, pp. 67–68; II, 1, pp. 87–88; II, 9–12, pp. 95–102; III, 10, 121; VI, 15, 211; *Tafsīr Mishlei*, 143.

when we arrive at the idea that there is a Maker or a Creator, but our language is poor, lacking one word to embrace all the three meanings. Nor is it desirable to create a word for the three ideas, as it will need explanations and we will gain nothing. But let no one think that these are three different concepts, because they all have one meaning, namely, a Maker.[12] Hence, no one of these three ideas introduces something distinct in the essence of God, which would imply variety, that is, pluralism. For God transcends variety. On the other hand, when we say Maker we do not express an addition to His essence. Similarly, the three terms—all of which mean only Maker—express no addition to His essence, but only that the world was made, that there is a Maker.

Let us cast a glance at the ideological background. The problem of attributes was involved in the efforts of Philo and Plotinus and the Gnostics to conceive of God as transcending thought, and even being, in order to safeguard His unity or His purity. But on the other hand, there were Christian thinkers who felt constrained to affirm divine attributes in order to provide a philosophical interpretation for the belief in the trinity; and in the hypostatizations they were probably influenced by Platonic idealism. When Islam came into being, Christians engaged in debates with the Arabs,[13] and as a result the Arabs began to see that the concept of attributes contradicts the concept of unity, that every attribute plus its subject make two. It was then that the Muʿtazilah arrived; and under the banner of unity (Ar. *tawḥid*) it rejected all essential or eternal attributes except eternity itself.[14]

But there were different groups among the Muʿtazilites, as described by al-'Ashʿari. One group was content with saying "God knows" instead of "God has knowledge" (which would entail dualism). The same is true of power. Another group thought it permissible to say "God has knowledge and power," but only in the sense that there is something known to Him or done by Him, always referring to an object of His

[12] Saadia, together with the Mutakallimūn, calls God a Maker, Agens, rather than a Cause or the First Cause, which would imply the eternity of the world, as the caused is coeval with the cause as cause. See *Moreh*, I, 69 (beginning) and Kaufmann, *Attributenlehre* 32, note 60. The ancestry of the term "Maker" goes back to Plato's use of the term τὸ ποιοῦν in *Philebus* 26e.

[13] See A. J. Wensinck, *The Muslim Creed* (Cambridge, 1932), 68, 71 sqq., 87, 146, 209; C. H. Becker, "Christliche Polemik und Islamische Dogmenbilbung" in *Zeitschrift für Assyriologie* XXVI (1912), 175–95.

[14] See Shahrastani, I, 30 (tr. Haarbrucker, 42).

action, always a description of His *action* but not of God Himself. A third group maintained that God has knowledge that is His essence, and life that is His essence, that is, never something added to his essence because of the involved pluralism. This third view is the one held by Abū Hudhayl and his school. A fourth group maintained: We must not say that God has knowledge, power, hearing, and seeing, and we must not say that He does not have these attributes.[15]

It seems that the second group, which explains divine attributes, though only those of knowledge and power, as attributes of action, comes nearest to Saadia's position. David Kaufmann, on the other hand, on the basis of a description by Shahrastani of Abū Hudhayl's view, identifies Saadia's position with the third group, led by Abū Hudayhl, and assumes that both denied additive attributes, that is, attributes added to His essence, but agreed that life and power and wisdom are not additive but the very essence of God, and all three attributes are one.[16] It is difficult to accept this identification and this explanation of Saadia. First, because, as we have seen, Saadia rejects all attributes, whether of substance or of accident, and where they do occur he says they must be taken as "extension of language." Second, because the main point of this Arab Muʿtazilite, that God Himself is life, is power, is knowledge—for which reason al-'Ashʿari taunted Abū Hudhayl by saying: "Why do you not pray: 'O knowledge, pray forgive me!'"[17]—is missing in Saadia. Saadia does speak of the attributes: living, omnipotent, and omniscient, but there is no hint in Chapter 4, in the very discussion of the problem of attributes, at their identification with God's essence.

15 See Wensinck, *The Muslim Creed*, 76–77.

16 Kaufmann, *Attributenlehre*, 33–37. Kaufmann believes that Saadia's words contain a dissenting hint at Abū Hāshim, who maintains, according to Kaufmann's explanation, that even though objectively the three attributes are one, *subjectively*, that is, as conceived by the human mind, they are different from one another. His source is Shahrastani, I, 34 (49). But in this source Abū Hāshim does not distinguish between subjective and objective aspects, and does not accept the opinion of Abū Hudhayl that those three attributes are God's essence, but, quite to the contrary, he assumes that they are beside His essence (ורא כונה דאתה), but he makes this admission to the Muʿtazilites, that he calls them not attributes but conditions (אחואל). Nor is there any such distinction in al-Baghdadi's account in his *Al-Farq bain 'l-firaq*, pp. 181–82 (in K. C. Seelye's English translation, pp. 201–203). All these three "conditions" are conceived objectively, according to Abū Hāshim, who differs from Abū Hudhayl. See also A. S. Tritton, *Muslim Theology* (London, 1947), 150–51.

17 Al-'Ashʿari, *Al-Ibānah ʿan Uṣūl ad-Diyānah*, 42 (tr. W. C. Klein, 95).

The whole intention of Saadia was different from that of Abū Hudhayl. It was not to push the attributes inwardly into the essence—which Shahrastani well designated as turning the substance into an attribute or the attribute into a substance—but to show that these three attributes, which are not three but one, do *not* describe His essence at all, because they are only explanatory words for the word "Maker." What is a Maker? Living—omnipotent—omniscient. And just as the word "Maker" does not describe God's essence but only asserts that the world was made by Him, "that there is here something made," so the word "living—omnipotent—omniscient" does not add anything to His essence, because it does not describe God but only asserts that "there is here something made." In other words, there are no essential attributes but only attributes of action,[18] which is essentially the view of the second group of the Mutakallimūn. All we know then of God's essence is in its outgoing, creative, aspect. The inner being of God remains inexplicable. This is the transcendence that Saadia tries to build up in the second treatise in general, and in the fourth chapter in particular, and it is the very opposite of the view held by Abū Hudhayl, at which he hints by concluding that chapter with a verse from Job: "And how small a whisper is heard from Him!"

True, in Chapter 5 Saadia seems to take a position similar to Abū Hudhayl's, apparently identifying the two attributes "living" and "wisdom" with God's essence,[19] as opposed to the Christians, "who thought that His life and wisdom are two things distinct from His essence," thus obtaining the doctrine of the Trinity. But a careful reading of the text reveals a different meaning. Essentially, we may discern here three arguments against Christianity. (1) If there is variety or plurality of aspects in God, He is corporeal. "And we have already established that these attributes [i.e., not His life and wisdom *and essence*, because essence was not discussed in the previous chapter at all, but only His life and wisdom] are one attribute" (and this too not as an attribute of essence but one

[18] See *Em.*, II, 12, 101; V, 7, 146. See also *Tafsīr Mishlei*, 143. The concept of ענינים עצמיים will be discussed later.

[19] So Jacob Guttmann, *Die Religionsphilosophie des Saadia*, p. 105. On p. 104, Guttman explains עצמו by "His being" and identifies the view cited here by Saadia with the Augustinian view and with the view reported by Shahrastani. See *ibid.*, note 2. But Qirqisani in his כתאב אלאנואר ואלמראקב formulates the Trinity exactly as substance, life, and wisdom. See Leon Nemoy's translation of pt. I and of ch. 16, pt. III, in the *Hebrew Union College Annual*, VII (1930), p. 365.

of action). But since to the Trinitarians there is plurality in Him, He must, by that definition, be corporeal. (2) "Any being whose life and knowledge are distinct from his essence must be created" (whereas, according to my view, His life and wisdom are not only not identical with His essence but do not exist at all as essential attributes). (3) The hypostasis of the attribute. Those people think that an attribute is its own being and its own cause, and therefore in God the attribute too must be God. Whereas we, "the community of monotheists," believe that an attribute springs from the essence and is caused by it. And even in the case of man we would say that he is "alive and wise because of his essence," were it not for the fact that we see him sometimes alive and sometimes dead, sometimes wise and sometimes otherwise. So that in the case of man we must look for external causes for these attributes. But in the case of God, He certainly is "alive because of His essence and wise because of His essence"[20] (though not identical with it). "The course that these people followed [i.e., the hypostasis of the attribute] becomes therefore nullified frcm the very root."

Thus this entire argumentation revolves around the plurality of attributes and their hypostatization, but not in the name of a Hudhaylic identification of attributes with essence—an identification that, according to Shahrastani, far from being the opposite of Christianity, comes very close to it, and that, far from rejecting attributes, presses them deeper inward. Saadia's whole intention is therefore to remove plurality from the concept of divinity. God's actions—including "living-powerful-wise" as an expression of action—spring not from attributes or powers or hypostases, but from the mystery of His essence alone. And in this Saadia is clearly echoed in Maimonides. "His actions are accomplished by His essence, not by any organ; and as undoubtedly 'forces' [i.e., attributes[21]] belong to the category of organs, He does not possess

[20] This is essentially the viewpoint of the Muʿtazilah, as we learn from Shahrastani, I, 30 (Haarbrücker, 42), and it is opposed to Abū Hudhayl's view, as again we learn from Shahrastani 34 (Haarbrücker, 49), which does not reject attributes nor the concept that these are the "persons" of Christianity or the states of Abū Hāshim: ואלפרק בין קול אלקאיל עאלם לדׄאתה לא בעלם ובין קול אלקאיל עאלם בעלם הו דׄאתה אן אלאול נפי אלצפהׄ ואלתׄאני אתׄבאת דׄאת הו בעינה צפהׄ או אתׄבאת צפהׄ הי בעינה דׄאת. ואן אתׄבאת אבו אלהדׄיל הדׄה אלצפאת וגׄוהא ללדׄאת פהי בעינהא אקאנים ללנצארי או אחואל אבי האשם.

[21] כחות, that is, attributes. Friedlander translates: "physical forces," which is not in the text and is disproved by the context. See *Shem Tob*.

any forces, that is to say, He has besides His essence nothing that could be the cause of His action, His knowledge or His will, for attributes are nothing but forces under a different name" (*Moreh*, I, 46, p. 65). "All the actions of God emanate from His essence, not from any extraneous thing superadded to His essence, as we have shown" (*ibid.*, I, 42, 74).

We have learned, therefore, that God is an indivisible unity,[22] that is, without attributes, and that He is "living-powerful-wise"—a term that does not intend to describe Him but only His creation. And now it is time to turn to the last of the "five attributes," namely that there is nothing that resembles Him. This question of resemblance (Ar. *tashbih*) began to lose its importance at the time of Saadia, so that even al-ʾAshʿari repudiated the doctrine of resemblance.[23] And it is perhaps for this reason that Saadia does not return to it for discussion, as he did to the three middle attributes. But in a sharper and more decisive form, undermining any attributistic school, it becomes the theme of Chapters 9–12, which intend to show that not one of the ten Aristotelian categories that embrace all existents can be predicated of God, or as he has already remarked: "It is out of the question and impossible to declare Him to be anything that He Himself created."[24] And since every human word bears a meaning of "what He Himself has created," the whole ground is removed from under "resemblance" and from under any doctrine of attributes. But before he begins this discussion, Saadia finds it necessary to introduce it with a short preface, which is not apparently linked with what precedes or follows, yet contains an echo of, and is continuous with, the exordium of the whole second treatise and warningly hints to the student not to think that the following repudiation of categories with reference to God, what the Arab orthodoxy calls *taʿtīl*, or emptying, really does empty this supreme concept. On the contrary. Water is thinner but also stronger than earth, and wind is more than water, and fire more than wind. "The finer one thing is in relation to another, the more powerful it is in proportion to the latter" (II, 8, 95).[25]

22 *Em.*, II, 7, 94: אחד נפרד; *Amānāt*, 91: אלואחד אלפרד.

23 *Ibānah*, 18 (63).

24 *Em.*, II, 8, 95. It should be observed that by the end of the tenth century this idea that God is neither substance nor accident entered also into the orthodox Kalām. See Wensinck, *The Muslim Creed*. p. 209.

25 *Ibānah*, 17, 36, 37, 42 (62, 87, 88, 94). See also David Kaufmann, *Attributenlehre*, p. 474, note 158.

Saadia enumerates the categories in an order somewhat different from that of Aristotle[26] and shows the transcendence of God. God is not substance, because He is the Creator of all substances in the five kingdoms of being: mineral, vegetable, animal, stars, and angels. Therefore, when the Scriptures state that God created man in His image, it only means in a *human* image pleasing to Him.

Nor is God quantity, because He is the Creator of quantity, or dimensions, and parts. Hence we must interpret figuratively the "ten corporeal words" with reference to God: head, eye, ear, mouth, lip, face, hand, heart, bowels, foot, and consequently we cannot ascribe to Him any action coming from these organs, such as seeing, hearing, speaking,

26 The order of categories in Aristotle's *Categories*, ch. 4, is substance, quantity, quality, relation, place, time, position, possession, action, passion. Saadia here and in his commentary on *Sefer Yeṣirah*, 20 follows Aristotle but cites possession before position. Baḥya, in *Ḥobot ha-Lebabot*, I, 7, follows Aristotle. Abraham ibn Daud, in *Emunah Ramah*, I, 1 cites position before relation. Maimonides in *Millot ha-Higgayon*, 10, counts time before place. It is interesting that in the exordium to treatise 2, p. 84, where Saadia traces the mental process of abstraction and refinement, quantity is the second step, higher than quality and coming after it; whereas Aristotle with reference to numbers, in *Metaphysics*, 1083a11, emphasizes that quality comes after quantity. Also Solomon ibn Gabirol in *Meqor Ḥayyim*, V, 42 thinks "that substance is more fittingly being than accident, and among accidents quantity is more being than quality;" and similarly in V, 19: "as quantity bears color and shape." Abraham ibn Daud too, in *Emunah Ramah*, I, 1, divides the accidents in accordance with their nearness to substance, so that quantity, quality, and position "rest in bodies and are revealed in them," and relation and place and time are near the other end, "very weak in being and concealed," whereas possession, action, and passion lie between the two extremes—which division resembles that of al-Farabi in his *Philosophical Treatises*, ed. Fr. Dieterici (Leyden, 1890), p. 91 (German translation, p. 150). Therefore, it may be that according to Saadia quality—and the qualities are particularly called accidents in *Em.*, 99 and in the Arabic text, 100—"rests more directly in the bodies and is revealed in it," and the mind must therefore free itself from it first in the process of refinement. From all these facts it appears that the principle of precedence in categories is: What *carries* comes first, what *inheres* comes second. Furthermore, it is seen that Saadia in *Em.*, II, exordium, pp. 83–84, putting quantity after quality in the process of abstraction and refinement, runs counter to Aristotle, Baḥya, ibn Gabirol and ibn Daud, and also counter to himself in II, 9 and 10.

Incidentally, the use of the term "accident" as opposed to essential attributes, as in *Emunah Ramah*, 42, 59, and in *Moreh*, I, 34, 51, 73, does not yet occur in Saadia. In other words, he knew the term as an Aristotelian category, in fact as any category other than substance, but not as a Porphyrian predicable, that is, as different from a property or a specific difference.

thinking, etc., except in a figurative sense.[27] Wherever you do find such anthropomorphisms, you must interpret them by a method called *ta'wīl*, that is, by trying to penetrate to their symbolic meaning. If, then, the prophet relates that he saw God in a human form, this form is a *special creation* for the sake of the prophet, a concept that we will discuss later in connection with Saadia's theory of the Second Air.

Nor is He quality, or the carrier of accidents, for He is the Creator of all accidents. Hence He does not love or hate, because love and hate are accidents. And if the Bible ascribes to God love of certain acts, it means only that He commanded us to do those acts or that we must love them, so that love is not an attribute of God but an attribute of action. On the other hand, things not to be done are regarded as hated by Him, because we must hate them. Similarly, God knows no anger or pleasure. These are only figurative terms.

Nor is there any relationship in God, because God is eternal, and if after creation He would *enter* into some relationship with a creature, it would constitute a change in His essence. Hence, expressions such as "king of the universe," "servants of God," "lovers of God," and "enemies of God" all are used figuratively.[28] In truth, there is no relationship of any kind between the Creator and His creation.

Nor is He in place, first, because He is the Creator of all places, and second, because there was no place before creation—how could He enter into place during it? Furthermore, only a material body requires place. Hence all placements of God, in heaven or in the Temple or in Zion, have no literal meaning. For the same reason, He is not in time, and hence expressions such as "from eternity," "before", and "after" are all only "approximate expressions" and refer to points of time in the life of the creatures. Nor is possession applicable to Him; because all creatures are His, so that expressions such as "the people of His property," "God of Abraham, Isaac, and Jacob," and "the God of the Hebrews" are all figurative. Nor, since He is incorporeal, does position apply, to

27 העברה מהלשון, העברה ושמוש, העברות ושמושים ורוחב הלשון (אמונות ב,ג,90) הקרבה והמשלה (ב,ח,95) העברה והקרבה (ב,יג,104). These terms, meaning figures of speech, are opposed to "true language" (לשון אמתי) on the one hand, and, on the other, to the understanding of a term corporeally (הגשמת המלה). See also II, 1, 88; II, 9, 96; II, 10, 97.

28 This applies also to the expression "Israel is My first born son" (*Em.*, II. 7, 94), as against Christological exegesis.

Him, and hence expressions such as "the Lord sitteth," "Rise up," "He stood," and "the Lord went" are all figurative. Nor does action apply to Him, because God's Will is His action, and consequently expressions such as "He made," "ceased," "rested," "spoke," "was silent," "remembered," is "merciful and gracious," and is "jealous and avenging"[29] do not describe God but the fate and destiny of His creatures. And lastly, passion does not apply, and here Saadia engages in a discussion of revelation, God's being perceived, since this too is a form of passivity, of being the passive object of the human eye. This question was debated between the Sunnites, who believed in the possibility of God being seen in this world, and certainly in the world beyond, and the Muʿtazilites, who denied such a possibility either here or in the hereafter. Saadia was not a Sunnite.

And so we have come "by way of speculation" to the height of divine transcendence, to a height where literally silence is praise. But suddenly we reach the last chapter of this second treatise and the atmosphere changes. If before God was above all space, now He fills all places and has a special place in the heart of man. And if we stood before without sight and speech before the mystery of His essence, we know now that "His essence is knowledge."[30] Indeed, He has a multitude of attributes that are even designated as "essential attributes," and one must praise Him in those terms. Does Saadia destroy here the high pyramids he has painfully built up? No, there are no contradictions, for there are two roads, one of reason and one of revelation,[31] and one must use

29 *Em.*, II, 12, 101. See also II, 10, 97: ואלו היינו באים לספר עליו בלשון האמתי היינו חייבים לעזוב ולהניח שומע ורואה רחום חפץ עד אשר לא יעלה לנו כ״א הישות בלבד. This seems to contradict II, 8, 95, where we read אל יטעוך המעיין בספר ויכניסו עליך הספקות מאמרך היה ומאמרך חפץ ומאמרך רצה וכעס והדומה לזה where a verbal tense of "to be" is also ruled out. The answer seems to be that Saadia distinguishes between being (Heb. היה, Ar. כאן) as a verbal tense and therefore time-limited and ישות (Ar. אניה), which is being or existence in the abstract. See כתאב אלאשאראת by ibn Sina (French translation by A. M. Goichon), pp. 304–305, note 3.

30 *Em.*, II, 13, 103. See also II, 8, 95: ובעבור זאת תמצאנה (כלומר, החכמה) לבדה מיוחסת אל הבורא, ה׳ בחכמה יסד ארץ ואומי בקו׳ רצתה נפשי אלי אלחכמה וכדׄלך כל נפש מצרוף אלי אלקדים. See also *Tafsīr Isaiah*, 122:

31 Among the attributes mentioned here in addition to living-powerful-wise, we find "ancient" (i.e., without a beginning) and "that He does nothing but good." The attributes "good" or "righteous and good" occur frequently in Saadia's other books, in accord with the moral approach of the Muʿtazilites, the "men of unity and justice." See, for example, *Tafsīr Bereshit*, 1, 3; *Tafsīr Mishlei*, 1, 2, 3, 161, 169;

both. But Saadia concludes this treatise with two warnings: first, that God is above and beyond all our powers of expression, and second, that one is to follow the principle (*shoresh*) stated, and regard words only as "figures of speech and approximations." So that reason prevails again.

3. REVELATION, THE SECOND AIR, THE WILL

Transcendence characterizes Saadia's *Emunot we-Deʿot* not only in an epistemological sense, namely, that God is above all attributes and above human thought, but also ontologically, that He is beyond all relationship and contact. In order to see this clearly, we must first glance at Saadia's stand on this problem in his commentary on *Sefer Yeṣirah*, which he wrote two years before the *Emunot*. In the commentary the general tendency is toward mystic immanence. The speculations about the two divine attributes, life and wisdom, accompany our author here too, but now life and wisdom denote aspects of God's relation to His universe. God is the "life of the world," the Stoic *anima mundi*, so that He fills the whole world, and no place, no rock or stone, is devoid of Him, Who is all its life. Nevertheless, just as the soul moves the body, so reason moves the soul; and as the reason of the world, He is above life, that is, above the world. Hence, though found everywhere, He is still above and beyond.[32] Thus Saadia tries to make peace between immanence and transcendence—an uneasy peace. The first tendency overpowers.

Let us dwell a little longer on the details of this immanence. Essentially, it is not God but His Will that fills the universe. Saadia makes a distinction between this Will, which is apparently created or emanated, as it is before actualization, when it is called "spirit" (*ruaḥ*), and the Will

---

Tafsīr Iyob, 1, 2, 6, 120. Here in the rationalistic *Emunot* the term wise, *ḥakam*, is more popular. See, for example, II, 6, 93; IV, 1, 126; V, 1, 137; V, 2, 139; V, 4, 142. See also III, 2, 108: "The wisdom of the Creator is above all," and III, 2, 109: "The wisdom of the Creator is above the grasp of human beings." As to the attribute of "place," see *Tafsīr Mishlei*, 94: ולדלך הם דעו המקום ברוך הוא אד הדא אעם [מן] אלאקסאם and his commentary on *Sefer Yeṣirah*, p. 26: אן אלחכים גל גלאלה אחאט באלכלק כלה מן גמיע גהאתה and also p. 28: לאנה גל ועז מתוסט אלכל בעד אלאחאטה בה.

32 Commentary on *Sefer Yeṣirah*, 69–70 (91–92). See also the fragment of the Hebrew rendering, Ms. Munich, cited by David Kaufmann in the additional notes to Barzillai's commentary on *Sefer Yeṣirah*.

as it is when already actualized, when it is called "the word" (*davar*).[33] This may be the origin of ibn Gabirol's distinction between the Will before action when it is one with God and the Will in action when it is apart from God. At any rate, this Will is conceived as a Creator and demiurgus. Saadia quotes the verses "By His spirit He hath garnished the heavens" (Job, 26, 13) and "By the word of the Lord the heavens were made" (Psalms, 33, 6). The "word" of the Lord is then the creative Logos. Here also is the source of ibn Gabirol's line in his poem "Crown of Royalty":

> Thou art wise and from Thy wisdom
> Thou hast set apart Thy appointed purpose [lit. will]
> Like a craftsman and an artist [tr. Israel Zangwill].

Thus, Saadia's Will is an artificer, a demiurgus. But it is also identified with the Second Air, which was the beginning of all creation, a subtle air penetrating and filling the whole world and called Glory (*kavod*), Divine Presence (*shekinah*), the Spirit of the Living God, the Throne of Glory. Out of this air there was carved "the created voice" (a concept that played an important part in later Jewish speculation), the voice that God especially creates for a prophet's ear, and from it came all signs and miracles and the wisdom and the power given to chosen men. And from it came also the "created light," called the Name or the Name of Glory, that penetrates into the "perceivable air" (*avir nir'eh*). It is also called the Holy Spirit, and the voice accompanying it is called Echo or *bat kol*. This is the doctrine of the Second Air, the first of creation, finer than fine, stronger than strong, through which God fills the whole of existence.

There are in this conception of immanence traces of Benjamin Nahawendi, who believed that before all creation God created Glory and the Throne, and that God created an angel who created and leads the universe and sends prophets and messengers and does wonders and miracles.[34] It can readily be seen that the created angel of Benjamin

[33] Commentary on *Sefer Yeṣirah*, 69: אלאול מנה משיה אללה יכון עאלם הי אול אלאשיא וסמאהא צאחב אלכתאב רוח עלי מא קאל אלכתאב ברוחו שמים שפרה. ותלך אלאראדה למא כרגת אלי אלפעל סמית כלמה כקולה בדבר ה׳ שמים נעשו. Comp. Solomon ibn Gabirol, *Meqor Hayyim*, V, 36.

[34] See *Eshkol ha-Kofer* by Yehudah Hadassi, sect. 46, p. 25: ויאמר אלהים נעשה בצלמנו כדמותנו למי אמר ויאמר באורו ויאמר מנפשו לנפשו ולחכמתו נעשה ולא אמר לא לחבר ולא ליועץ ולא לברואי אחד מן המלאכים. See also *Em.*, V, 8, 147: כאשר סוברים בפר׳ נעשה אדם בצלמנו וחשבו כי מלאך ברא אדם וכל העולם.

Nahawendi is the Second Air of Saadia's commentary on *Sefer Yeṣirah.* Qirqisani says that a certain sect called Magharians transferred the divine attributes from God to the created angel and that this is similar to the view of Benjamin Nahawendi.[35] Saadia too transfers divine attributes to the Second Air. So that the development of this doctrine can be traced from Philo's Logos through the Angel of the Magharians and Benjamin Nahawendi to Saadia's Second Air, with the addition of a tendency toward Stoic immanence.

But very little of this concept, which Saadia presents in his commentary to the *Sefer Yeṣirah*, did he admit into his later *Emunot*. The idea of the Will, which is one of the seven essential attributes in the Moslem Creed, he left out entirely. God is living-powerful-wise, but not willing; and not because the Will indicates a want and a lack,[36] but because the hypostatization of the Will is connected with the concept of an intermediary or a Logos. Here we touch upon the underlying cause of Saadia's abandonment in the *Emunot* of what he built up in the commentary, and this cause is antichristological. Something similar to the Logos, and under its influence, underwent a development among the Arabs in their concept of the eternal Koran, or the Word of God.[37] But it is not against the Logos of the orthodox Arabs that Saadia directs his criticism; his discussion of the Logos and its identification with Biblical terms occurs as a part of his polemic against Christianity in treatise II, Chapters 5–7.[38]

35 See Leon Nemoy, "Al-Qirqisānī's Account of the Jewish Sects and Christianity," *Hebrew Union College Annual*, VII (1930), 364. See also Harkavy, "Leqorot ha-Kitot be-Israel" in Graetz's *Geschichte der Juden* (Hebrew translation by S. P. Rabinowitz) (Warsaw, 1916), III, pp. 496–98, and "Ḥadashim Gam Yeshanim," *ibid.*, V, 16.

36 Kaufmann, *Attributenlehre*, p. 27 note 54. See also Z. Diesendruck, התכלית והתארים בתורת הרמב"ם, in *Tarbiš* I, 4; II, 1, p. 38, note 1.

37 Wensinck, *The Muslim Creed*, pp. 77–79.

38 *Em.*, II, 6, 93: ומצאתי קצתם חושב ענין ה׳ קנני ראשית דרכו (משלי ח,כב) שלבורא מלה קדמונה לא סרה ברואה (ער׳: לם תזל מעה תכלק). Kaufmann, *Attributenlehre*, p. 47, translated: *ein ewiges ungeschaffenes Wort*, but this is incorrect. The meaning of לא סרה ברואה is that it always was created, though ancient, that is, without a beginning. The allusion is to Eastern Christianity, as it was formulated by John of Damascus, that the Son was γενητός (born) but ἀγενητός (ancient). It is to this doctrine that Saadia alluded by saying that the Logos was always created, that is, beginningless but always in a relation of a created one to its Creator. See Wensinck *The Muslim Creed*, p. 150. Also, Origen taught that Jesus was ancient but always born. "The Father did not beget the Son a one-timed begetting, but He constantly

Saadia rejects in its two aspects the idea of a Logos: as a self-existing being or person, which contradicts the doctrine of unity, and as a demiurge or a tool in creation. He therefore emphasizes in various places that wisdom is no substance by itself and did not serve as a creative tool.[39] He tries to show that the biblical terms "spirit," "word," "the spirit of God," "the word of God," "image," 'name," "the name of the glory," and "the name of the glory of the kingdom,"[40] all of which were applied to the divine Will and to the Second Air, do not imply a different divine being, and that a sufficient knowledge of Hebrew will always suggest to the reader their true meaning.

Only the two ideas of the Created Voice and the Created Light[41]

---

begets him." This was also the view of Athanasius. See A. C. McGiffert, *A History of Christian Thought,* I (New York, 1932), 219, 254, note 1.

[39] *Em.*, II, 6, 93.

[40] רוח, מלה, רוח אלהים, דבר ה׳, כבוד, צלם, שם, שם כבוד, שם כבוד מלכותו. See these terms in their order in the following references. *Em.*, II, 3, 90; II, 5, 92–93; II, 13, 104; V, 8, 147. Also in his discussion of the term צלם in II, 6, 93; V, 8, 147, Saadia aims to reject the theory of a Logos, that is, the angel who created man and the whole world, according to Philo and Nahawendi. See Harkavi, "Ḥadashim Gam Yeshanim," in the Hebrew translation, by S. P. Rabinowitz, of Graetz, *Geschichte der Juden*, pt. 5.

[41] Concerning the "created voice" (Heb. קול נברא), see *Em.*, II, 5, 92; II, 12, 101. Concerning the "created light" (Heb. אור נברא), see II, 10, 98; II, 11, 100 (אור הנברא הנקרא שכינה וכבוד), 101; II, 12, 102; III, 10, 123. An expression such as כי יש לבורא אור בראהו (II, 12, 102) does suggest the Second Air, but the *Emunot* never states that the light fills the universe, that is, that it is immanent. It is noteworthy that those expressions with which Saadia describes the Second Air in his commentary on *Sefer Yeṣirah*, he transfers in his *Emunot* to God. Thus in his commentary, p. 73, he describes the Second Air as follows: והו אללטף מן אללטיפה̈ ומע דלך אקוי מן כל קוי, and in *Em.*, II, exordium, 84–85; II, 6, 94–95, he uses the same terms about God. In *Amānāt*, 90 and in various places in his commentaries on the Bible he sometimes uses the word "light" for God, as in the phrases נור אללה and אלנור (Tibbon: הכבוד), in order to avoid anthropomorphism. Saadia's concept of a "created voice," which is Philonic—see Professor Louis Ginzberg, *Legends of the Jews*, I (Philadelphia, 1909), 39—was literally taken over by Yehudah Halevi (comp. *Em.*, II, 21, 102 with *Kuzari*, I, 89), and his idea of a "created light" was accepted by Maimonides in *Moreh*, I, 10; I, 64, although with veiled reservation in I, 5. Among the Arabs the idea of a "created voice" is essentially contained in the teaching of the Muʿtazilites about a created Koran, and especially in the assumption of Abū Hudhayl that there is a word that went out to no object and from the mouth of no subject. See Baghdadi, *Al-Farq bain 'l-firaq*, 109 (131). See also Goldziher in *Revue des Études juives*, XLVII, 184. Al-Jubbai believed in a "created glory." See A. S. Tritton,

remain. And to this Light he now transfers the epithets he first accorded to the Second Air, namely, Glory and Shekinah.[42] But without the element of immanency, they serve to emphasize even more the divine transcendence and the distances that only the religious approach, described in the last chapter of this second treatise, can leap over.

4. ANGELS AND PROPHETS

This anti-Christological transcendence will also explain Saadia's views concerning angels and prophets.

Arabic orthodoxy thought man to be more excellent than angels, and the proof is the following: (1) Allah commanded the angels to bow down before Adam. (2) Adam's knowledge as giver of names is greater than that of angels. (3) Man through struggle can rise, while angels are fixed. (4) Various verses in the Koran show this to be true. On the other hand, the Muʿtazilites declared the angels to be higher than man: (1) Angels are pure spirits, without passion. (2) Prophets learned from angels. (3) Various verses in the Koran show this to be true. Al-Gazali accepted the orthodox view, for (1) angels have fixed rank, while man can rise, and (2) sometimes man asks angels and receives no response, then he asks his heart and is answered.[43] It is clear that the arguments on both sides are rationalizations, for orthodoxy aimed at the exaltation of its prophet, and hence of all believers, while the Muʿtazilah had to take exception to such a view, because of rationalism, but mainly out of an anti-Christological fear that placing man higher than angels might endanger unity (as they feared also the concept of an eternal or pre-existent Word of God).

Now *prima facie* we find Saadia again in the Muʿtazilite camp. He enumerates "five principles": the mineral, the vegetable, the animals, the stars, and the angels,[44] showing that man belongs to the third rank and angels to the fifth. Elsewhere he says, "man must strive to attain to the rank of angels, the spiritual animals."[45] "Someone might wonder,"

Muslim Theology, p. 142. Thus did Arab and Jewish thinkers arrive in parallel ways at the same concepts.

42 *Em.*, II, 10, 98: II, 11, 100; III, 10, 123.

43 See E. E. Elder, *Saʿud al-Din al-Tiftizani* (New York, 1950), pp. 168–69; M. Schreiner, *Der Kalam in der jüdischer Literatur*, 14, note 8.

44 *Em.*, II, 10, 98.

45 *Tafsīr Mishlei*, 195. Ar. אלחיואנין אלרוחנין. It is noteworthy that in the *Emunot*

he writes, "how it happened that the Creator should have caused His light to abide among men and have abandoned the pure angels. Our reply would be: How dost thou know that the angels are without such divine light, when it is possible that God caused many times as much light to dwell in their midst as he had put among men?"[46] All this shows that angels are more excellent than men. But as against this, Abraham ibn Ezra cites an instance in which Saadia claims that man is higher than angels,[47] because man can rise to perfection by his deeds, whereas angels cannot change their rank; and ibn Ezra takes exception to this view because he thinks that man is below angels, as is shown by Joshua falling prostrate before the angel. It is easy to see that Saadia's argument, as cited by ibn Ezra, is the first argument of al-Gazali and the third argument of Arab orthodoxy, while ibn Ezra's argument is a refutation of orthodoxy's first argument.

One should also note Abraham ibn Ezra's comment on Isaiah, 48, 16: "And now the Lord God hath sent me, and His spirit." Ibn Ezra maintains that "His spirit" means an angel, but he quotes disapprovingly Saadia's view that "and His spirit" means "by His spirit." One can see here too, underneath the difference in exegesis, the controversy between ibn Ezra and Saadia concerning the comparative ranks of angels and men.

True, in the *Emunot* no such Arabic orthodox view, which ibn Ezra ascribes to Saadia and which Maimonides too combated (*Moreh*, III, 12, 15), is expressly stated. It may only follow from his emphasis that man is the aim of creation.[48] But if so, this swerve from the Muʿtazilah to orthodoxy can be explained only in that the anti-Christological fear entertained by the Muʿtazilites lest man may be elevated to Godship is overpowered by the anti-Gnostic fear that an angel may be raised to a demiurgus. Such an apprehension is indeed stated: "As some think in connection with the verse 'Let us make man in our image' that an

---

Saadia uses the term רוחניים only for intermediators, which he rejects, for example, the Logos (II, 6, 93). See also I, 3, 64, 72; X, 7, 204. With reference to God, he uses the negative term, "incorporeal," בלתי גשמי.

[46] *Em.*, III, 10, 123.

[47] See ibn Ezra on Gen, 1, 2, and the shorter text on Gen,. 23, 20. See also M. Friedlander, *Essays on the Writings of ibn Ezra* (London, 1877), p. 115, note 1, and H. Malter, *Life and Works of Saadia Gaon*, p. 212.

[48] *Em.*, IV, 1, 125.

angel created man and the whole world,"[49] alluding to Benjamin Nahawendi or to a Mandaean view that Gabriel the angel is the demiurgus.[50] Hence, although he accepts, like the Muʿtazilites, the existence and the exalted rank of angels, he refrains from admitting them into his philosophical system because of the fear of intermediation and pluralism.

This same motive dominates Saadia's conception of prophecy. The doctrine of "protection" (Ar. *ʿismah*) current among the Arabs, perhaps under the influence of the Shiites, maintained that the prophets are guarded against sin, and the extreme Shiites believed that God was incarnated in the prophet. This again constituted a danger of border-effacement between the Creator and creation through intermediary beings belonging to both realms. Hence Saadia was emphatic that prophets are in all respects like men (in mortality, in need for food) and are subject to all physical wants and ailments, except for the fact that they are sent on a mission by God. This view was opposed by Yehudah Halevi, who was interested in finding a higher stratification for Israel.[51] And with reference to sin, Saadia steered clear of the doctrine of "protection," stating not that they are above it or guarded against it, but that God chooses those whom He knows in advance to be loyal to their mission.[52] We shall return to the subject of prophecy later in our discussion of dogmas in Judaism.

Thus Saadia drew in his *Emunot* a sharp line between the above and the below and avoided all intermediates, pre-existents, and spirituals.

49 *Em.*, V, 8, 147. See also II, 6, 93.

50 See Israel Friedlander in *Journal of the American Oriental Society*, XXIX, pp. 84–85. See there the passage from Irenaeus, ending with "Let us make man in our image."

51 An opposition to Saadia's view we may note in Yehudah Halevi's *Kuzari*, I, 41–43: אמר החבר ואם ימצא אדם שיבא באש ולא יוזק בו ויעמד מבלי מאכל ולא ירעב... ולא יחלה ולא יחלש... עם ידיעת העבר והעתיד. אמר הכוזרי אבל המעלה הזאת אלהית מלאכותית אם היא נמצאת... אמר החבר אלה קצת תארי הנביא.

52 *Amānāt*, 228. See also *Em.*, III, 5, 112.

Chapter Five

TELEOLOGY

THE SECOND part of the book may be said to begin with the third treatise, that is, the justification of God, in keeping with the Muʿtazilite method of dividing works into two parts, divine unity and divine justice, so that the Muʿtazilites are called "men of unity and justice" (Ar. *ahl al-tawhid wal-ʿadl*). This second part offers a moral vindication of the Creator and Administrator of the universe and deals with the following subjects: the Torah (third treatise), free will (fourth treatise), this world (fifth treatise), the hereafter (seventh, eighth, and ninth treatises), and the ethical life (tenth treatise). The sixth treatise, concerning the soul, apparently comes as an introduction to the three treatises following. On the place of the tenth treatise, we shall speak later. This theodicy therefore revolves around four subjects, but we must add to these a fifth, the purpose of creation—a subject to which Saadia did not devote a separate treatise but one that he discusses in various places, and with it we shall begin.

1. THE PURPOSE OF CREATION

At the end of treatise I, Saadia offers three answers to the question of why God created the world:

[1] He had created all existents without any motive, and yet it would not be considered a wanton act, because only man acts wantonly when he does anything without a motive, inasmuch as he would thereby be neglecting his own benefit, but such a thing is far removed from the Creator.... [2] To reveal and make manifest His wisdom.... [3] To benefit His creatures... so that they may obey Him.

Prima facie, the first answer cancels out all the rest, because it rejects all teleology. Furthermore, it belongs to a different Arabic school from the rest. For the second and third answers, which are essentially one, that is, the abundance of divine goodness, reflect the Muʿtazilite view that God is wise and good, that he *cannot* do evil, whereas the first answer comes apparently from the Ashʿarite school, which emphasizes the absolute Will of God unbounded by eithei wisdom or justice. It seems, however, that Saadia's meaning in his first answer, that God created the world "without any motive," is that He created it without any *personal* motive. And in his second and third answers—and also in other sections, as will be explained—he emphasizes the benefits of existence for creatures, so that there is no cancellation but rather mutual completion.

There were some who noticed such a cancellation or contradiction[1] in *Moreh*, III. For in Chapter 13 Maimonides says: "We remain firm in our belief that the whole universe was created in accordance with the Will of God, and we do not inquire for any other cause or object" (which is apparently the orthodox, Ashʿarite view), whereas in Chapter 25 he states:

There are thinkers that assume that God does not create one thing for the sake of another, that existing things are not to each other in the relation of cause and effect; that they are all the direct result of the Will of God, and do not serve any purpose. According to this opinion we cannot ask why has He made this and not that; for He does what pleases Him, without following wisdom. Those who defend this theory must consider the actions of God as purposeless, and even as inferior to purposeless actions.

So there seems to be a contradiction. But in Chapter 13 Maimonides opposes only anthropocentric teleology, only the view that all creation is for man. In what is apparently a satirical reference to Saadia, he writes: "And so they think that the purpose of the whole existence is the existence of the human species, so that it may serve God." But he also believed that there is wisdom in creation, only we cannot grasp it.[2] Even at the end of Chapter 13, where he sharply criticizes teleology and posits the divine Will, almost like one of the Ashʿarites, he links the two apparently contradictory terms: "existence which depends on the Will of God, or, if you prefer, on the Divine Wisdom." And in Chapter 25 he is even more explicit: "Most of our wise and learned men believe that the creation was not the exclusive result of His will, but His wisdom, which we are unable to comprehend, made the actual existence of the universe necessary." Thus between Saadia and Maimonides there are both a correspondence and a difference. The difference relates to the world as a whole: Saadia felt that the purpose was man,

1 See שביל האמונה on *Emunot,* end of first treatise.

2 See *infra* "Nature and Spirit in Maimonides."

whereas Maimonides believed the supreme purpose to be incomprehensible to man. The correspondence is with reference to things within the world among which there is a relative purpose, with man occupying the highest rank, even though not as high as the spheres according to Maimonides and not higher than the spheres according to Saadia.

More explicitly, Saadia's teleological conception is as follows: The world is not a child of chance nor of necessity but created by Word and Will, that is, by design. This design manifests itself in the wisdom that characterizes all parts of existence. "Whoever sees them will testify that a wise being made them."[3] It manifests itself also in the "justice" (Ar. *ʿadal*) of the world, that is, the *harmony* of the universe in which the earth is at the center and the sphere is all around it, and springs of water break from underneath, and dew and rain come down from above,[4] a harmony symbolized in the commentary on *Sefer Yeṣirah* by ten fingers, "five against five," and also in the *moral* justice of commands and prohibitions and reward and punishment—in all of which there is symmetry and measure. And the final aim of all this design, of the earth and the spheres and the luminaries, is man. For there is a general rule that all important things are in the middle, the yolk of the egg, the heart of man, and the *spiritus visus* of the eye. And since the earth is in the center of all spheres, it must have been the purpose of the spheres.[6] And on the earth there are the minerals, the vegetables, the animals, and man, so it is certain that the intention was the last creation, man. It is "like a person who builds a palace and, after having furnished and decorated it, brings the owner into it."[7]

The question, of course, arises if, in opposition to Maimonides' view, the whole world was created for the sake of man, why was man created?

[3] *Em.*, II, 6, 93.

[4] *Tafsīr Mishlei*, 29.

[5] Commentary on *Sefer Yeṣirah*, 25.

[6] *Em.*, IV, exordium, 124–25. See also introd., 5, 46; I, 3, 64; IX, 1, 185. On the origin of this rule, that all important things are guarded in the center, see my *Ancient Jewish Philosophy* (Wayne State University Press, 1964), p. 61 and note 60. Saadia cites an opinion on the basis of this rule that there exists another world, so that fire, which is more important than the earth, would be located in the center, and he argues against this view (introd., 5, 46; I, 1, 57). Thus also Abraham ibn Ezra on Gen., 1, 2 writes: והנה ראיות גמורות לאנשי שיקול הדעת שאין שם רק ארץ אחת. This is Plato's view in *Timaeus*, 30, as against the Milesian view that there are many worlds.

[7] *Em.*, IV, exordium, 124–25; VI, 4, 155; IX, 1, 185.

Here the answer cannot be *ʿadal*, justice, neither in its Greek-esthetic, nor in its moral, sense. What moral injustice could there be if man were not created? The answer requires something more than harmony and more than justice, and the concept that came to Saadia, as it came to Plato in answer to this question in *Timaeus*, 29E, was the *good*—the good and the gracious. It is the way of the good to do good; that is why there was creation. The first kindness of God was to grant being, because to exist is a good in and of itself. More than this, it is the greatest possible kindness.[8] But there are other kindnesses as well. There is life, there is divine rule, there are commands and prohibitions. There is the possibility to give praise and thanks to God—all these constitute grace and bounty.[9] And there is "the complete happiness and perfect bliss"—the world to come. True, God could have granted man his portion in the hereafter without commands, but "graciousness by way of reward is greater than by way of kindness."[10] In short, the purpose of the world is man, "the axle of the world and its foundation," and the purpose of man is serving God, because thereby he attains eternal life in the time of reward.[11] That is to say, the ultimate purpose of this world is the world to come. This is the aim and drive of divine goodness. But Maimonides, who has a different view of reward, argues:

Even if the universe existed for man's sake, and man existed for the purpose of serving God, as has been mentioned, the question remains, What is the end of serving God? God does not become more perfect if all His creatures serve Him and comprehend Him as far as possible. It might perhaps be replied that service of God is not intended for God's perfection; it is intended for our perfection.... But then the question might be repeated, What is the object of being perfect?[12]

[8] *Em.*, III, exordium, 105; *Tafsīr Iyob*, 2; *Tafsīr Mishlei*, 1. See also Maimonides, *More Nebukim* (Wilna), III, 12 end: כי המצאתו הוא הטוב הגדול הגמור and also ch. 25, p. 39: כי המציאות טוב בלי ספק. Comp. Plato, *Timaeus*, 30, where divine goodness is similarly taken as the cause of creation.

[9] *Em.*, III, beginning: גוד ופצ̇ל. In *Tafsīr Iyob*, 2–3: פצ̇ל ואחסאן.

[10] *Em.*, III, 1, 105; III, 3, 141; IX, 1, 185.

[11] Beginning of Treatise on Resurrection, Arabic text as published by S. Landauer. See also *Em.*, 1, 4, 82. The phrase "the axle of the world and its foundation" (Heb. קטב העולם ומכונתו, Ar. קטב אלעאלם וקאעדתה) occurs in IV, 1, 125. Perhaps there is a veiled slur here on Sufism: not only the head of the Sufi hierarchy, but man as such, Saadia seems to say is *Qutb*, the axle of the world. See our last chapter in this discussion of Saadia's philosophy on his relation to Sufism.

[12] *Moreh*, III, 13, p. 18.

Saadia's particular conception of God as the good, although abundantly supported in all strata of Hebrew literature,[13] identifies itself with the rationalistic Muʿtazilite idea of God as the best, the kindest (Ar. *aṣlaḥ*), that God who is wise can do nothing but good.[14] Al-Ashʿari[15] cites a controversy regarding divine goodness. According to Abū Hydhayl, God's goodness is complete and entire, and there can be nothing better. Others maintain one cannot ascribe completeness to God's goodness, for it is infinite. From Saadia's introduction to his commentary on the book of Job, which he calls *kitab al-taʿdīl*, "The Book of Justification," it seems that he takes the latter position that "His kindness and grace are higher than the spheres and wider than the world and have no end." And arguing against Arab orthodoxy, which refuses to believe that God created all and leads all only for the sake of man[16] and emphasizes the absolute will and power of God, Saadia states that God "cannot do the absurd, for example, changing Himself" (*Emunot*, I, 3, fourth theory) or "cause five to be more than ten... to put the world through the hollow of a signet ring... [or] to bring back the day gone by," and that instead of these absurd encomiums one must "praise Him for His essential attributes... that He deals out unto His servants only what is best [Ar. *alaṣlaḥ*] for them."

The question then may be raised: If so, if the epithet "all-powerful" is limited, and on the other hand the "good" is without limits, why is not the good counted among the five attributes of God? For in Plato this is the divine appelation, ἀγαθός, and it is not uncommon in Hebrew literature as a name for divinity.[17] The answer seems to be that the good is included in the wise. This is the rationalistic approach in the field of ethics, which is essentially the Socratic doctrine identifying virtue with knowledge, and which characterizes the Muʿtazilite view that, according to Shahrastani, the recognition of good and evil comes through reason. But here we come to the next subject in Saadia's theodicy.

13 See, for example, *Menaḥot*, 53b: מטוב זה הקב״ה דכתיב טוב ה׳ לכל. See also my *Ancient Jewish Philosophy*, pp. 60, 67, and note 51.

14 Shahrastani, I, 30 (43).

15 Wensinck, *The Muslim Creed*, p. 80.

16 See Wensinck, *The Muslim Creed*, p. 267. Concerning al-Ashʿari's debate with his former teacher, al-Jubbai, on the fate of three that died, a believer, an infidel, and a child—a debate that was intended to reduce *ad absurdum* the idea that God intends in His administration of the universe only the good of man—see W. Spitta, *Zur Geschichte Abu'l Ḥasan al-'Ashʿaris* (Leipzig, 1876), 41 ff.

17 See my *Ancient Jewish Philosophy*, pp. 67, 173, note 51.

2. THE RATIONALITY OF THE LAW: THE INTELLECTUALISTIC APPROACH TO MORALS ACCORDING TO SAADIA AND MAIMONIDES

The third treatise, entitled "Command and Prohibition," aims to offer a rational defense of the sources of religion. The subjects dealt with in this treatise are the rationality of the Torah, the miraculous revelation to the prophets, the importance of tradition, the irrevocability of the Torah, and the explanation of certain verses that contain contradictions or apparent irrationalities. We select for discussion the first subject, the rationality of the Law.

There are, Saadia says, three demands of reason: thankfulness, refraining from insults, and refraining from crimes against society. And from these demands of reason, Saadia maintains, all rational laws can be deduced. But reason also "deems it proper for a wise man to give employment to an individual... and offer him a wage for it, merely... in order to confer a benefit upon him;" and this fourth consideration is the basis of all the other laws that are non-rational—those laws that are revealed and whose object is only to reward the faithful. But if we examine even these laws carefully, we will find that they have "partial uses" or reasons. In Chapter 2, Saadia tries to show how reason demands that one man must not hurt another, must not murder, commit adultery, steal, nor lie, and here he also attempts to illustrate the partial uses of some revealed laws.

This defense of the Law agrees with the Muʿtazilite viewpoint that good and evil are intrinsic, and that we recognize them by way of reason, whereas the orthodox Ashʿarite viewpoint claims that all moral laws are divine *decrees*, and we know them through revelation only.[18] Also,

[18] Concerning the Muʿtazilite attitude, see Shahrastani, I, 31 (44): ואתפקוא עלי אן אצול אלמערפה̈ ושכר אלנעמה̈ ואג̇ב קבל ורוד אלסמע. ואלחסן ואלקביח יג̇ב מערפתהמא באלעקל ואעתנאק אלחסן ואג̇תנאב אלקביח ואג̇ב כד̇לך. See also *ibid.*, 55 (82), and also Julian Obermann, *Wiener Zeitschrift*, XXX, p. 68. As to the Ashʿarite view, see Shahrastani, I, 73 (110): קאל(אלאשערי) ואלואג̇באת כלהא סמעיה̈, ואלעקל ליס יוג̇ב שיא, ולא יקתצי תחסינא וקביחא. About the terms שראיע עקליה̈ (Heb. מצוות שכליות) and שראיע סמעיה̈ (Heb. מצוות שמעיות), which Saadia introduced from Arabic into Jewish literature, see Jacob Guttmann, *Die Religionsphilosophie des Saadia*, p. 135, note 2. See also references in Joseph I. Gorfinkle, *Eight Chapters of Maimonides* (New York, 1912), p. 77, note 3. That Saadia, in opposition to the Ashʿarites, takes the Socratic view that reason has the power to decide between good and evil, we find also in *Tafsīr Iyob*, 11.

in the introduction to his *Tafsīr Mishlei*, Saadia maintains that reason has this moral jurisdiction, and he divides the commendments into "righteousness and judgments" (*ṣedaqah u-mishpat*), which are the rational laws, on the one hand, and "statutes" (*ḥuqqim*), which are revealed laws, on the other hand—a division the source of which is Talmudic, in Yoma, 67b.

Now Maimonides, in the sixth of the *Eight Chapters*, says: "They are called commandments about which the Rabbis said, 'If they had not already been written in the Law, it would be proper to write them.' Some of our later sages who were infected with the sickness of the Mutakallimun called these rational laws." This derisive remark against Saadia is surprising. Maimonides himself in the *Moreh*, II, 2b, accepts the Muʿtazilite view that all the commandments have their uses, "some of them we know their usefulness, like the prohibition of murder and stealing, while there are others whose usefulness is not clear," and he divides the commandments exactly as did Saadia or the Talmud into "judgments" (*mishpaṭim*) and "statutes" (*ḥuqqim*), that is, those of understandable benefits and those whose benefits we do not understand. What wrong then did Maimonides find with the term "rational laws" that Saadia introduced?

In order to understand wherein Maimonides takes issue with Saadia, and incidentally to clarify various aspects of the nature of the religio-ethical command, we must turn to Aristotle. There are three places in his writings that concern this subject. In *Ethica Nicomachea* (tr. W. D. Ross), V, 7, 1134b20, Aristotle divides political justice into two categories, natural and legal. "The natural is that which everywhere has the same force and does not exist by people's thinking this or that," and the legal is "that which is originally indifferent, but when it has been laid down is not indifferent, for example, that a prisoner's ransom shall be a mina or that a goat and not two sheep shall be sacrificed."[19]

It is clear that the "legal laws" correspond to the revealed laws, and

19 According to Diogenes Laertius, *Lives of Eminent Philosophers*, III, 86, Plato divides laws into those written and those unwritten. The second type is custom (κατὰ ἔθη), for example, not to walk in the streets naked or in a woman's dress. Aristotle too, in *Rhetoric*, I, 13, 1373b2, brings forward this division and includes as examples of the second kind the rewarding of kindness with kindness and the repaying of a gracious act—examples that Saadia includes among the demands of reason and that other medieval thinkers classify as *meforsamot*, conventions.

the "natural" to the rational laws. The word "natural" here means intrinsic, independent of man's agreement, in contradistinction to the "legal," the whole authority of which is the lawgiver, the legislator. Thus in this Aristotelian passage we have a point of contact between Aristotle and the Talmud, and a source of the Mutakallimun's and Saadia's view that there are *rational* laws, that is, those whose authority is immanent and the approach to which is reason. Moral values therefore have two characteristics: (1) their authority is natural, that is, intrinsic, and (2) they are discovered through reason. Reason discovers reason in a monism of man-world, which ultimately originates in the reason of God. This is the Saadianic theodicy. We may add a terminological remark that in the meantime a Stoic influence entered and joined together the natural and the rational, and hence we have the term "rational laws." So also Maimonides in *Moreh* II, 14 (end), dealing with the Aristotelian method of proving the belief in the eternity of the universe, says that "it appears natural [i.e., rational], not assumed."[20]

But in the *Topics* (tr. O. F. Owen) I, 1, we can trace the source of a different tendency. There Aristotle differentiates between the demonstrative syllogism whose premises are "things true and primary which obtain belief *not through others but through themselves*," and the dialectic syllogism "which is collected from probabilities... those which appear to all, or to most men, or to the wise, and to these either to all or to the greater number, or to such men as are especially renowned and illustrious," that is, that obtain their belief not by their own power but by the power of agreement, or whose authority is extrinsic and whose recognition is through agreement. Now the term "probabilities" (τὰ ἐνδόζα) does not denote particularly religio-ethical ideas but rather all general observations that intuitively come near the truth. But its Arabic translation, *mashūrāt* (Heb. *meforsamot*), conventions, came to denote, as early as in al-Farabi, *moral laws*. These conventions are less than rational laws. They convince, as Averroes argues, only because of human agreement, but they cannot convince through their own power. Thus the idea developed that, in spite of Aristotle himself, *all* moral laws are convential, without any intrinsic force, as against the *Ethica Nicomachea*, which posits also a class of *natural* justice having intrinsic authority independent of human agreement. It is from the second source

20 שהענין טבעי לא מונח.

that Maimonides drew, as Munk has already observed, his emphatic distinction between conventional truth (Heb. *meforsamot*) and rational, that is, scientific, truth (Heb. *muskalot*) in *Moreh nebukim* I, 2.[21] And therefore, true to his system, which places reason above morals in the scale of human perfection, Maimonides sharply opposes the term "rational laws" applied to morals, because all morals are only conventions, and reason is not involved in their essence or authority nor in our approach to them. And therefore, in the beginning of the *Moreh* (I, 2), in his interesting explanation of the Biblical account of the tree of knowledge, Maimonides moves the knowledge of good and evil from the category of rational truth into the category of conventions, because by reason we know the true and the false but not the right and the wrong. The whole distinction between rational laws and traditional laws in the religio-ethical realm, or between the natural and the legal in Aristotle's *Ethica Nicomachea*, fades away in Maimonides' philosophy. All religious laws become revealed laws and have only extrinsic authority, through revelation or human agreement, as opposed to intrinsic, scientific laws. True, Maimonides too seeks "causes for the laws," but these are not to be perceived by theoretical reason but only by practical reason, which deals with the contingent and belongs to the power of the imagination.[22] Saadia, on the other hand, speaks about "rational commands" and their explanation by way of reason (Heb. *muskal*), which calls forth the sharp reservation of Maimonides, because he believes this confuses the stages in the perfection of man.

But there is also a third place that serves as a source of compromise. In *Rhetoric*, I, 13, 1373b (see also 10, 1368b), Aristotle differentiates between peculiar and universal laws:

the peculiar law being that which has been marked out by each people in

[21] See Solomon Munk, Maimonides, *Le Guide des égarés*, I, 3, note 1. As to *meforsamot*, in the sense of moral foundations, in al-Farabi, see my edition of Maimonides' *Millot ha-Higgayon* (New York, American Academy for Jewish Research, 1938), introd., p. 19. See also *ibid.*, ch. 22, where I remarked that the source of the term מפורסמות, or in Arabic: משהוראת, may be the Stoic κοιναὶ ἔννοιαι and *consensus gentium*.

[22] See *Emunah Ramah*, 13; *Shemonah Peraqim*, ch. 1 (end); *Millot ha-Higgayyon*, ch. 14. The author of *Ruaḥ Ḥen* writes explicitly: יקראו מצוות השכליות לפי ששכל המעשי אשר באדם, והוא מן המדמה מקבל אותם, לא שיהיו נודעות מצד השכל העיוני שהוא שכל על דרך האמת. Aristotle too, in his *De Anima*, III, 10, identifies imagination with the epitactic or practical reason. See also his *Ethica Nicomachea*, VI, 10, 2.

reference to itself.... I call that law universal which is conformable merely to the *dictates of nature* for there does exist naturally an universal sense of right and wrong, which, in a certain degree, all *intuitively divine* [Gr. μεντεύται τὶ πάντες], even should no intercourse with each other, nor any compact have existed; which sentiment the Antigone of Sophocles enters uttering, that it was just, namely to bury Polynices, though denounced, since this by *nature* was a deed of justice.

Here too is the emphasis on the natural, intrinsic, authority of justice' in spite of the opinion of men, but the novel element here comes from the standpoint of recognition. The universal law is *divined intuitively*. True, according to Thomas Aquinas, in his commentary on *Ethica Nicomachea*,[23] Aristotle intended also to mean that justice is natural insofar as the mind grasps it naturally, that is, intuitively, as it grasps axioms. But the influence of that source on Arabic and Jewish circles was in terms of its literal sense; and the thought explicitly expressed that ethics is grasped not rationally-discursively but intuitively draws it near, as Thomas remarks, to axioms, but on the other hand, this relates it also to conventions, insofar as they are not the result of demonstrative reasoning.[24] Indeed, Joseph ibn Zaddiq and al-Gazali tend to link conventions with axioms or to include axioms among conventions because in both cases recognition is immediate and independent. Only ibn Rushd draws a sharp line between axioms, which convince intrinsically, and conventions, whose power is only human agreement. This, as we have seen, is also Maimonides' view. On the other hand, Abraham ibn Daud, who is apparently influenced by the third source, joins the two classes. Thus he writes in his *Emunah Ramah*, p. 75:[25]

[23] Sections 1017–18, 1277.

[24] See S. Horovitz, *Die Psychologie bei den jüdischen Religions philosophen des Mittelalters* (Breslau, Jahresbericht des jüdisch-theologischen Seminars, 1898), p. 49, note 1. See also *Emunah Ramah*, 69, where Abraham ibn Daud also equates conventions (*meforsamot*) with rational laws (*muskalot*), and traditions (*mequbbalot*) with perceptions (*muḥashot*). See the following note.

[25] The whole passage is interesting because it clarifies terminological differences between the Aristotelians and the Mutakallimūn, among whom ibn Daud may have included Saadia: ומדתות מהם מפורסמות בלשון בעלי ההגיון, ואצל בעלי חכמת הדבור דתות שכליות מפני שהם מתיחסות אל המושכלות התיחסות מה וזה כמו שהיושר טוב והעול רע ושבח המטיב טוב... ומהם מקובלות בלשון בעלי ההגיון והם בלשון חכמת הדבור דתות שמעיות כמו שמירת השבת ואיסור אכילת בשר החזיר... ואשר יקראום שכליות לא תתחלף בהם אומה לאומה ולא יתכן זה ואפילו יטען טוען חלוף דבר מהם עד יתיר העול אוהב בגידה (קרי: או הבגידה) או בדומה לזה נפסדה הדת שלו ובוטל סדרה.

mong laws some are conventions [Heb. *meforsamot*] in the language of philosophers, and rational laws [Heb. *datot sikliyyot*] among the Mutakallimun, because they bear a *certain relation* to laws of reason, for example, justice is good and injustice is bad, and praising a kind person is good, and to deceive one who seeks protection is wrong.... And some of the laws are traditional [Heb. *mequbalot*] in the language of the philosophers and revealed [*shimʿiyyot*] among the *Mutakallimun*, like the observance of the Sabbath and the prohibition of eating the meat of the swine.... As to what they call rational laws, no people is different from another, and no difference of opinion is possible. And if one would come and permit injustice or treachery or the like, his law would be absurd and its order invalid.

This is an echo of Aristotle's remark about Antigone. Thus the moral law is objective, immanently authoritative, but man comes to know it in a non-rational way. He does not create it by agreement as he creates the conventions but discovers it as he discovers the axioms, by an immediate power, which Aristotle describes as "mantic," or intuitive divination, and to which ibn Daud refers as "a certain relation to laws of reason." One can also see from this quotation from *Emunah Ramah* that ibn Daud would have agreed with Maimonides in calling Saadia, who designated moral conventions (Heb. *meforsamot*) as rational laws (Heb. *sikliyyot*), not a philosopher but a Mutakallimūn.

In short, there are three different opinions regarding moral laws, and they all derive from Aristotle. (1) Saadia's opinion is that they are of intrinsic authority—as opposed to revealed laws—and are rationally recognized. (2) Abraham ibn Daud's opinion is that they are conventions, but their recognition is *mantic*, like that of axioms to which they have a "certain relation." Joseph ibn Zaddiq and al-Gazali also tend in this direction. (3) Maimonides' opinion is that they are entirely conventional, that is, of external human authority, and that they are recognized as conventions only and have no relation to axioms, which exist only in the realm of science. Saadia belongs to the Muʿtazilite school. The orthodox Asharite school, maintaining that all morals are only revelations, even the primary laws of ethics, has no representative in Jewish philosophy, although in his negation of an intellectualistic-intrinsic authority in the moral laws there is a strange rapprochement between Maimonides and Arab orthodoxy. The great rationalist among these thinkers is Saadia, who demands the support of reason in all our spiritual life, while the great guardian of the height and purity of reason is Maimonides.

The world's thought followed the path of separation between science and values, the way of Maimonides and ibn Rushd, and science made astounding progress, but values have not. And one may wonder whether it would have been better if the world had chosen the Saadianic way of seeking the union of the true and the good.

Chapter Six

FREE WILL

1. IS THE WILL A RATIONAL FORCE?

THE FOURTH treatise, entitled "Obedience and Rebellion," deals with predestination and justice, that is, with man's power of choice between serving God and rebelling against Him, a power that in Muʿtazilite terminology is called "justice," meaning divine justice, because, if necessity ruled over the deeds of men, all commands and prohibitions would be useless and all reward and punishment unjust. Here in particular we will have to keep an eye on the Arabic background and its influence on Saadia's philosophy.

Let us first clarify the concept of free will as it is used in Saadia's discussion. It seems that the power that chooses, or the will, is not reason, because in his psychological proof for the freedom of will, Saadia says that man "is not conscious of the existence of any power that might prevent him from carrying out his will. All he has to do is to allow his *nature* to be led by the *intellect*. If he does so, he is wise. If not, he is foolish" (IV, 4, 129). It therefore appears that the will, or the leader, stands apart from the struggle between nature and reason and juridicates between them. Evidently, Saadia conceived the dynamics of choice to be somewhat different from Aristotle's version. According to Aristotle, the will is desire under the leadership of reason, and evil is the result of the corruption of reason (although elsewhere Aristotle asserts that reason cannot err).[1] Thus, according to Aristotle we have two active powers in the process of choice: reason and nature or desire, and the leadership of reason is the will and the freedom to make the choice between the alternatives that the will may impose. Yet according to Saadia, the will stands beside these two forces; and man's balance or decision in favor of reason or desire is the will, so that there are three powers involved in choice.

[1] See E. Zeller, *Die Philosophie der Griechen*, 2^2, pp. 598–600.

2. POWER

But this third force, the will, needs power[2] in order to go into action, to be free. Saadia does not explain the nature of this power, but we find comments on it among the Arabs. Thumāma thinks of it as all the physiological health necessary for the execution of the will, while Hishām extends the concept of power to include five elements: health, absence of deterrents, time, tools, and motive,[3] that is, physical and intellectual powers and favorable circumstances. Now when Saadia states that God gave man "the power and ability to execute what He had commanded him and to refrain from what He had forbidden him," he cannot have included motivation, for then it would constitute divine intervention and the will would not be free, as we shall soon see. But it seems he did include under power all physical factors and appropriate circumstances to make possible a free choice. This then is Saadia's conception of a free will: the decision between reason and nature and the necessary tools to execute that decision.

Looking at the history of this question, we find that Plato and Aristotle affirmed the freedom of will.[4] The Stoics tried to reconcile causality with possibility by distinguishing between approximate and main causes. The approximate cause is the outside push, whereas the main and responsibility-imposing cause is the internal assent which is in our own power, Man is free to obey or to refuse obedience to the laws of the world. although he cannot avoid them or change them. *Ducunt volentem fata,*

[2] Saadia uses the following terms for free will: (1) קדרה̈, Heb. יכלת in *Em.*, IV, 1, 125. (2) קדרה̈ ואסתטאעה̈, Heb. כח ויכלת, and again אסתטאעה̈, Heb. יכולת, in *Em.*, IV, 3, 127. (3) אכ̇תיאר, Heb. בחירה in *Em.*, IV, 3, 128. See *infra*, "Philosophical Terms in the Moreh Nebukim," s.v. יכולת גמורה, where it is pointed out that *qudra* is the physical power necessary for the action, while *istitaʿa* has also a psychological power, that is, motive, so that *istitaʿa* is *qudra* plus *ikhtiyar*. See also references to free will in *Tafsīr Mishlei*, 82, 115.

[3] See A. S. Tritton, *Muslim Theology*, pp. 77, 99. See also Thumāma's view in Shahrastani, I, 49 (end): ומנהא קולה אלאסתטאעה̈ הי אלסלאמה̈ וצחה̈ אלג̇וארח וכ̇ליתהא מן אלאפאת והי קבל אלפעל. See also *ibid.*, p. 35 (51), 44 (66), 60 (90), 100 (151). At-Ṭaḥawi, in his ביאן אלסונה ואלג̇מאע, gives a definition of power similar to Thumāma's. See *the Macdonald Presentation Volume* (Princeton University Press, 1933), p. 141.

[4] About Plato, see his *Timaeus*, 42b; *Republic*, X, 617E; 619b. About Aristotle, see E. Zeller, *Die Philosophie der Griechen*, 2^2, 588–92. But see Theodor Gomperz, *Greek Thinkers*, IV, 537.

nolentem trahunt, said Seneca.[5] In the Muslim world this question became an issue at first between the necessetarian Jabariya and the free-willist Qadariya, and afterward between the Muʿtazilites, who emphasized divine justice and therefore free will, and the Ashʿarites, who refused to bind the all-powerfulness of God, not even with the claims of ethics and logic, and therefore maintained a belief in the doctrine of necessity or predestination. Saadia, of course, found support for his doctrine of free will in the Bible and in the Talmud, but the Muʿtazilah exerted an influence on the course of his discussion.

In the beginning of his discussion, we encounter an idea borrowed from the Arabic background, indeed from the Koran itself. Saadia proves that God gave man the power to do what He commanded, because "the All-Wise does not charge any one with aught that does not lie within his competence or which he is unable to do." This echoes the verse in the Koran (3, 286): "Allah imposes not on any soul a duty beyond its scope." But it became a point at issue between the Muʿtazilites and the Ashʿarites. The Muʿtazilites, as al-Ashʿari states, accepted such a view, whereas the Ashʿarites and also al-Gazali rejected this limitation on God's Will and maintained that religion may be above the competence of man, that God may demand what is beyond man's powers.[6] Saadia, reflecting the Koran, sided with the Muʿtazilites.

Then there is a second question: When does power come: before, after, or during the act? A strange question, but again the two camps argued. The Muʿtazilites, who strove to prove that man is master of his acts, argued that power comes before the deed, it being the ability to do that deed or the reverse of it, whereas al-'Ashʿari, who rejected man's freedom of will in order to maintain God's limitless power, held that really a man cannot do his deeds at all, that he only *acquires* (Ar. *kasb*) his deeds through a power that is created in him together with the act, suffi-

[5] See E. Vernon Arnold, *Roman Stoicism*, pp. 210–13. For Seneca's saying, see his *Epistulae Morales*, 107, 11.

[6] *Em.*, IV, 3, 127, and *Amānāt*, 150: אלחכים לא יכלף אחדא מא ליס פי טאקתה. See also *Tafsīr Bereshit*, 3: אלעדל לא יכלף עבאדה מא לא יטיקון and comp. Koran, 3, 286: לא יכלף אללה נפסא אלא וסעהא... רבנא ולא תחמלנא מא לא טאקה̈ לנבאה. See also al-'Ashʿari' *Maqālāt*, 230; At-Ṭaḥawi in the *Macdonald Presentation Volume*, p. 141; A. J. Wensinck, *The Muslim Creed*, p. 157; Walter C. Klein, *Al-Ashʿari's, Al-Ibānah ʿan Uṣūl ad-Diyānah* (New Haven, 1940), 108.

cing for that act alone.[7] Thus, Abū Hanifa states in his *Fiqh Akbar*, I, 11, *Usūl al-din*, dogma 12: "We believe that power is created at the same time as the act, neither before nor after, because if it were created before the act man would not be in need of God... nor could it come after the act, for then the act would be created without power."[8] In this way, the orthodox Arabs tried always to maintain the sense of man's dependence upon God. And therefore Muhammad ibn Karrām was right in remarking that the assumption that power comes with the act is nothing but determinism.[9]

Saadia discusses the various possibilities as to when the power comes in relation to the deed, and agrees, of course, with the Muʿtazilites. It cannot come simultaneously with the act, because if so, then either there would be a mutual relation of causality between them (since neither one preceded the other) or there would not be any relation of causality. Both possibilities are absurd, because power must serve as a cause (an efficient cause). Nor could it come after the act, because in that case—Saadia's reasoning here is sharper than that of Abū Hanifa—man could reverse, or "unact," his act (i.e., since power is by definition the ability to act or not to act). We must therefore conclude that power comes before the deed, so that man is free and responsible.[10]

3. GOD AND MORAL EVIL

So much about man's possession of his acts. What portion of these acts does God possess? The orthodox view among the Arabs is that they are all His, whether good or evil, belief or heresy. And all is predetermined. All was written in the beginning with a pre-existent pen on a preserved tablet. Saadia, together with the Muʿtazilah, opposed this view. He adduces two proofs that God has no influence on human deeds. First is the psychological proof. Man feels conscious of his ability to speak or to remain silent, to seize or to let go,[11] and is not conscious of any deterrent. Second, there are five rational considerations. (1) One act

[7] Al-Ashʿari, *Maqālāt*, 229–30; Klein, *Al-Ashʿari's Al-Ibānah ʿan Uṣūl ad-Diyānah*, 180.

[8] Wensinck, *The Muslim Creed*, p. 128.

[9] Tritton, *Muslim Theology*, p. 110.

[10] *Em.*, IV, 3, 127.

[11] *Em.*, IV, 4, 129: שהאדם שוער בנפשו שיוכל לדבר ויוכל לשתק. Similarly Yehudah Halevi in *Kuzari*, V, 20: כי אתה מוצא עצמך יכול על הדבור ועל השתיקה.

cannot have two authors, and how can we affirm determinism without affirming double authorship? Nor can we divide the act, saying that one part is man's and the other belongs to God, without admitting at least a part as being wholly man's. (2) If God decrees, why does He command and prohibit? (3) If God decrees, why does He reward and punish? (4) On the contrary, He should reward both saint and sinner for carrying out His decrees. (5) The heretic can exonerate himself by saying that he could not overpower God.

But this severance of human acts from divine responsibility presents two difficulties. First, if moral evil—physical evil Saadia discusses later—does not come from God, Who does not desire sin, its existence in the world means that there is something in God's world that God does not desire—how can that be? Of course, the Ashʿarites plainly admit sin into the mystery of God's infinite will. But if, as the Muʿtazilites believe, God is just and wise, how can there exist injustice and folly? Saadia's answer is not easily understandable. God, he says, does not hate sin—and social sins are explicitly included—in and for itself, but only for our sake, because it brings us harm. And therefore it is not hateful to God in and of itself but only because of His mercy upon us.[12] The answer does not accord with a strictly moral view of sin, that sin is inherently, autonomously, evil, not because of ulterior considerations but because God Himself is hurt, as it were, by the occurrence of sin in the world. But it is consistent with Saadia's transcendentalism, and even reference to His mercy should be taken figuratively.

And the second difficulty of "freedom-being given" lies in the idea that "all is foreseen." First, God's justice is thereby affected, for how can He decree and yet punish? Second, why is man sinful, for "inasmuch as God knows what is to be before it happens, He must also know that man will rebel against Him; and in that case man cannot but rebel, since otherwise God's foreknowledge is not realized."[13] The answer again reflects thoughts and explorations from the Arabic background. What does divine foreknowledge mean? And how does it relate to the foreknown event? The Ashʿarite belief is that God's Will accompanies His knowledge. All that He knows, good or evil, He wills, and all that He wills happens. This does not solve our difficulty, namely, how can a

12 *Em.*, IV, 4, 129–30.
13 *Em.*, IV, 4, 130.

human act be a sin when foreseen and willed, and why it is punished; but the Ashʿarites flatly deny human freedom and ignore the question of justice. There is a second view, endorsed even by some Muʿtazilites, namely, that the whole creativity of God is in His foreknowledge,[14] which intensifies our difficulty. But there is a third view. In *Fiqh Akbar*, II, fifth dogma, we find an orthodox conciliatory solution: God foreknows, and nothing can happen except what is written on the preserved tablet. "But His knowledge is descriptive, not decisive"; and later on in the same dogma: "He knows the non-existents in their state of non-existence and also in their future state of existence. He knows existents in their state of existence and also how in the future they will cease to exist."[15] Thus His knowledge is spread out over all time: before being, during being, and after being, and there is never a change in His knowledge. It is this view that constitutes Saadia's answer. God's knowledge is "no cause for the being of things." That is, it is descriptive in advance but not causative, because, if we assumed that His knowledge is a cause, as the Ashʿarites believed that His knowledge is accompanied by Will, or as some Muʿtazilites held that His knowledge is creative, "then all things would have been ancient," that is, without a beginning, "because His knowledge of them is ancient." "But," Saadia adds, "we think that He knows things in their true being." What is this knowledge, which is not creative or which holds back its creativeness? It is a knowledge of future things not as existing but as as yet non-existent, so that *ipso facto* such a knowledge does not include the creation of existents or a will toward the existents. "What He will create He knows that He *will* create it; what man will choose, He knows that man *will* choose it." This is historical knowledge, a knowledge of before and present and after, and the knowledge of before can never kindle its creative fire as long as the thing is also, as with knowledge, in a state of before. Hence, things are not "ancient,"[16] and His knowledge is not cause. It is descriptive, a knowledge of things "in their true being," and therefore not causative.

[14] Wensinck, *The Muslim Creed*, pp. 144–45, 211.

[15] *Ibid.*, p. 190.

[16] *Em.*, IV, 4, 130. In *Shemonah Peraqim*, ch. 8, Maimonides discusses the possibility of another deterministic influence, for example, the stars, and repudiates any belief in astrology. Saadia does not even admit it into the discussion. But in ch. 13 of this treatise, he explicitly opposes fatalism and astrology. See also ch. 7.

But people ask about passages in the Bible that seem to contradict he conception of God as justice and wisdom. Saadia deals with these questions in Chapter 5. To one of these questions he gives an answer that involves a philosophical idea. People ask, he says, concerning Sennacherib and Nebuchadnezzar, who brought death and destruction to the world, how could God refer to the one as *My* scourge, and to the other as *My* sword? Does not this mean determinism? The answer is, God only gave them power, but they acted out of choice, for which they deserved punishment.[17] Here essentially is the Stoic idea mentioned before, that no matter what the external "pushing" cause may be, man is responsible for his assent.

And in Chapter 6 Saadia considers those many expressions in the Bible that seem to imply determinism and divine intervention. Saadia divides them into eight classes, naming each class by the method of its interpretation in line with freedom: (1) prohibition, that is, as expressed in terms of prevention, (2) obstruction, as if it were compulsion, (3) giving courage, as if it were a hardening of the hearts, (4) assignment of rank, as if it were an exercise of influence, (5) forgiveness, as if it were compulsion, (6) human nature, as if it were inspiration and influence, (7) hyperbole, as if it were a creation of a special faculty, (8) creation of means, as if it were compulsion and intervention. This last class is of three types: delivering man from his enemies so that he becomes *free* to act, clearing man's mind, and offering miracles for the sake of inspiration. Let us again select one example of some philosophical-historical importance. It is discussed as an illustration of the fourth class, that of assignment of rank. It is the verse in Is., 63, 17: "*Why dost Thou make us err from Thy ways*," and is interpreted to mean only "Do not make us rank with men that err," or "Do not judge us as belonging to those that err." Now this is exactly the explanation of most Muʿtazilites on some verses in the Koran. Thus, 'Al-Ashʿari remarks in his *Maqālāt*, 261–62: "Most Muʿtazilites assume that the verses that speak of God's causing man to err mean only *applying names* to men and *passing judgment* on them as having erred."[18]

[17] *Em.*, IV, 5, 132. This reconcilation of causality and freedom finds some expression also in Yehudah Halevi's *Kuzari*, V, 20: והבחירה מכלל הסבות האמצעיות ולבחירה סבות משתלשלות אל הסבה הראשונה. The Stoics call choice, that is, the *ascent* to the cause, the main cause.

[18] See Klein, *Al-Ashʿari's Al-Ibānah ʿan Uṣūl ad-Diyānah*, p. 121.

God then does not cause man to err, nor in fact does He guide man at all. Some Muʿtazilites opposed the Christian idea of grace (Ar. *luṭf*), that God sometimes grants faith to a man as a gift of grace, although some others accepted it.[19] Saadia apparently belongs to the first group of Muʿtazilites, in that he opposed such a belief because that too would conflict with the doctrine of freedom. Hence he endeavors to eliminate all hints of determinism even from such a verse as *Incline my heart unto Thy testimonies* (Ps., 119, 36) and even hints of "influence and instruction" from such a verse as *Show me Thy Ways, O Lord, teach me Thy paths* (Ps., 25, 4).[20] All this exegesis illustrates Saadia's rationalistic stand on man's freedom.

19 Wensinck, *The Muslim Creed,* p. 82; Klein, *Al-Ashʿari's Al-Ibānah ʿan Uṣūl ad-Diyānah,* p. 108.

20 *Em.*, V, 6, 135.

Chapter Seven

MERITS AND DEMERITS

1. STAINS ON THE SOUL

THE FIFTH treatise, entitled "Merits and Demerits," aims to show that there is a direct connection between man's degree of moral goodness and his degree of physical happiness, although the contrary may sometimes appear to be true. This stirs questions as to why the good suffer, but through certain assumptions and categorizations Saadia attempts to remove some of the pain of these eternal questionings.

To begin with, Saadia postulates that deeds make an impress on the soul—either they polish the soul until it is bright and luminous or they soil and darken it until it becomes the sad record of its misdeeds. The soul's lightnesses and darknesses reveal the story of its struggles, those that triumphed and those that ended in defeat. But this book is open only to God, for the impress is of a spiritual substance, and no human eye can see it.[1]

This ethico-poetic conception apparently sprang from Muʿtazilistic exegesis. According to al-'Ashʿari, in his *Maqālāt*, 259, the Muʿtazilites interpreted those Koranic verses that speak of God's "sealing the hearts of men" as referring to black stains, like sword-rust, which God puts upon the human heart, but they do not imply that He sealed up in them the spring of faith, that He deprived them of this power in the future. The Muʿtazilites therefore advanced the theory of the darkness of the heart in order to explain away passages of determinism in the Koran. Saadia, however, uses the same doctrine as a descriptive explanation of providence. The Muʿtaziliṭes add, according to al-'Ashʿari, that God makes those marks on the human hearts so that the angels can tell God's friends from His enemies.[2] Saadia, who generally minimizes the role of angels, says that the marks are revealed to *God*, and also that the deeds themselves stain the soul, rather than that God put the stains

1 *Em.*, V, 11, 136–37.

2 Walter C. Klein, *Al-Ashʿari's Al-Ibānah ʿan Uṣūl ad-Diyānah*, p. 114. See also A. S. Tritton, *Muslim Theology*, p. 149, who quotes this belief in the name of al-Jubbai.

upon it. All this is in the direction of greater rationalism and anti-anthropomorphism.

2. THE CATEGORIES

From the standpoint of psychic light and darkness, that is, merits and demerits, men may be classified, says Saadia, according to ten categories, namely, "pious and impious, obedient and disobedient, perfect and imperfect, sinful and corrupt, renegade and penitent." There is also another category, one without a counterpart, namely, "the equal," that is, one whose merits and demerits are balanced, whom God in His mercy will join with the pious. Thus Saadia opposes the Muʿtazilite viewpoint that there is an intermediate place between heaven and hell for the equal.[3]

As to the first pair of categories, the difference between the pious and the impious does not lie in the comparative sum total of *all* the deeds but in the sum of *most* of them. The pious is one whose deeds are mainly merits, and the deeds of the impious are mainly demerits. "If a man has to his credit two hundred and one acts, one hundred of which are good and another hundred are evil, which would render his record evenly balanced; then, if the additional single act is good, he is called pious, and, if it is evil, he is called impious."[4] It may be that this view was influenced by Akiba's statement in Abot, 3, 15: "And all is according to the amount of the work," which Rashi explains as meaning "most of the work." Maimonides' explanation, which differs from that of Rashi, takes the term *rov*, translated as "amount," to mean frequency, or the number of times of a good deed, which gives it a stronger hold. Against this, Arab orthodoxy, believing that all is written in advance on the "preserved tablet," thought that all is according to the *final* work, that a man may follow the law all his life, yet in his last days he will be caught by his fate and corrupt himself and enter hell.[5] Al-Tahāwī, too, believed

[3] *Em.*, V, 2, 138–40. See also V, 6, 145. Saadia here opposes Abū Hāshim, who set aside this intermediate place for "equals." See Tritton, *Muslim Theology*, p. 155; C. Snouck Hurgronje, *Mohammedanism* (New York, 1916), pp. 75–76.

[4] *Em.*, V, 3, 141.

[5] Wensinck, *The Muslim Creed*, p. 55. On the other hand, Abū Hāshim thought that the retribution for the minority acts is subtracted from the majority of the acts, and the remainder is man's destiny in the hereafter. See Tritton, *Muslim Theology*, p. 155.

that only the final acts are taken into account.[6] It is because of such a view that al-Gazali spoke of the fear of the end or the conclusion.[7] Saadia who consistently rejected determinism, was free from the fear of the end and from the frightful thought that one final act can cancel out a whole life dedicated to goodness, Thus the doctrine of freedom inspires man with the feeling of calm and security.

The "obedient" is one who devotes his whole life to one particular command, and the "disobedient" is one who rebels against one particular command. The "prefect" is the completely righteous. Saadia the rationalist, who believed in the Socratic identity of reason and virtue and in the *infinite* goodness of God, had to believe that the idea of a completely righteous person is in the realm of possibility. And even though the Bible asserts *For there is not a just man upon the earth that doeth good and sinneth not* (Ecc., 7, 20), this only means that there is not a just man who has not the ability to sin too, for ability is two sided, the power to do and to refrain from doing.[8] The "imperfect" is one who is negligent in regard to the positive commandments. The "sinner" is one who transgresses negative precepts, such as are however not of a serious nature, for example, eating unlawful flesh, wearing mixed fibers, soothsaying and augury, etc. The "corrupt" (Ar. *al-fāsiq*) is he who commits serious transgressions, such as are punishable by various forms of death, for example, incest, desecration of the Sabbath, eating on the day of atonement, eating leavened bread on Passover.[9] The "renegade," or "infidel" (Ar. *al-kāfir*), is he who abandons the basic

6 See *the Macdonald Presentation Volume* (Princeton University Press, 1933), p. 136.

7 Al-Gazali, *Iḥya,* I, 114–17; Wensinck, *The Muslim Creed,* p. 139.

8 *Em.*, V, 4, 142. In V, 19, 214 Saadia says שיאמין האדם שאיננו נמלט מחטא. We must then there too refer to the "yekolet," to the *ability* to sin.

9 *Ibid.*, In IX, 9, 195, Saadia illustrates serious violations by murder, stealing, and adultery. This idea that there are lighter and more serious commandments, Saadia emphasizes also in *Tafsir Mishlei,* 115. So also in *Tafsīr Iyob,* 39, where he differentiates between robbers and the corrupt and the renegade (אלט̇אלמין ואלפסאק ואלכפאר); and the question arises of why the robbers are not included among the corrupt, since according to *Em.*, IX, 9, 195. stealing is regarded as a serious violation. The answer is that the stealing that is of a serious nature is stealing of human beings, punishable by death. See Sanhedrin, 86a. The term כבאיר, which Saadia uses for mortal sins is not according to Hebraic uses, which is קלות וחמורות, and not גדולות וקטנות. This term, which the Khārijites emphasized in particular, is taken from Arabic theology. See Wensinck, *The Muslim Creed,* p. 39.

principle of the faith, the belief in the Creator. The "penitent" is he who repents.

Saadia's distinction between the "corrupt" and the "renegade" should be considered against an Arabic background in which there raged a fierce controversy on this point, a controversy not unstained with blood. According to the Kharijites, who were religious zealots, the "corrupt" person, that is, one who transgressed serious (Ar. *kabāyir*) commands, is like a "renegade," that is, he is outside the Moslem fold, and the conclusion is practically that it is proper to kill him, and theoretically it means that faith is not a fixed entity but is, rather, affected by the acts. The Murjites, on the other hand, opposed the theoretical aspect of joining the "corrupt" with the "renegade" and removed the moral element from faith. They taught the solidity of faith, that it cannot be affected by the nature of one's deeds. In this controversy orthodoxy supported the Murjites, whereas the Muʿtazilites took a middle road, namely, that the corrupt is neither a believer nor a renegade. True, he must abide forever in Fire, for there are only two divisions in the next world, heaven and hell; yet his punishment is not as severe as that of the renegade.[10] What was Saadia's opinion on this question? He certainly was not a Kharijite, since he assigned the corrupt and the renegade to two different categories. From his assumption that at the time of retribution there will be only two groups of men, the righteous and the evildoers (V, 7, 146), to the exclusion of a third, and furthermore that in the next world no one is transferred from one status to another, that each group remains eternally in its particular position (V, 2, 139), we may infer that here too Saadia tended toward the Muʿtazilah, though the latter sought a more lenient solution, But he also agreed with the Murjites as to the fixity of faith.

As to the punishment for an evil thought, Saadia tended to be more lenient than the Muʿtazilites, who held that an evil thought has the status of an act, for he differentiated between "guilt of intent" and "guilt of action" and held that there is no punishment for intention or conviction except for that of denial of a Creator.[11] On the other hand, he maintained the greater severity of a misdeed when repeated, thus agreeing with al-Jubbai who said that the stealing of one drachma is a light transgression,

10 מנזלה בין אלמזלתין. See Duncan B. Macdonald, *Muslim Theology*, p. 130.
11 *Em.*, V, 8, 147.

whereas the stealing of five drachmas is severe, and that if a man steals but one drachma from each one of five persons he is guilty of a severe transgression, because deed is added to deed.[12] Similarly, Saadia taught that "it is worse if one robs a thousand men of a sum total of a thousand drachmas than if one robs five hundred men of that amount, as Scripture says: *By reason of the multitude of oppressions they cry out*" (Job, 35, 9).[13] And it may be from Saadia that Maimonides derived the idea for his above-mentioned explanation of Abot, 3, 15. *And all is according to the amount of the act*, that is, according to its frequency.

3. DOGMAS IN JUDAISM

This category of the *kafir*, the renegade, who denies a principle of faith, raises the question of what Saadia regarded as a "principle," or a dogma. The problem of dogmas, it is true, was more crucial among the Arabs than among Jews during Saadia's time and also for many years before. The reason for this was probably psycho-political. A new religion coming up within the mass and friction of peoples and faiths needs self-definition, both for its followers and against its opponents; whereas an older faith is not required to look into itself until challenged by circumstances. Hence in the period of the *hadiths*, or traditions concerning the sayings and actions of Mohammed, the following six dogmas became crystallized among the Arabs:

1. Belief in God.
2. Belief in His angels.
3. Belief in His books.
4. Belief in His messengers.
5. Belief in the hereafter.
6. Belief in predestination.[14]

A further stimulus to dogmatism was perhaps provided by the Kharijite group, which arose thirty years after the death of Mohammed and which placed emphasis on human action, declaring, as we have seen, that he who is guilty of severe transgressions is regarded as a renegade, thereby coming into conflict with the Murjites, so that for a long time the discussion was kept alive as to what is faith, and what is Islam. In Saadia's time the Arab orthodox party, under the leadership of al-'Ash'ari,

12 Klein, *Al-Ash'ari's Al-Ibānah 'an Uṣūl ad-Diyānah*, p. 22.

13 *Em.*, V, 7, 146.

14 Wensinck, *The Muslim Creed*, pp. 23, 35.

provided a further impetus to the question of what must a man believe. What is the theological border beyond which man leaves his fold? This was the atmosphere in which Saadia lived, and these questions certainly confronted our pioneer of medieval Jewish thought when he came to write his *Emunot we-De῾ot*. What were his answers?

First, we must not, together with some scholars, regard the very division of the book into its various treatises as an enumeration of dogmas.[15] This idea was essentially noted earlier by Israel Halevi Kitover in his introduction to the Yosefov edition of our book, where he speaks about "the Division of the Book, its Treatises, and its Chapters." But did Saadia really regard every view that he expressed and substantiated in this book as a dogma or "root" in Judaism? It not, where does the root end and the stem or the branch begin? We must examine Saadia's words in the book itself and also in his other books, and then we will have a more definite idea as to what he regarded as dogma.

In the first place, in his commentary on Genesis (ed. Joseph Derenbourg), p. 3, Saadia enumerates the roots of faith[16] from the standpoint of reason only, that is, prior to revelation—deistic dogmas, which are as follows:

1. Belief in Creation.
2. There is an Eternal Creator, One and Without Resemblance.
3. The Creator is Wise, foreknowing.
4. The world was created without matter.
5. The Righteous imposes on His servants no burden they cannot bear.[17]

There is no reference here to the Torah or to the heareafter; these roots all antedate the Torah. But, according to Saadia, no rational principle can lose its validity at the giving of the Law.

In various places in *Emunot* we find attempts at the formulation of dogmas in *Judaism*. In V, 4, 142, Saadia defines the *kāfir*, or renegade,

15 For example, my master, Solomon Schechter, in his *Studies in Judaism*, First Series (Philadelphia, 1896), p. 162, and David Neumark in his תולדות העיקרים בישראל (Odessa, 1912), p. 98. Neumark therefore struggled with difficulties on p. 99 in the arrangement of dogmas 5, 6, and 9.

16 Ar. אצול אלאמאנאת. Comp. *Amānāt*, V, 177 ואמא אלכאפר פהו אלתארך אלאצל. Heb. (V, 4, 142) אבל הכופר הוא העוזב העיקר.

17 Comp. *Em.*, IV, 3, 127 and Koran, 2, 286, and see above ch. 6, note 6. Comp. *Em.*. I, 3, 63 where Saadia counts as "roots" creation, a Creator, *creatio ex nihilo*.

as one who abandons the "root" (*al-aṣl*, Heb. *ha-ʿiqqar*). This abandonment may take three different forms: the worship of someone else than God, the worship of no one ət all, or being in doubt about faith. In V, 8, 147, Saadia say about those who explain *Let us make man in our image* as meaning that an angel created man and the whole world, that they belong to the category of renegades, or *kāfirin*. And in IX, 9, 195, he joins renegades and polytheists in the one category designated as "the men that have rebelled against Me." From all this it seems that the belief in one God Who created all is a "root "or dogma. And apparently there are no more. For in VII, 1, 163, he says:

Whoever denies the resurrection of the dead... will be compelled likewise to deny the miracle of the transformation of the staff into a serpent, and water into blood... and all the other marvelous miracles... to make liars of all God's messengers... to reject the doctrine of *creatio ex nihilo*, with the result that he would deny the existence of the Creator Himself and thereby exclude himself from the community of believers.

It would seem from this passage that until then, that is, until he denies the divine existence, man does not exclude himself from the community, even if he rejected resurrection and miracles and creation from nothing.

It appears however that the "self-exclusion form the community of believers," which characterizes the denial of the divine existence, is a special category, as will be noted later, and that the other beliefs mentioned in this passage are indeed dogmas. For in VII, 1, 175, he calls redemption a dogma (Ar. *aṣl*, Heb. *shoresh*). And in VII, 3, 167, he says about one who rejects resurrection that "he is not deserving to meet the face of the Divine Presence," that is, that he has no portion in the hereafter, in accordance with the Mishnah in Sanhedrin 90a. And in VII, 6, 170, he combines these four dogmas, that is, the existence of God, the unity of God, resurrection, and redemption, and he adds to these retribution. Thus he quotes the verse *See now that I, even I am He* (Deut., 32, 39) and comments:

The verse quoted last contains a reply to four different types of heretics (Ar. מכדּבין, Heb. מכחישים]. The first are those who affirm there is no Creator.... The second group is made up of those who assert there is a Creator but that He had an associate in the work of creation.... The third group is that of those who reject the doctrine of resurrection.... The fourth group consists of those who deny there will be a reckoning and a punishment in the here-after.

All these four groups are called "heretics." And there are other dogmas, for in VII, 5, 170 he says that he who explains away allegorically creation and miracles and, in general, revealed commandments "excludes himself from the Jewish religion." Consequently, miracles and the authority of revealed laws—about rational laws there are no disputes—are also roots.

It is possible, therefore, that Saadia differentiated between the expression "he excludes himself from the category of believers" and the expression "he excludes himself from the Jewish religion," just as the Arab tradition distinguished between "faith" as a sum of doctrines and "Islam" as a system of practical laws. And by the expression "he excludes himself from the category of believers" Saadia might have meant that he who disbelieves in God excludes himself not only from the Jewish religion but from any kind of religion, from faith, for in Saadia's conception, as we have seen, there is faith prior to the Torah.

At any rate Saadia's Jewish dogmas seem, therefore, to be the following eight:

1. The existence of a Creator.
2. Creation out of nothing.
3. The Creator had no associates.
4. The authority of revealed laws.
5. Belief in miracles.
6. Belief in reckoning and retribution.
7. Belief in resurrection.
8. Belief in redemption.

So that we have here, at the beginning of the Middle Ages, a full account of Jewish dogmatics, which, when added to some of the rational "roots" that are prior to the Torah, contains almost all of the thirteen dogmas of Maimonides. But in order to understand the significance of this "almost," we must first see what Saadia omitted from the previously listed dogmas of the Arabic creed.

He omitted the following three dogmas: angels, messengers (i.e., prophets), and predestination. The last he omitted obviously because he rejected it as a concept. But why the omission of angels and prophets? The answer lies in his transcendental tendency, which shrank, as we have seen, from all thought of mediation because that is apt to blur the boundary between God and the universe, or, in other words, endanger the principle of unity. The belief in angels contains the danger of identifying the angel with the demiurge, as the Magharians and Benjamin

Nahawandi did, and as did Philo, according to Harkavy, long before them.[18] There was also a Gnostic thought that angels created man and the universe and that they said *Let us make man in our image.*[19] Saadia himself quotes this interpretation and calls it heresy,[20] as we have seen. Hence he refrained from giving the belief in angels the status of a dogma, and even maintained that man is higher than angels.[21]

For the same reason he refrained from making prophecy a dogma, so that people should not be led to the deification of the prophet, as he was deified by the Shiites. On the contrary, he tried to show that the prophet is subject to all biological laws that rule over all men, and, in opposition to the doctrine of *ʿiṣmah* that was current among the Arabs, namely, that the prophet is *guarded* against sin, he maintained that the prophet can sin like all men.[22] The prophet, according to Saadia, is only a tool for the working of miracles, and in this aspect he is included in the dogma of miracles.

Saadia's exclusion of belief in angels as a dogma was accepted by all Jewish thinkers who came after him, except Abraham ibn Daud.[23] Maimonides too, who devoted much space in his discussion to angels, who regarded them as means for prophecy and providence, and felt therefore that belief in them is prior to the belief in prophecy,[24] eliminated the belief in angels from his creed, apparently for the same reason, the fear of assuming associates with God in creation. In fact, he warns against this "association," mentioning angels in particular in his fifth dogma.

But Saadia's second elimination was not accepted. And Maimonides records as his sixth dogma the belief that man can rise to a supreme degree of moral and intellectual development, that his mind may unite with the Active Intellect, which union constitutes prophecy. He also

18 Harkavy, לקורות הכתות בישראל in Graetz's *Geschichte der Juden*, translated into Hebrew by S. P. Rabinowitz, V, 16. See Leon Nemoy, "Al-Qirqisani's Account of Jewish Sects and Christianity," in *Hebrew Union College Annual*, VII, p. 364.

19 See Professor Israel Friedlander, "The Heterodoxies of the Shiites, etc," in *Journal of the American Oriental Society*, XXIX, p. 84.

20 כופרים. *Em.*, V, 8, 147. See also II, 6, 93.

21 See Henry Malter, *Life and Works of Saadia Gaon*, p. 212, and above, ch. 4, p. 4.

22 *Em.*, III, 4, 111, and above, ch. 3 (end).

23 See Neumark, תולדות העיקרים בישראל pp. 121, 124. See also David ben Yom-Tob Bilia, quoted by Prof. Schechter, *Studies in Judaism*, p. 166.

24 *Moreh Nebukim*, III, 45.

posits a seventh dogma, that Moses rose above humanity to an "angelic station." Saadia would have winced at such an exaltation. Nor could he include the doctrine of the Active Intellect into his system, most likely because he regarded it, as he regarded all intermediating "spirituals," with absolute negation. Yehuda Halevi, who likewise rejected the belief in the Active Intellect, thought that the prophet unites with the "divine essence" itself and rises above biological-human conditions to an angelic stage higher than that of other men as other men are higher than animals.[25] Saadia, however, as we have seen, aimed not to emphasize the prophet's superiority and supernaturalness but rather his naturalness and equality with all men—all in order to guard divine transcendence. Hence, despite the Arab ideas all around him, he did not include the belief in the prophets in the dogmas of Judaism.

4. WHY THE GOOD SUFFER

One of the main discussions in this fifth treatise revolves around the problem of why good people suffer, since this suffering contradicts the division of men into the various categories of good and bad. How can a sufferer be called good or righteous without thereby implying a protest against the ways of God and a destruction of all theodicies?

True, concerning the very existence of evil, Saadia has already given his explanation. God did not create evil, but man, endowed with free will, can turn into evil things that are not originally so. In his wisdom, he eats and drinks to satisfy his needs; in his folly, he crosses the border to his own misfortune.[26] This means that essentially there is no evil; it is man himself that creates it. The problem however is more limited—not pain in general, but the pain of the righteous and the *wise*. For virtue and wisdom are identical in Saadia as well as in Socrates, so that folly cannot serve as the final answer. We must therefore conclude that there is evil that is sent down from above and that is nevertheless good. How is this possible? This is what Saadia tries to show in Chapters 2 and 3 of this treatise.

The explanation of those facts that seem to deny the principle of moral causality—the principle that goodness brings reward, evil causes punishment—is already implied in the concept of the "majority of acts." This

[25] *Kuzari*, I, 41–42.

[26] *Em.*, I, 3, 71. This is the third kind of evil according to the *Moreh*, III, 12. In *Em.*, VI, 4, 156, suffering is either folly or punishment.

concept, we will recall, says that since retribution comes in the next world, where there is no transference from one compartment into another, from reward to punishment or the reverse, "where every one stays forever where he is,"[27] it must be the *dominant* good or evil of a man's acts that receives its retribution there, whereas the smaller part of his action is paid for here in this world. It is therefore possible that a good man should suffer all his life and a wicked man should wallow in pleasure, because they are being paid off for their minor acts. One must also consider the element of regret, which completely upsets a man's moral account, because it cancels out merits or demerits stored up for him in the next world; so that it is possible that a good man who receives his penalties in this world for the sinful minority of his deeds should suddenly regret his merits, and since there are some merits that even heresy cannot destroy, he will be given his reward for them in this world; and he who looks on will stand astonished: This good man suddenly rotted, whereupon he became a successful man! Thus Saadia delves into the mechanism of destiny, into the complex laws that rule over human life. And the conclusion is that the treasures stored on high are not after all permanent possessions but may momentarily evaporate because of an evil thought or emotion, so that even Saadia's philosophy is not altogether free from the fear of the end—if not of the final act, then of the final thought that may come up like a wave and wipe off all. Yet obviously, as against this fear of the danger that confronts a good man, there is also the hope that beckons to the wicked man, the hope of penitence. Thus nothing is after all final and sealed until the day of death.

This is the first reason for the sufferings of the righteous. They are the penalty for the evil minority of their acts. This penalty is called a purification (Ar. *tamḥīḍ*), a purging of the sins. Hence in truth suffering is a loving kindness.[28] The second reason for suffering is trial,[29] a testing when the Tester knows that the one who is to undergo it will stand it and hence inflicts it upon him in order to reward him and to demonstrate that he was not chosen in vain. Such suffering may be sent upon a perfectly righteous person and upon innocent children who will undoubtedly

[27] *Em.*, V, 2, 139: כל אחד מהגמולים עומד תמיד במה שהוא בו.

[28] תמחי׳ץ. *Tafsīr Iyob*, 3, 104; *Em.*, 3, 140; VI, 4, 156.

[29] Concerning this twofold reason, penalty or trial, see *Em.*, V, 3, 140 and also IV, 5, 132; VI 4, 156; *Tafsir Mishlei*, 28, 96; *Tafsīr Iyob*, 4.

be rewarded for their pains. Al-'Ashʿari tells in his *Maqālāt*, 253[30] that, according to the Muʿtazilites, God sometimes brings pain upon children in order that they should serve as an example to older persons, and He rewards them for it.[31] Nor is the trial by suffering without immediate benefit, for it strengthens man against the lure of sin.

As for the well-being of the wicked, there are several explanations, in addition to the one that they are obtaining their reward in this world for their few merits. (1) God knows that the wicked will regret. (2) The wicked man is to beget a righteous son. (3) He will serve as an instrument for punishing malefactors who are worse than he. (4) A righteous person prays for him. (5) His punishment in the hereafter may thereby be made more severe.

And trial too is loving-kindness. Therefore man must bear his pains, because they are either atonement or a test.[32] For all things are due to God's wisdom, even pain.[33] Sickness has its good side.[34] So does suffering of all kinds.[35] Man should not therefore wish his pains upon others, only his pleasures.[36] Here Saadia went to the extreme of the Talmudic dictum "Sufferings are dear" (Ber., 5b), joining also Arab orthodoxy, which maintained that the evil deeds of the sufferer are not weighed in the balance in the hereafter, and his reward is paid at once, so that those who had lived happily will wish that their bodies had been cut with scissors.[37] But Jewish literature too wreathed golden crowns for sufferers. It is enough to mention Ps., 94, 12; Pr., 3, 12; Job, 6, 17, and the statement in the *Sifrei* on Deut., 6, 5: "Sufferers are dear to God, for the glory of God rests on one who suffers, for as the Bible says, *The Lord thy God chasteneth thee.*"

Maimonides rejects the theory of trial or "visitations of love" (Heb. *yissurim shel ahavah*), even though it is maintained by some sages in the Talmud,[38] and explains suffering as either punishment or the result of unwise choice. The difference between Saadia and Maimonides in

30 See Klein, *Al-Ashʿari's Al-Ibānah ʿan Uṣūl ad-Diyānah*, p. 112.

31 Wensinck, *The Muslim Creed*, p. 81.

32 *Tafsīr Mishlei*, 96,

33 *Ibid.*, p. 83.

34 *Em.*, IV, 2, 126.

35 *Tafsīr Iyob* (ed. Derenbourg), 3, 104.

36 *Ibid.*

37 Wensinck, *The Muslim Creed*, p. 171.

38 *Moreh Nebukim*, III, 17; III, 24.

this respect can be characterized as follows. In so far as Maimonides lays the whole responsibility for action on man, his view is more ethical; and in so far as Saadia sees divine intervention in human life as irrespective of moral causality, his view is more theological.

We have then two kinds of suffering: penalty and trial. There is still another kind, suffering as "chastisement and instruction,"[39] "toil and effort and practice," which accompany each process of learning. Saadia perhaps thought here of the Talmudic statement in Berakot, 5a concerning the three gifts that God gave to man, all of them to be acquired through pain, and among them is the gift of the Torah. This kind of suffering Saadia regarded as of the highest importance, higher than punishment and trial. It may be that this kind too, like the suffering of trial, Saadia regarded as "visitations of love," for in connection with it he cites the verse in Ps., 3, 12: *For whom the Lord loveth he correcteth*, so that there are only two causes for suffering, penalty and love.

And even though Saadia sometimes thinks that man is after all incapable of understanding why the good suffer, and that all the energies he expends in this direction may be in vain,[40] still he devotes to this problem his commentary on Job and calls it "The Book of Justification" (Ar. *Kitab al-Taʿdīl*). Five characters appear in Job, and Saadia's interpretation of them is as follows. On the one hand there are the three friends, who believe that God sends suffering only upon the sinner, and so Job must have sinned. Job, on the other hand, demonstrates his innocence, but does not censure the Deity. On the contrary, he maintains that God can inflict pains on the good and confer happiness on the bad simply because man is His possession and reacts to His will. And the truth is represented by Elihu, who is noticed only later on. A man, according to him, can cleanse his way with three things: with repentance, with merits, even a few, even "a single angel, an interpreter, one among a thousand," and with suffering of trial, the highest degree, for the sake of reward.[41]

If now we compare the three Joban views as Saadia sees them with those in Maimonides' interpretation in *Moreh*, III, 17, it will appear that Job, who believes that God is Will, unbound by chains of justice, belongs to the Arab orthodoxy called Ashʿariya, which is the third view

[39] אלתאריב ואלתפהים. See *Tafsīr Iyob,* 3.
[40] See *Tafsīr Mishlei,* 184; *Tafsīr Iyob,* 97.
[41] *Tafsīr Iyob,* 4–6.

in the Maimonides interpretation. The three friends take the fifth view of Maimonides, the view of the Torah that suffering is punishment. Whereas Elihu, that is, Saadia himself, who introduces the idea of suffering as trial, is only a Muʿtazilite.

And Maimonides, as the sharp critic of the Muʿtazilah, and the opponent of the idea of "visitations of love," was compelled, in *Moreh*, III, 23, to change the ideological roles. Job was not an Ashʿarite but an Aristotelian who believed that divine providence does not descend into the sublunar world. Eliphaz represents the view of the Torah; Bildad, the Muʿtazilah. Zophar, the Ashʿariya; and Elihu, the view that the divine administration of the universe belongs to divine mysteries. Almost all the interpretations, that is, except the Aristotelian, that Maimonides finds in the book of Job were already found by Saadia; only the players are different. But one issue stands out between Saadia and Maimonides. Saadia lifts divine trial to the highest degree as being of the greatest merit, whereas Maimonides sees in it an infringement upon justice; and though it is mentioned in the Bible and has some support in the Talmud, he rejects it.

Chapter Eight

THE SOUL

1. THE SPLIT IN THE SOUL AFTER PLATO

THE OPENING of the sixth treatise surprises us with its presentation of the idea that "man's soul has its origin in the heart simultaneously with the completion of the formation of its body,"[1] that is, that God creates the soul within the embryo when its form is finished, as it is written *And formed the spirit of man within him* (Zech., 12, 1). This is surprising because it contradicts Talmudic statements that there is a storehouse of souls in heaven, called Body or *guf*, and that "the son of David will come only when all the souls in the *guf* are exhausted (Yeb., 62a).[2] Plato too taught the pre-existence of the soul. Aristotle thought differently, and we shall discuss his views later, but why did Saadia reject a view so fostered by the Talmud and also supported in Greek philosophy and endeavor to prove the opposite? Is it only on the basis of that verse in Zechariah? Could he not find other verses to prove the soul's pre-existence?

Also surprising is a contradictory interpretation of Saadia, recorded by Abraham ibn Ezra, who writes in his commentary on Isaiah, 48, 16: "The Gaon said that here is a hint that the soul antedates the body," that is, that the soul originated in the six days of creation. It seems therefore that when Saadia wrote his commentaries, he still followed the Talmud and Plato. Why did he abandon this view when he began to work out his philosophical system? The problem is interesting because the attempt at its solution will raise other problems in connection with

[1] *Em.*, VI, 1. See also *ibid.*, ch. 3: והפסד שיהיה דבר קדמון זולתי הבורא... אבל הבורא בורא אותה עם שלמות צורת האדם כאמרו בקרב. Comp. Sanhedrin, 91b where Antoninus asks Rebbi when the soul is given, at the time of divine visitation or at the time of formation, and Rebbi answers: at the time of formation; but there the question is not when the soul was created but when the soul was *given*. Justin Martyr and Origen, among the Christians, taught the pre-existence of the soul, but the church declared their view heretical in 540.

[2] See Moise Ventura, *La Philosophie de Saadia Gaon* (Paris, 1934), p. 236, note 49.

the meaning of the soul, and will incidentally reveal how he molded his system, looking before and after, examining conclusions from what preceded and foundations for what followed.

According to Plato the soul enters the body from the outside. It is immaterial and immortal, and longs to leave the body in which it is imprisoned and to return and dwell with God. After death it receives its reward and punishment for a limited time, whereupon it enters into the eternal cycle of transmigration.[3]

Aristotle opposes this view, taking the soul to be the perfection, or "entelechy," of a natural body. And this is how Saadia defines it in VI, 1, 149. Although Yehudah Halevi is more explicit, defining it in *Kuzari*, V, 12 as the perfection of a natural organic body, both Jewish authors follow the Aristotelian definition. This means that the soul is not a separate substance but rather an immanent principle that organizes the body, that imparts to it its "natural form," its life and essence. Furthermore, the soul does not act alone but always within and through the body. Hence, if the question is raised of who is the agent and where is the seat of the self—is it in the soul or in the body?—the Aristotelian answer would be: in both together inseparably.[4] Hence Aristotle scoffs at the thought of the soul's transmigration. It "is very much like saying that the carpenter's art clothes itself in flutes, whereas an art employs its own instrument just as a soul employs its own body."[5] But this emphasis on the inseparability of body-soul notwithstanding, there are places where Aristotle speaks of the Active Intellect as a separate element, coming from the outside, "beginningless and eternal."[6] This contradiction in his psychological system gave rise to various theories.

Alexander of Aphrodisias accepted Aristotle's view concerning the tight entity of body-soul and described the soul as a "form-within-matter" (ἔνυλον εἶδος), but nevertheless endeavored to prove that the soul is not only a form, or an entelechy, but also a substance. The proof of it is that it entertains opposite accidents, which argument is a basic departure from Aristotle. Now in this substance there is implanted an intellectual power, the "passive intellect," which, as only a power, perishes together with the body. But when this passive intellect is actualized

3 *Timaeus*, 34E; *Phaedo*, 80, 94; *Phaedrus*, 246 ff.

4 See Aristotle, *De Anima*, I, 408a 34–408b18; II, 2, 414a19.

5 *Ibid.*, I, 3, 417a26; II, 2, 417b17.

6 *Ibid.*, V, 3.

through the Active Intellect, which, according to Alexander, is God, it becomes an "acquired intellect," which joins the Active Intellect and lives forever.

Simplicius separated this substance entirely from the form and introduced two intellects. He began by pointing out a logical difficulty in Aristotle's definition. For if the soul is a perfection of a natural organic body, it is the soul of what already has a soul, a perfection of what is already perfect, because a natural organic body is *ipso facto* something that has a soul and perfection. We must therefore say that there is a second perfection in terms of a moving force. The flute, for example, has an immanent perfection without which it is not a flute but a piece of wood. But the player is the *mover* of the flute's perfection, and he is a separate, external power. So the soul is the second, trascendent perfection that moves the first organic perfection, and we have a return to Plato.[7]

Thus the soul was torn apart after Plato, and the tear is between the passive and active intellect (Aristotle), or between the passive intellect as form and the active intellect as substance (Alexander), or between the first and second entelechies (Simplicius), or between knowledge and feeling (Plotinus)—all because of a desire to maintain the two opposites: immanence and transcendence, or interiority and union on the one hand and exteriority and immortality on the other. Saadia knew these Aristotelian and post-Aristotelian speculations and nevertheless refused to accept the tear and return to Plato.

2. THE IMMANENT SOUL

He did not return to Plato, probably because he did not favor any thought that posits any "spiritual" or beginningless substance other than God, on account of Christological suggestions. Thus he opposed the assumption of a Logos or any hypostatization of spirit or word or soul in relation to God, and he introduced this opposition in his discussion of Christianity.[8] Indeed, the pupils of an-Naẓẓām, perhaps under the influence of Gnosticism, spoke of two Creators, one as God, and the other, which is created, as God's Word.[9] It is perhaps because of

[7] For the views of the post-Aristotelian thinkers, see F. Rahman, *Avicenna's Psychology* (London, 1952), pp. 3–8.

[8] *Em.*, III, 5.

[9] כלמה̈ אללה, אלמסיח עיסר. See Professor Israel Friedlaender, "The Heterodoxies of the Shiites," in *Journal of the American Oriental Society*, XXIX, pp. 90–92.

these anti-christological considerations that Saadia spoke little of angels, thought that man ranks higher than angels, and did not include angels, unlike the Mohammedans, into his conception of dogmas, as we have seen in our previous discussions.[10] It is also noteworthy that among his listed eleven views of the soul, only the first four regard the soul as pre-existent, and it is these four that also assume its "spirituality" or even its divinity. It seems, then, that to Saadia every view that affirmed the pre-existence of the soul was a threat to divine unity, and therefore "it would be wrong to ascribe eternity to aught except the Creator."[11]

It is apparently for this reason, in order to differentiate between the Creator and His creatures, that he also rejected the view of Plato and Plotinus that the soul is an immaterial substance. For these two orders of being must be sharply distinguished. All things fall into the ten categories of substance, quantity, quality, etc., except the Deity.[12] Hence, the soul too must be subject to these forms of existence with accidents. "The soul is the bearer of many accidents. One speaks for example of an ignorant and a knowing soul and of a pure soul and a wicked soul,"[13] and every substance endowed with accidents must be material, according to Saadia.[14] The very ideas of pure and dark souls point to something material.[15] And so in the difference of opinion between Schreiner and Horovitz as to Saadia's view,[16] we must agree with Schreiner that for Saadia the soul was a material substance. True, it is purer, subtler, and simpler than the spheres and the stars,[17] and is even called an "intellectual substance."[18] Nevertheless, Saadia's emphasis on the resemblance between the substance of the soul and that of the spheres[19] and on the soul being endowed with accidents proves materiality.

Nor did Saadia accept platonic pessimism, the view that the body is

10 See above, ch. 4, 4; ch. 7, 3.

11 *Em.*, VI, 3 (beginning).

12 *Em.*, II, 8.

13 *Em.*, VI, 6.

14 *Em.*, II, exordium.

15 *Em.*, V, 1. See also VI, 5.

16 Ventura, *La Philosophie de Saadia Gaon*, p. 237, note 51.

17 *Em.*, VI, 7; V, 1 and 5.

18 עצם שכלי in *Em.*, V, 1.

19 *Em.*, VI, 3, 153: וידעתי כי הספרים לא דמו אלה בגלגלים המזהירים ואלה בפחות מהגלגלים סתם, אלא שהיא מכמו זה העצם.

a grave (σῶμα σῆμα),[20] the source of pain and filth and sin.[21] "To him who asserts that it would have been best for the soul if God had left it in a state of isolation, so that it would have been relieved of sin and defilement and pain, I will make it clear and evident that if such an isolation had been the best thing for the soul, its Creator would have fashioned it in such a state." Sins come not from the body but from choice. As for defilement, "the body of man contains no impurity by and of itself." And pain is born of error, or comes as punishment or trial, in which case it is loving-kindness.[22] Nevertheless, Saadia knew also the Platonic sadness of the soul in this world, its restlessness and longing for "an abode that is superior to all the excellencies of its present dwelling."[23] He used it as a psychological argument for the existence of the hereafter, but not to prove a *metaphysical origin* of the soul.

Saadia, then, rejected the Platonic theory of the soul's pre-existence and transcendence, but neither could he accept Aristotle's view that the soul is only "a perfection of a natural body," and this for two reasons. (1) An accident—Saadia did not yet differentiate between form and accident—cannot be the source of great wisdom.[24] This anti-Aristotelian argument is borrowed from Plotinus. (2) No accident can occur on top of another accident,

> and we find that the soul is the bearer of many accidents. One speaks of an ignorant and a knowing soul and of a pure soul and a wicked soul. Thou dost also ascribe to the soul love and hate and good will and anger and other well known traits. Possessing these characteristics, it cannot possibly be construed as being a mere accident. On the contrary, since we note that it is susceptible to such opposite attributes, it is more likely that it is a substance.

Here we have a blending of two proofs: one is from the soul being susceptible to opposite accidents, as a wise soul and an ignorant soul—taken from Alexander of Aphrodisias—and the second, from the soul's reception of contrary desires—taken from Plotinus.

3. SOUL-BODY

We are therefore compelled to say that the soul is a material substance and that it is not pre-existent but created in the embryo at the time of

20 Plato, *Cratylus*, 400 C.

21 Plato, *Phaedo*, 66, 81.

22 *Em.*, IV, 4.

23 *Em.*, IX, 1.

24 *Em.*, VI, 1.

the completion of its form. The question now is, what is the relationship between the two, between the soul and the body, while they are interconnected in life. Saadia rejects the Platonic dualism of soul and body with their mutual hostility and accepts Aristotle's idea of soul-body, the welded personality as an active unit. Saadia needed this view for two reasons. First, for systematic consistency. Even in his first treatise, in his struggle with Manichaean dualism, he tried to prove that two agents cannot be the authors of one act,[25] a principle that was a subject of dispute in the Arabic background. The orthodox Sunnites, who repudiated the doctrine of free will and believed that God commits the human act and man *acquires possession* of it—the so called Arabic theory of *kasb* or *iktisāb*—said that in this case two commit one act. Al-Baghdadi[26] tells that al-Murdār, the Muʿtazilite, rejected the view of the Sunnites but nevertheless thought that it is possible for two agents to do one deed by way of *tawallud*, that is, that the first agent begins and the second automatically continues. Al-Shaḥḥām freed himself entirely from this rule that there cannot be two agents of one deed, but his pupil, al-Jubbai, reinstated the rule. Saadia had argued against Manichaean dualism on the basis of this principle. If he would now accept Platonic dualism in relation to soul and body, he would always have two agents with one deed. And if we suppose that only the soul is the subject of all action, there would arise the difficulty, why should the body receive reward and punishment. Thus anthropological dualism endangers the belief in resurrection. And hence Saadia emphasizes, as did Aristotle, that "the soul and body are together one agent"[27] and censures those, like the Arab an-Naẓẓām,[28] who think that only the soul acts, as well as those who credit only the body with all action.[29]

It follows that together with Aristotle Saadia should discard the Platonic theory of transmigration of souls,[30] because that theory is based on the thought that the soul enters from the outside, that it is not created

25 *Em.*, I, 3, fifth view. Comp. the Talmudic rule שנים שעשוהו פטורין (Shabbat, 3a).

26 Al-Baghdadi, *Al Farq bain 'l-firaq*, 152 (172). In Shahrastani, I, 48 (71) אלמונדאר in place of אלמורדאר. Concerning al-Shaḥḥām, see Tritton, *Muslim Theology*, p. 141.

27 כי הנפש והגוף יחדו פועל אחד (או״ד ו, 7), את כל מעשה רוצה בו הגוף והנפש יחדו (או״ד ו,ז). See Aristotle, *De Anima*, I, 4, 408b11.

28 Al-Baghdadi, *Al Farq bain 'l-firaq*, 118 (140).

29 *Em.*, VI, 4.

30 *Em.*, VI, 8. Called הישנות and also העתקה (Ar. כר and also תנאסך. On the argumentation against metempsychosis, comp. Abraham ibn Daud, *Emunah Ramah*, I, 7.

in the mother's womb. And indeed, it is the concept of soul-body as a tight unit that also motivates Aristotle's opposition to metempsychosis. The soul cannot enter another body, especially that of another species, any more than the art of a carpenter can clothe itself in a flute.[31] Saadia saw clearly that transmigration is connected historically or ideologically with the idea of the independence of the soul, its separateness and pre-existence originating in "the viewpoint of the dualists and spiritualists." We have explained in Chapter 3 that the "spiritualists" were the Pythagoreans, and they indeed are the source for the belief in transmigration according to Aristotle as well.[32] Here Saadia departed from the camp of the Muʿtazilites, who accepted transmigration out of a sharp sense of justice and retribution, since the suffering of children can only be explained, they thought, on the basis of sin in a previous life. It was because of such an explanation that some of them abandoned the concept of the hereafter, since man can receive his retribution in transmigration.[33] Hence Saadia tried to clarify again that suffering is not always for the past but may come on account of the future, that is, as a trial for the sake of greater reward.

What is of main importance is that Saadia's psychological theory is free from that split of the soul that arose among the Greeks as a result of their conception of immanence *vis à vis* the longings for immortality, so that they were compelled to rend the soul into two parts, one for the body and the other for the hereafter. Saadia too conceived the soul as immanent, yet not as intrinsic—the way the Aristotelian scholiasts conceived it—but as a *creation.* Hence at separation it goes out, not as a half-soul, as according to Alexander, Simplicius, and Plotinus, but wholly, because from the very beginning it was not *organically* connected with the body as its perfection but created and joined to it for a limited time only. The supernatural element in the inception of the soul saves its wholeness. Saadia therefore rejects the view that the soul "is of two parts, one intellectual and indestructible, dwelling in the heart, and the other vital, extending over the whole body and therewith coming to an end." He tries to explain, together with Plotinus, that the intellectual element participates in all perception, that "it is the soul

31 Aristotle, *De Anima,* I, 3, 407b26; II, 2, 414a16.

32 *Ibid.*

33 Friedlander, "The Heterodoxies of the Shiites," in *Journal of the American Oriental Society,* XXIX, pp. 45, 63, 64, 74.

that provides the various sense-organs with their sense-faculties,"[34] that there is no sharp border line between reason and perception, or as he writes in his commentary on Job, 12, 12: "When the soul wants to perceive colors and forms, it turns to the eye; and when it wishes to know voices, it takes its power toward the ear; and when it aims to feel taste, it applies to the palate. So we find that when it wants to understand, it takes its power toward reason." That is to say, all is one power and the difference lies in the organs. Nor is there validity for Saadia in the distinction Plotinus himself made between the higher soul of knowledge and perception and the lower soul of passion, such as fear, anger, hate, and love. All the three powers, reason, appetition, and anger (i.e., "spirit," courage) manifest themselves only through the soul's union with the body, through the use of the body as an instrument. But the soul is essentially one,[35] as Aristotle emphasized, and when it leaves the body there is no division.

4. MAN'S APPOINTED TERM

The belief in "the end of the days of one's life,"[36] which Saadia affirms, namely, that every man is granted at his birth a fixed number of years, is found in the Koran, 7, 32; 63, 11, and it was the subject of controversy among the Arabs. Al-'Ashʿari thought that when a man is killed, it is the end of his appointed time, for if he had not been killed he would have met his end in a natural way. Most of the Muʿtazilites, among them Abū Hudhayl, agreed with this view. Saadia, however, proves from the Scriptures that when a man dies in a plague, it is not at the end of his appointed term,[37] thus siding with the Muʿtazilite

[34] *Em.*, VI, 1, 150; VI, 3, 153.

[35] *Em.*, VI, 3, 153: ג׳ כחות כח ההכרה וכח הכעס וכח התאוה... נפש רוח ונשמה... טעה מי ששמה שני חלקים אך השלשה לנפש אחת. The Arabic names for the three powers are: קוה̈ אלתמייז וקוה̈ אלשהוה̈ וקוה̈ אלעֿצֿב. The order for the last two powers in Tibbon does not correspond to the Arabic. Comp. *Em.*, X, 2, where the order follows the Arabic in *Amānāt*, 284. The Ar. word עֿצֿב means violence, force, and compulsion, as well as anger, rage, or in Hebrew כעס. These are the three Platonic faculties of the soul: the rational, the spirited, and the appetitive. See Plato, *Republic*, 44 A, B; *Timaeus*, 69, 70. For the Aristotelian criticism of Plato's division of the soul into three distinct parts, see Aristotle, *De Anima*, II, 2, 413b11. Saadia here follows Aristotle.

[36] *Em.*, VI, 6, 157: קץ ימי החיים Ar. אגֿל.

[37] *Em.*, VI, 6: המגפה זולת קץ הימים.

minority, whom al-'Ash'ari called "ignorant members of the sect."[38] But whereas among the Arabs the concept of *ajal*, or appointed term of life, carried a suggestion of predeterminism, Saadia confers upon it a rationalistic-psychological aspect. The "end" is the measure of strength given to the body. Yet God can add or detract years through a plague. It depends on merits and demerits. It follows then that man has power also over his duration of life.

It should be remarked that this concept of the measure of strength or duration given to man at birth is a physiological application of Saadia's general, physical theory, discussed above at the beginning of Chapter 4, that the duration of anything is not due to inertia, or causeless continuance, but rather to the presence of an active force, called in I, 1, 56, "the force that maintains."

[38] See Duncan B. Macdonald, *Muslim Theology, Jurisprudence and Constitutional Theory* (New York, 1903), pp. 298, 311; Walter C. Klein, *Al-Ash'ari's Al-Ibānah 'an Uṣūl ad-Diyānah*, p. 115, note 458.

Chapter Nine

ESCHATOLOGY

1. NATIONAL MOTIVES

SAADIA'S eschatology obtains its direction and dramatic tenseness from the idea of two resurrections, one at the time of Messiah, destined for the righteous of Israel, and the other, in the world to come, for all men.[1] This idea is entirely absent in Islam, since Islam generally is not a Messianic religion. It is mentioned in Talmudic literature only implicitly and in a late midrash called *Tena debei Eliyahu*, although there may be hints about it in a saying by Rabbi Eleazar of Modin and in a controversy with Samuel who, said, "There will be no difference between the present and the Messianic days except the oppression of governments."[2] Still, Saadia states that most Jews, in his day, had adopted this belief and that only "a minority of the nation do not accept two resurrections but only one, namely in the world to come."[3] It can

[1] Eschatology is discussed in treatises VII–IX. The world to come is called עולם הגמול, העולם האחר (V, 1, 138), עת הגמול (V, 7, 146; VI, 7, 159), as against this world, called עולם הטורח (IV, 2, 126), עולם המעשה (V, 1, 138), and as against the Messianic era, called עת הישועה, עת הגאולה (VII, 1, 162; VIII, 1, 175). Another term for גמול is תמורה, Ar. עוץ̇, אלתעויץ̇. See, for example, *Em.*, IX, 2, 188 and *Tafsīr Iyob*, 102, 103. In *Tafsīr Iyob*, 71, the day of resurrection (יום אלקיאמה̈) is called יום עברות, *dies irae*.

[2] In תנא דבי אליהו, I, 5: תחה״מ להקב״ה בעוה״ז כדי לקדש שמו הגדול וכן תחה״מ להקב״ה כדי ליתן דין וחשבון. See *Mekilta* (Lauterbach), II p. 120: ר׳ אליעזר המודעי אומר אם תזכו לשמור את השבת עתיד הקב״ה ליתן לכם שש מדות טובות ארץ ישראל ועוה״ב ועולם חדש ומלכות בית דוד וכהונה ולויה. As to the controversy with Samuel, see *Berakot*, 34b. See also Joshua Finkel's essay on מקאלה̈ פי תחה״מ להרמב״ם in *Essays on Maimonides*, ed. Salo W. Baron, pp. 98–102, 116, and M. Waxman, גלות וגאולה, 271.

[3] *Em.*, VII, 1, 162. The Arabic text of this seventh treatise, as translated by Judah ibn Tibbon, was published by Wilhelm Bacher in the *Festschrift zum achtzigsten Geburtstage Moritz Steinschneiders* (Leipzig, 1896), pp. 98–112. It should be noted that Abraham bar Ḥiyya in his *Megillat ha-Megalleh* (Berlin, 1924), pp. 84–89, offers proofs for two resurrections, but states that many of his generation in Spain and France did not accept this belief.

be seen from Saadia's reply that the opposition of this minority rested on a rationalistic refusal to believe in a supernatural event in a natural, that is, this, world. And although he himself frequently joined the rationalists, he now found it necessary to oppose them, for the reason that he gives in the beginning of the seventh treatise.

Thereupon I shall note it down for our nation in order that it may serve it as a guide, helping it to serve our Lord and endure patiently what it has to suffer in exile. I followed therein the course enjoined by God in recommending patience, when He said: *Strengthen ye the weak, and make firm the tottering knees. Say to them that are of a fearful heart: Be strong, fear not, behold your God etc.*

This passage teaches us much concerning the spirit and the mood of the time of Saadia. There was "forcing of the Messianic end," growing impatience, and despair.

It should be noted here that the national *motif* takes a most prominent place in Saadia's thinking, as it does in the philosophy of Yehudah Halevi. Saadia's well-known saying, "Our nation of the children of Israel is a nation only by virtue of its laws"[4] is not a denial of what we would call nationalism but quite the reverse, an appeal to the eternity of Israel as a proof for the eternity of its laws. And the land of Israel is "the land which the Creator had appointed to be the seat of prophecy," the "distinguished land."[5] And the nation, poor and despised, has a Joban role in the world.[6] It fell many times and rose, unlike the other nations of the world.[7] And exile is indeed long and harder and more scattered than the exile in Egypt, but it is partly punishment and partly trial, both parts being a loving-kindness.[8] But there are complainers and grumblers, and Saadia tells them that "their distress is no excuse for disloyalty to their faith, but that they must be patient, as Scripture says: *Let him give his cheek to him that smiteth him, let him be filled with reproach*" (Lam., 3, 30),[9] and that they should hold on to the

4 *Em.*, III, 7, 115: כי אומתנו איננה אומה כי אם בתורותיה.

5 *Em.*, III, 5, 113: הארץ אשר יעדה הבורא שתהיה בו הנבואה... הארץ המיוחדת. Ar. אלבלד אלכ̇אץ. Comp. *Kuzari*, II, 14. The term אלכ̇אץ also means a royal favorite, private property, hence equals סגולה.

6 *Em.*, III (end), p. 124.

7 *Tafsir Mishlei*, 137.

8 *Em.*, VIII, 1, 175.

9 *Em.*, V, 8, 148; VIII, 1, 178.

belief in the Messianic resurrection. It is this belief that can strengthen the power of patience,[10] without which the people would be unable to bear the hardship of exile,[11] and that promises, as historic justice, additional reward, that is, greater glory, for the people that suffered more than all others.[12]

Hence he is also emphatic that all the Messianic hopes, which he describes with national pride as well as with national anger—see, for example, VII, 9; VIII, 2—should be accepted literally and not by the allegorical method (Ar. *ta'wīl*). We infer, then, that those who belonged to the minority and did not believe in the Messianic resurrection were also men of *ta'wīl*. Indeed, Abraham bar Ḥiyya, in his *Megillat ha-Megalleh* (pp. 48, 49) states that *many of his generation* in Spain and France who believed in the resurrection that is to take place in the world to come denied that there will be a first resurrection in the Messianic era, and they explained those references in the Bible to an earlier resurrection by way of *ta'wīl*. And there were the Karaites, such as Yeshuah ben Yehudah and Yefet ben Ali,[13] who also engaged in this manner of interpretation. It is also true that Saadia himself used this Muʿtazilite method in order to explain away Biblical anthropomorphism. But the others, both Rabbanites and Karaites, were more extreme in this method of exegesis. Also in the Arabic world, we find the Ismāʿīlians allegorically explaining every verse in the Koran that refers to resurrection in general and to retribution. And al-Gazali states that *al-falāsifa* (philosophers) thought that those verses, in their literal sense, were good for the masses; whereas for the wise who penetrate to the deeper meaning, resurrection denotes the transference of the soul from a state of ignorance to one of knowledge of the essences of things. And the Shiites even explained all the practical commands in terms of allegory.[14] Saadia felt therefore constrained to limit the use of this method to four cases: (1) when the literal meaning is against the testimony of sense, or (2) of reason, or

[10] *Em.*, VII, 1, 162; VIII, 1, 176.

[11] *Amānāt*, 222.

[12] *Amānāt*, 226.

[13] See Finkel, *Essays on Maimonides*, p. 121 note 58.

[14] For the Ismāʿīlians, see Finkel, *Essays on Maimonides*, p. 107. For al-Gazali, see his *Tahāfut al-falasifat*, ed. M. Bouyges, pp. 354–55; De Boer, *Widersprüche der Philosophie, nach Al-Gazzali*, (Strassburg, 1894), p. 91. As for the Shiites, see Prof. Israel Friedlander, "The Heterodoxies of the Shiites, etc.," *Journal of the American Oriental Society*, XXIX, p. 107.

(3) of other verses, or (4) of tradition.[15] All other uses he considered invalid. Particularly, one must not apply the allegorical method to revealed laws, to the account of creation, and to miracles.[16] He did more than merely combat the application of *ta'wīl*. He made the belief in resurrection one of the dogmas of Judaism, which he who rejects will forfeit his portion in the world to come.[17]

We must add that the meaning of this doctrine of two resurrections is not that man will come to life twice, once in the Messianic era and once again in the hereafter. It means that there will be two periods for resurrection. The righteous of Israel will arise in the Messianic era and will no more die, but will be *transferred* to the world to come when it comes, while the others, Jews and non-Jews, will arise only in the hereafter.[18] In this Saadia's view is different from those of Abraham bar Ḥiyya and Abraham ibn Ezra (in his comment on Dan., 12, 2), both of whom believed that the righteous of Israel will die and revive twice. Saadia's view is also different from that of Maimonides, who held that they will die twice but will not arise bodily twice; rather they will enter after their second death into a psycho-spiritual eternal life.[19]

2. SECOND RESURRECTION

This world will end when the number of human beings destined to come to life will be exhausted.[20] Here we think of the Talmudic dictum: "The son of David shall not come until all souls in the *guf* [the Talmudic name of the storehouse of souls in heaven] are exhausted" (Yeb., 62a). Yet Saadia does not mention this Talmudic passage, for two reasons. First, because that statement is based on the Platonic theory—which he rejects—about the pre-existence of souls; and second, because the end of the number of souls to be created marks, according to Saadia, the end of this world and the beginning of the next, and not the coming

15 *Em.*, V, 8, 147; VII, 2, 165; IX, 3, 189; *Amānāt*, 213, 217.

16 *Em.*, VII, 5, 169.

17 *Em.*, VII, 3, 167; VII, 7, 171; *Amānāt*, 226. In all these places, the reference is to the first resurrection.

18 *Amānāt*, 223, 224, 228, 229; *Em.*, VII, 8, 172.

19 See מקאלה פי תחה״מ להרמב״ם, ed. Finkel, American Academy for Jewish Research, IX, pp. 16–17. Comp. Tanḥuma, quoted by Rashi on Gen., 46, 30, where there seems to be a suggestion of a fourth view: two deaths for the sinners, and one for the righteous.

20 *Em.*, V, 1, 138; VI, 1, 149; IX, 1, 185; *Amānāt*, 211.

of the Son of David, which belongs to this world, since during the Messianic era there will continue to be marriage and birth (VII, 8, 172). It is therefore surprising that Professor Henry Malter, in his *Life and Works of Saadia Gaon*, pp. 230, 231, writes that, according to Saadia, the Messianic era is to begin when the number of souls to be created is completed. Nor does he seem correct in stating that at the end of that era all the souls will be *transported*, including the wicked souls, since the wicked souls will not be transported but will *arise*, for the first time, in the world to come in order to receive their retribution.

When we come to the second resurrection, that is, the world to come, we re-enter the general background, and Arabic discussions re-echo in Saadia's work. The association known as "Sincere Brethren" (Ar. *Ikhwān as-Safā*) scoffed at the belief in bodily resurrection—a belief that is good, they thought, only for women and children. Better than this is the belief in a separate soul and transmigration. But the truth, they stressed, was that the soul enters the body only to develop its powers, and then it awakes from sleep and longs for the transcendent world from which it came, and the lower world becomes strange to it, appearing like a storm of passions. But the soul knows that its confinement is temporary, that it will depart from the body, for death is revival.[21] These thoughts on the soul and its longings and on death are permeated with the Neoplatonic spirit, and particularly with the philosophy of Plotinus. There is no bodily resurrection, only the survival of the soul, only immortality. True resurrection is awakening *from* the body, not with the body.[22] The Muʿtazilites, on the other hand, endeavored to prove through logic that bodily resurrection was necessary as a prerequisite for reward and punishment.

Al-Farabi and Avicenna agreed with the Sincere Brethren. But al-Gazali showed the failures in the reasoning on both sides. Against the argument on the side of immortality—that even God cannot entirely destroy a soul,[23] he answers that one should not limit divine power. But there are also arguments against resurrection. In general, he says, there are three views. (1) Man is body, the soul being an accident, and after death the body-parts are preserved to be collected in the hereafter

21 Finkel, *Essays on Maimonides*, pp. 100, 102–103.

22 Plotinus, *Ennead*, III, 6, 6.

23 Essentially this is ibn Sina's argument and is taken from Plotinus. See F. Rahman, *Avicenna's Psychology*, p. 108.

by God and reshaped by Him into a new life. The counter-argument to this view is that this is a new creation, not a restoration, at all events not a restoration of the same man. (2) The soul is not an accident and survives, and in the hereafter God will rejoin the two. The counter-argument here is that the person may be eaten up by worms or beasts and, in some places, by human beings;[24] to whom then will belong the eaten parts? (3) Man is the soul, and the soul returns without caring to what body he returns. But where will there be so many bodies for all the returning souls? Furthermore, this view is nothing but transmigration, a soul with two bodies. Al-Gazali is inclined toward the last view, that the returning soul will find a new and more suitable body.[25] Now what is Saadia's view?

The view of the Sincere Brethren and the Neoplatonists is not valid for him. Life is not a prison, and death is not an emergence from the grave. There are, to be sure, some pessimistic Neoplatonic notes in Saadia, for example, the proofs for the hereafter: that since *here* even the good is not free from evil, there must be a world that is purely good; or that since here the soul is sad and restless, there must be a world that draws it, for which it longs.[26] But more characteristic and consistent is his effort at theodicy and a defense of the body.[27] For if life is an imprisonment, for what sins was the soul imprisoned? And, if there are prenatal sins, we have again a theory of transmigration. Indeed, this is how Saadia argues against the transmigrationists at the end of his treatise on the soul. Saadia's view, then, is opposed to Neoplatonism and is based on justice. Life is action, and the hereafter is the necessary retribution; and since in action the body and the soul are one agent,[28] in the hereafter the body too must be revived. Saadia therefore maintains that there will be full, that is, bodily, and not merely

24 Averroes also brings forward this objection, and he therefore assumes the soul's resurrection in a *new* body. See Louis Gardet, *La Pensée religieuse d'Avicenne* (Paris, 1951), p. 86; Finkel, *Essays on Maimonides*, p. 107.

25 *Al-Ghazzali*, *Tahāfut al-falasifat*, ed. Maurice Bouyges (Beyrouth, 1927), p. 357; De Boer, *Widersprüche der Philosophie, nach al-Gazzali*, p. 94.

26 *Em.*, IX, 1, 185.

27 *Em.*, IV, 4, 155–56.

28 *Em.*, VI, 5, 157; IX, 5, 190. See also *Amānāt*, 224; *Em.*, VI, 1, 149; IX, 6, 192–93. This was also the opinion of David ha-Babli, as quoted in Barzillai's commentary on *Sefer Yeṣirah*, 153.

spiritual, resurrection, not mere immortality of the soul, as claimed by the Sincere Brethren, *al-falāsifa*, and also Maimonides.

As to the three views of the return of the soul discussed by al-Gazali, Saadia does not accept the first—that the body returns, the soul being an accident—nor the third—that man is his soul and does not care to what body he returns. His is the second view. Man is a body-soul. And when the question is raised, what if the body is eaten or burnt, Saadia's answer is that there is nothing that can so destroy a thing as to change it to nothing, except God.[29] In this he agrees with al-Gazali and disagrees with those who believe in only spiritual immortality because even God cannot annihilate a soul.

The philosophers' argument against the first view is that if man is a body, what do we gain by saying that God regathers the same parts when it is not the same man. This argument also applies partly to the view that man is a body-soul. On the other hand, Avicenna emphasizes that the soul after death retains its individuality,[30] to which however al-Gazali is right in replying, how can the soul endure in its individuality when all its being is wrapped up in that tight relationship of body-soul?[31] Saadia is more consistent in assuming the survival of individuality through a continuation of that same relationship in the hereafter.

> Each one of them [i.e., of the dead] will, when he comes to life, know for certain that he is the person who has been alive and has died, and that it is he himself who has come back to life again... for he who will awake will relate, when he awakes, what he has seen in his sleep and will be aware of the fact that he is the person who has been asleep and waked up.[32]

It is interesting that Saadia's approach is frequently internal, psychological. So here, so in his arguments for the existence of a hereafter, and so in his proofs for the freedom of will (IV, 4, 129).

In his *Iḥyā ʿUlūm al-Din*, al-Gazali describes those who ignore the simple meaning of the Koran, those who follow the extremism of Aḥmad ibn Ḥanbal in opposing *ta'wīl*, and those groups that seek a middle road: the Ashʿarites who permit the application of the method of *ta'wīl* to anthropomorphic passages but condemn any deviation from the literal meaning in the eschatological passages; the Muʿtazilites who turn into

29 *Em.*, VII, 1, 163–64; *Amānāt*, 220–22.

30 Rahman, *Avicenna's Psychology*, pp. 106–107.

31 De Boer, *Widersprüche der Philosophie, nach Al-Gazzali*, p. 90.

32 *Em.*, VII, 4, 167–68. See also VII, 8, 172.

figures of speech the punishment in the grave, the scales, the bridge, the open book, but not the bodily resurrection, the garden and its physical pleasures, and hell with its physical tortures; and the philosophers who go further, denying also bodily resurrection, so that it is all a metaphoric reference to the immortality of the soul whose reward and punishment are spiritual only. And al-Gazali weighs in his mind which indeed is the middle road between unlimited *ta'wīl* and strict Ḥanbalism and decides that only the divine light illumines that road.[33] Saadia deviates from the Muʿtazilah in apparently accepting the belief in the punishment in the grave and belief in the open book. But as to the general question raised by al-Gazali: which is the right road regarding the application of *ta'wil* to eschatological passages, it was not, according to Saadia, the road of *al-falāsifa* nor the road of the Ḥanbalites. He was nearer to the Muʿtazilah, except for the assumption of two resurrections. In this respect Maimonides differed, making a compromise between the Mutakallimūn and *al-falāsifa* in assuming one bodily resurrection in the Messianic era and another, entirely spiritual resurrection in the world to come.

3. THE WORLD OF RETRIBUTION

The purpose of creation is man, the purpose of man is the worship of God,[34] and the purpose of the worship of God is to provide a just claim on God's goodness in the hereafter.[35] "Death is the way of the journey to the world to come which is the ultimate goal." It is for this goal that the soul longs while still in this world, which accounts for its sadness and restlessness[36]—a Neoplatonic note not entirely in accord with Saadia's other expressions about the rank and value of the body.

Candidates for punishment in the hereafter are the renegades, the polytheists, and those guilty of severe transgressions who have not

[33] Saadia mentions the punishment in the grave (דין הקבר, חיבוט הקבר) in *Em.*, VI, 7, 159. See also *Tafsīr Iyob*, 14, 20. For the views of the Jahmiya and the Muʿtazilah, see Wensinck, *The Muslim Creed*, pp. 104, 119, 195. As to the "open book" also rejected by the Muʿtazilites (see E. E. Elder, *Sa'ud al-Din al-Tiftizani*, p. 103), Saadia rationalizes it in *Em.*, V, 1, 138; IX, 3, 188.

[34] See Maimonides' critique of this teleology in the *Moreh*, III, 13, p. 18.

[35] *Em.*, III, exordium, 105; IX, 1, 185. See also III, 7, 116: כי המות היא דרך הנסיעה אל העולם הבא אשר היא הכוונה.

[36] *Em.*, IX, 4, 189.

repented; while those who have committed only minor sins will be forgiven.[37] Saadia propounds this Muʿtazilite law and adds:

Should someone ask, on what ground they are pardoned, seeing that no repentance has taken place, we would answer: Is it not our basic assumption that these individuals are charged solely with lesser transgressions? That in itself is proof that they have guarded against sins of a grave character. Now how could they have kept aloof from them except by doing the opposite: namely, instead of denying God's existence, believing in Him; instead of going astray, being led aright; instead of committing murder and theft and adultery, doing what is right and just and fair.

The questions, which essentially remains unanswered, and the long rhetorical reply demand comment. It appears as if Saadia were arguing here with someone in the background. Now the Muʿtazilites were stricter in their attitude toward punishment than were the orthodox, for the latter thought that the Prophet's intercession in the hereafter will cause forgiveness even for grave transgressors, while the Muʿtazilites rejected all intercession because it interferes with the character of strict justice,[38] and they therefore maintained that he who enters hell will never depart therefrom. Hence, after Saadia, like a strict Muʿtazilite, ruled that those who sinned gravely are doomed for hell and no prophet or angel can obtain for them atonement, he found it necessary to answer the question with respect to lighter sins—how will *they* be atoned? Indeed, there is no atonement for these actions, but the refraining from graver ones is enough.

And all animals will receive compensation for the pain inflicted upon them, as in slaughter[39]—again a Muʿtazilite doctrine, the acceptance of which by "some one of the last of the Geonim" Maimonides censured in *Moreh*, III, 17. Furthermore, together with the Muʿtazilites, Saadia emphasizes the reward in the hereafter for children who died sinlessly.[40] Moreover, the pain and death of these children prove the existence of a hereafter. As an example Saadia mentions the children of the generation of the Flood and the children of the Midianites whom God com-

37 *Em.*, IX, 9, 195. This was also the Muʿitazlite view. See Elder, *Saʿud al-Din al-Tiftizani*, pp. 111–12.

38 Wensinck, *The Muslim Creed*, pp. 61, 180–82.

39 *Em.*, III, 6, 122. See al-Ashʿari, *Maqālāt*, I, 243 ff.

40 *Em.*, VIII, 2, 176; IX, 2, 188. See also Walter C. Klein, *Al-Ashari's Al-Ibānah an Uṣūl ad-Diyānah*, p. 112.

manded to kill, proving that there must be reward for them. From this, incidentally, one may infer that Saadia rejected the view of ibn Ḥanbal and al-'Ash'ari that the children of heretics must go to hell.

As opposed to the materialistic description of the hereafter in the Koran,[41] Saadia emphasizes that "life in the world to come consists exclusively of light, and that eating and drinking and fatigue and procreation and buying and selling and all other mundane occupations are eliminated from it, the reward of the righteous there being only the enjoyment of the light of the Creator;[42] and therefore "there is no need there of fields or plants or rivers or valleys... or aught that resembles them." And heaven and earth will be effaced, there will be no air for breathing, space and time will cease; only a center and an environment will be created for them by God as it will please Him.[43] What is this "light of the Creator," which will be the reward of the righteous? It is the Second Air previously discussed, a subtle air that was the beginning of creation and is called Glory, Shekinah, and Holy Spirit. But that substance will then have two powers, a light for the righteous and a fire for the wicked. It may also be, Saadia suggested, perhaps in order not to materialize this light too much, that these powers will not reside in that substance itself but will be due to some qualities in man: the righteous will have the power to absorb the light and the wicked will be receptive to the fire only. At any rate, that light is the Garden of Eden, and that fire is Gehenna.[44] In all these descriptions, which have a foundation in the Talmud (Berakot, 17a), there is felt an effort to strip the concepts of the world to come and retribution and the Garden of Eden and Gehenna of their materiality, so that Saadia's view comes close to that of Maimonides as well as to that of Plotinus and the

[41] Koran, 52, 19–20; 36, 56; 13, 23; 40, 8.

[42] *Em.*, IX, 4, 189: אבל גמול הצדיקים מכבוד הבורא Ar. נור אלכֹאלק, for which see above ch. 5, note 40 and *infra*, ch. 10, note 26. See also *Tafsīr Iyob*, 96: ...והוא אלאור הו תֿואב אלצאלחין.

[43] *Em.*, IX, 6, 192–93. The Arabic for "center and environment" is מרכז ומחיט, and Yehudah ibn Tibbon looked for a Hebrew word for the Ar. *markaz*, and translated the phrase by מתקע ומקיף. His son Samuel used the Arabic term; see his comment in his *Perush meha-millot zarot*, while Harizi used the Hebrew עמוד. Prof. Louis Ginzberg in his notes on my *Philosophical Terms in the Moreh Nebukim*, s.v. מרכז, states that Abraham bar Ḥiyya was probably the first to use this Arabic term in Hebrew.

[44] *Em.*, IX, 5, 191.

Sincere Brethren and *al-falāsifa*, so that verily there is no room there for the body. But Saadia was compelled to maintain the survival of the body because of his view, already discussed, that soul and body are one agent and therefore must be one at the time of retribution, and perhaps even more because of his general refusal to accept a spiritual substance other than God—an anti-Christological attitude that the Muʿtazilites shared.

Nevertheless, there are sections in which his descriptions of the suffering and loneliness of the wicked take on a Dantesque appearance, especially in IX, 9, 196, where the righteous see from a distance the suffering of the wicked and say "Praised be He that saved us from this torment," and those destined for punishment never meet "on account of their separation produced by their sufferings and their preoccupation with themselves."

Characteristic is Saadia's view that divine worship will continue in the hereafter, and the commandments will be valid, since "sound reason will not permit itself to be completely divested of commandment and prohibition," and some revealed laws will be observed, such as designating a place to which the souls will be required to travel at appointed seasons for divine worship. But alas, the wicked will be exempt from worship so as not to leave their place of torment (IX, 10). And this worship too will receive its reward. Saadia, then, differs from Abū Hudhayl, who taught that in the world to come there is no free will, and hence there is no reward for service there.[45]

That other world—does it already exist? There are differences of opinion among the Arabs on this question. According to al-Taḥāwī, the Garden and the Fire preceded creation,[46] and this was the orthodox view, current also in Jewish literature. But according to most Muʿtazilites, they will be created after the day of Judgment: since if they were already in existence they would have to be destroyed at the end of the world, for according to the Koran all will come to an end.[47] Saadia

45 K. C. Seelye, *Al-Baghdadi, Al-fark̦ bain ʿl-firak̦* (New York, 1920), 106 (128).

46 Aṭ-Ṭaḥāwī, *Bayān al-Sunna wa-'l-Jamāʿa*, tr. E. E. Elder in *The Macdonald Presentation Volume* (Princeton, 1933), p. 141; Wensinck, *The Muslim Creed*, p. 166; Professor Louis Ginzberg, *Legends of the Jews*, VII, pp. 213, 360.

47 *Al-Baghdadi, Al-fark̦ bain 'l-firak̦*, ed. and tr. Kate Chambers Seelye, 150 (170); E. E. Elder, *A Commentary on the Creed of Islam* (New York, 1950), p. 105. But see A. S. Tritton, *Muslim Theology*, pp. 98, 148, 155. See also Edward Sell, *The Faith of Islam* (London, 1896), p. 233.

sides with most Muʿtazilites, certainly not because of the verse in Koran, but because he refrains from ascribing pre-existence to aught except God. Hence he says: "This latter world will be brought into being by Him when the entire number of rational beings the creation of which has been decided upon by His wisdom, will have been fulfilled." "This reward and punishment will take the form of two very fine substances that our Master will create at the time of retribution."[47]

The Arabs are also divided as to how long the Garden and the Gehenna will exist. Al-Taḥāwī thought that they will never end, and again this was the general orthodox opinion; whereas the Jahmites and the Muʿtazilites opposed such a view. "The Garden and the Fire will cease," said Jahm, "and Allah will again be alone as at the beginning." Similarly, Abū Hudhayl maintained that the world to come, together with the pleasures of the righteous and the suffering of the wicked, will turn into a frozen silence.[49] On the other hand, the opinions were arranged in reverse order as to whether the divine verdict was forever, that is, for the duration of heaven and hell. The orthodox said the wicked will leave Gehenna and enter Paradise; and the Muʿtazilites, who were stricter in questions of punishment, thought that he who enters Gehenna never departs.[50] Saadia here divided his loyalty, maintaining with the orthodox that the Garden and the Fire will be endless, and holding with the Muʿtazilah that he who enters never leaves.[51]

48 *Em.*, V, 1, 138; IX, 5, 190.

49 Aṭ-Ṭaḥāwī, *Bayān al-Sunna wa-'l-Jamāʿa*, p. 141; al-Baghdadi, *Al-farḳ bain 'l-firaḳ*, pp. 102–104 (125–26); Shahrastani, 61 (91); Elder, *A Commentary on the Creed of Islam*, p. 106; Wensinck, *The Muslim Creed*, pp. 106, 119, 165–66; Duncan B. Macdonald, *Muslim Theology*, pp. 126, 138, 146; Friedlander, "The Heterodoxies of the Shiites, etc.," *Journal of the American Oriental Society*, XXIX, pp. 15, 74.

50 According to Aṭ-Ṭaḥāwī, *Bayān al-Sunna wa-'l-Jamāʿa*, p. 139, grave sinners will not remain in fire forever, if only they believed in divine unity, but will enter the Garden. See also Elder, *A Commentary on the Creed of Islam*, p. 114; Wensinck, *The Muslim Creed*, pp. 61–62; Sell, *The Faith of Islam*, p. 229.

51 גמולם בלי תכלית ובלי הפסק... ע״כ שם היסורין באין תכלית (או״ר ט,ז,193), שהוא מתמיד לעד... שהוא מותמד לנצח (או״ר ט,ז,ח,194), לא יתכן להעתיקם בעולם ההוא ממדרגה אל מדרגה, כי כל אחד מהגמולים עומד תמיד במה שהוא בו (או״ר ה,ב,139) החיים התמידים (או״ד ח,ג,177), חיים המתמידים (או״ד ד,ב,126; ט,א,185). See also *Amānāt*, 211: אלחיוה̈ אלדאימה̈ פי דאר אלגזא. This was also the opinion of Saadia's contemporary, David ha-Babli. See Barzillai's *commentary on Sefer Yeṣirah*, 152, and compare the quotation with *Em.*, IX, 7, 193.

Chapter Ten

ETHICS

THE TENTH and last treatise of Saadia's *Emunot we-Deʿot* is devoted to the problem of human conduct, apart from the specific commands and prohibitions dealt with in the third treatise. The problem here is purely ethical, with a psychological background—How man can wisely arrange his life pattern in view of the variety of tendencies to which he is subject. Saadia's answer is an affirmation of all the thirteen human tendencies or "loves," but with some reservations. We shall try to deal (1) with a classification of these "loves," (2) with these reservations as compared with the Aristotelian doctrine of the mean, and (3) with the place of this treatise within the general pattern of this book, a place about which some doubts have been raised. This third issue will involve Saadia's attitude toward Sufism.

1. THIRTEEN LOVES

According to Saadia, the good life is never one-sided, never dominated by any single tendency. A sound ethical theory should allow harmonious gratification of all human desires. "Even the heavens are not illuminated by just one star—so too man's conduct cannot be based on just one motive."[1] In this demand for an all-around pattern of life, Saadia follows Aristotle, as against the Cynics who regarded the moral good as the only good, and also against the Stoics who looked upon all things beyond morality as devoid of value, even if "desirable."[2] True, there is in his defense of the many-sidedness of the good life an implication of approval of the Stoic doctrine—to live according to nature.[3] But essentially Saadia is faithful to his own system with its Muʿtazilite theo-

[1] *Emunot* (Yosefov, 1885), X, 1, 198: גם השמים אינם מאירים בכוכב אחד, כן האדם לא יתנהג כל ימיו במדה אחת.

[2] Concerning the concept of ἀδιάφορα, see E. Vernon Arnold, *Roman Stoicism,* 289, 315.

[3] See Diogenes Laertius, VII, 85: "This is why Zeno was the first (in his treatise *On the Nature of Man*) to designate as the end life in agreement with nature."

dicy. First, if God is one, then creatures must be many, that is, each creature must be plural, not only in physical composition but also in his psychological make-up, in his drives and impulses. Secondly, if God is good, then all these drives and impulses that he implanted in us must also be good,[4] and "no wise man would say of what was made by the Creator: All is vanity."[5] This treatise of Saadia is therefore a critique of all ethical theories that wish to limit life and reject instincts in the name of ethical monism.

First he discerns in Ecclesiastes a reference to three ways of life, and he apparently connects them with the three faculties of the soul according to the Platonic division, so that wisdom stems from the rational faculty, rejoicing from the appetitive, and habitation of the world from the spirited faculty, that is, from the intermediate power that gives rise to anger, striving, love of honor, and other strong emotions.[6] But he soon gives us a richer classification of human goals into, what he calls, "thirteen loves." Yet it seems that these too are arranged by Saadia according to Plato's tripartite division of the soul, except that he begins with abstinence, which is not in keeping with this division, but which, as will be shown later, is the aim of the those treatises, being the corrector and regulator of the psychic mechanism whenever any drive gets out of control.

Thus from the lowest faculty, that is, appetition, stem the first four loves, that is, from the second to the sixth desire: eating and drinking, sexual intercourse, eroticism, and accumulation of money. This classification is Platonic, and the reason for the inclusion of money under

[4] *Emunot*, X, 1, 199: כי שנאת דבר אחד והגברתו אלו היה יותר תקון לא היה נוטע הבורא במדות האדם אהבת שאר דברים.

[5] *Emunot*, X, 3, 200. Not all these "loves" are regarded as of equal rank. Some are higher than others. The highest apparently are knowledge and worship, and the rest are subsidiary. The lowest are dominion, vengeance, and laziness. See also *Tafsīr Mishlei* 20, 29.

[6] Concerning the division of the soul into הכרה כעס ותאוה see *Emunot*, 153, 199 and *Tafsīr Iyob*, 1, 6. The Ar. Terms, are אלפכר ואלגצ̇ב ואלשהוה̈; and in Greek: νοητιχόν, θυμοειδές, ἐπιθυμητικόν. See Plato, *Republic*, 435–42 and *Timaeus*, 69, 70. The Heb. term כעס is a translation of the Ar. גצ̇ב, which translates only one of the meanings of the Greek Term θυμοειδές. Plato uses this term in the wider sense of "high-spirited," "courageous." But see Plato, *Republic*, 580D: Τὸ μέν, φαμέν, ἦν ᾧ μανθάνει ἄνθροπος, τὸ δὲ ᾧ θυμοῦ ται ("One part, we say, is that with which a man learns, one part is that with which he feels anger").

appetition is given by Plato: "because money is the chief instrument for the gratification of such desires."[7] Similarly, Saadia refers to some who claimed that "food and drink and sexual intercourse, which are the basis of physical existence, are made possible by money."[8] From the intermediate faculty, spirit, stem the five intermediate loves: children, habitation of the world, longevity, dominance, and vengeance. And from the highest faculty, reason, come forth the three highest loves: knowledge, worship, and rest. The last, which he particularly censures as a dominating motive, is not a sensuous desire, nor yet the child of spirit or conation of which it is indeed the opposite. It must be, therefore, a philosophical attitude toward life, hence stemming from reason together with the two previous desires. What is this philosophical attitude? It seems that it is the Stoic apathy, an inner peace obtained through the expulsion of worry and the neutralization of all will and striving, or Pyrrhonistic ataraxy (ἀταραξία) resulting from an utterly skeptical position toward all knowledge and enterprise. If we compare this thirteenth love to the thirteenth theory of creation in the first treatise, which too is the theory of Pyrrhonistic skepticism, we will see that the love and cosmogony come from the same school of thought. There Saadia says: "These however are more senseless than all those previously mentioned," and here too he says: "Now I examined the view of the proponents of this theory and I found that they were the most senseless of all men." Saadia could brook no doubts or hesitancy either in knowledge or in action. There is still a more inherent reason for this grouping of rest with worship and for Saadia's negative attitude, but this will be discussed later.

2. SOVEREIGNTY OF THE INTELLECT AND THE DOCTRINE OF THE MEAN

Thus all inclinations implanted in the human heart are good. How then can we achieve an inner harmony? Here we are reminded of the idea of the middle road as propounded by Aristotle. Malter remarks that Saadia was the first Jewish thinker in the Middle Ages to introduce this idea into ethics, but Saadia's conception is essentially different.

[7] See Plato, *Republic*, 580E.

[8] *Emunot*, X, 8, 206. Hence Bacher's Translation ורדיפת ממון for the last two words in Saadia's *Tafsīr Iyob*, 1, 6: ואמא קוה̈ אלגצ̇ב פהי אלתי ילחק אלחיואן בהא אלאקדאם ואלאנתקאם ואלג̇ראה̈ ואלחקד ואסתיפא אלטואיל seems to be incorrect and should be rendered ורדיפת יתרונות.

Let us first note three points in Aristotle's ethical theory. First, Aristotle criticized Socratic intellectualism, which identified the good with knowledge ("to know the good is to do the good") and ignored the irrational part of the soul, such as instinct and character.[9] He therefore defined the ethical goal as giving reason power over nature. Secondly, the ruling reason chooses a middle road between extremes, between too much and too little, both of which are bad. Thirdly, this middle path is not determined by arithmetical calculation, as six for example is the mean between two and ten, but is subjective and relative, all according to the nature and circumstances of the person. Hence we need a "man of practical wisdom" (φρόνιμος) to define the mean for us.[10]

Now as to the first point, Saadia emphasized it in various places. Reasonable man, he says, allows his natural impulses to be ruled by his intellect.[11] He took full cognizance of this irrational element, which he called "nature." He saw the two opposite characteristics of human nature: on the one hand, the characteristic of sloth that seeks to avoid all that costs effort and pain—to avoid even some vital needs such as food, clothing, and shelter, and *a fortiori* that quest for knowledge; and on the other hand, the passions that run after immediate pleasures without looking at consequences. Therefore reason must be given power over nature through exercise, until the good becomes nature.[12] Sometimes Saadia points to the tripartite division of soul into reason, spirit, and appetite, and defines the good as the rule of the highest faculty over the two others, and evil as the revolt of the other two against the highest.[13] And this is what differentiates the discipline of the wise from the discipline of the foolish, if the latter may be called discipline.[14] Thus knowledge, according to Saadia as according to Aristotle, is not enough to effect good conduct: one must struggle and overcome dark nature.

But as to the doctrine of the "mean," Saadia makes no use of any such term, nor of the term "extremes," from an ethical viewpoint, in

[9] See Aristotle, *Magna Moralia*, I, 1, 1082a20. See also *Ethica Nicomachea*, VI, 13, 1144b8; VI, 6, 1140b22.

[10] *Ethica Nicomachea*, 1106a26–1108b13; 1133b32 (in the Loeb Classical Library, II, vi, 15).

[11] *Emunot*, IV, 4, 129: אין הדבר כי אם שהוא מנהיג טבעו בשכלו ואם יעשה כן יהיה משכיל ואם לאו יהיה סכל. See also Saadia's introduction to his *Tafsir Mishlei*.

[12] *Tafsir Mishlei*, I, 33.

[13] *Emunot*, X, 2, 199; *Tafsir Job*, I, 6.

[14] *Emunot*, X, 2, 199–200; *Tafsīr Iyob*, I, 6; *Tafsīr Mishlei*, I, 7; 22, 15.

any place in the *Emunot*. He had the idea, because he mentions it in the *Tafsīr Mishlei*,[15] but he does not use it in the systematic discussion of the problem. Here the viewpoint is basically different. To Aristotle, the human inclinations were parallelograms of forces, where the resultant is to be located somewhere between the lines of force; whereas to Saadia these inclincations were divine suggestions or even commands, each one waiting for a situation, or a "place," where it is to find its fulfillment in a proper measure, just as rational commands, such as human gratitude to God or laws of marriage and commerce, require, according to III, 3, divinely prescribed measure and form. For Saadia does not consider extremes to be evil, as Aristotle does, because every "love" is implanted by God in the human heart and therefore cannot be but good. Only, one must know the "place"—which includes time and measure—"because for each of our loves and hates there is a place where we must use it; and when we find the place, we must use it in the full measure required for the completion of the act." "I will mention in the case of each love the place where it must be used, and for which it was created and set."[16] Thus as against Aristotle's mean, Saadia posits "place" (Ar. מוצׄע; Heb. מקום), and there is a thoroughgoing difference in conception. The Aristotelian man always seeks to escape from evil extıemes and finds refuge in the mean; whereas the Saadianic man is full of good inclinations and always seeking situations for which they were "created and set." Paradoxical as it may seem, there is more struggle with sin in the man of the first kind than in the man of the second kind.

But the third point in Aristotle's ethics, Saadia fully accepts. He too emphasizes the relativity of the measure, not only in each one of the

[15] In *Tafsir Mishlei*, 30, 9, the author states: ואלאצלח ללעבד אן יכון מתוסטא פי נעמתה but this does not refer to the mean from an ethical standpoint. Yet it is clearly stated on 27, 2 אן יכון מנע אן ימדח אלמר נפסה לאסתקבאחה דׄאך ומע צׄלך לם ילזמה אן ימנע אלנאס מן אן ימדחוה בל גׄעלהא חאלא מתוסטהׄ לילא יטׄן בעצׄנא אן מנע אלמדיח כלה אצלח. Baḥya in *Hobot ha-Lebabot*, IX, 3 uses for the mean the term חדׄ אלאעתדאל (Heb. הדרך השוה), also תוסׄטוא חדוך אלזהד (Heb. שהלכו בדרך הגדר הבינוני).

[16] כי לכל אחד ממה שהוא אוהב ושונא מקום ראוי שישתמש בו, וכאשר יראה המקום אשר ראוי להשתמש בו במדה ההיא ישלחנה בשיעור עד שישלים המעשה ההיא (י,ב,199) ואזכור בכל אחד מהם המקום אשר ראוי להשתמש בה אשר לו נברא והושם (י,ד,201). Concerning the concept of "measure," see also X, 17, 212 and X, 19, 214, where the element of time is also noted, as in Aristotle, *Ethica Nicomachea*, 1106b17. See also *Tafsīr Mishlei*, 20, 29.

thirteen loves but also in their combinations and fusions. "Man's behavior is a combination of his likes and dislikes in varying proportions." "It is not right to select equal parts from each of the thirteen; one should rather take from each kind the proper measure as is prescribed by wisdom and the Torah." "It is not proper to take equal parts of each."[17] Since then no mechanical calculation can aid us, Saadia, like Aristotle, finds need for the "man of practical wisdom." This is the meaning of Saadia's remark: "Having stated in the introduction to this treatise that need requires a sage to arrange for us the likes and the hates and to show us how we should conduct ourselves with reference to them, I will say that I find the sage Solomon, the son of David, who dealt with this problem in order to inform us what is good!"[18] Here in this passage the first mention of the sage does not refer to God, as some take it, but to the Aristotelian "man of practical wisdom." But elsewhere he says: "And if man is left to himself in order to understand what to choose in moral conduct, nature would keep him away from his goal. Therefore the All-Wise, blessed and exalted be He, had to write in this matter a book by the hand of the wise Solomon, the son of David, peace be upon him."[19] Here ethics ceases to be autonomous and becomes subservient to "wisdom and the Torah."

3. CONTRA SUFISM

Some maintain that this last treatise has no connection with the preceding treatises and is no part of the general pattern, that it must have been originally composed as a separate work and was joined afterward.[20] This opinion seems without foundation. The treatise is well-connected, but some matters require clarification.

The treatise deals, as we saw, with thirteen loves, or objects of human desire, and begins with abstinence, or asceticism, as practiced by those

[17] כן מהתקבצות מדות האדם באהבה ובשנאה על רב ומעט ישלם לו תקון ענייניו (י, א, 198). ואין ראוי ג״כ שיוקח מכל אחד מהם חלק משלשה עשר בשוה, אך יקח מכל מין מהם השיעור אשר הוא ראוי לקחת כפי מה שתחייבהו החכמה והתורה... ולא יתכן שיקחו אותם חלקים שוים (י, ז, 212–213).

[18] וכיון שהקדמתי המאמר הזה שהצורך מביא אל חכם שיסדר לנו האהבות והשנאות איך נתנהג בענינם אומר שמצאתי החכם שלמה בן דוד שהתעסק בזה להודיענו מה הוא הטוב (י, ג, 200). The word חכם here does not seem to refer to God, but to the Aristotelian φρόνιμος, the prudent man.

[19] *Tafsīr Mishlei*, introd.

[20] See Henry Malter, *Life and Works of Saadia Gaon*, 247 and notes 456, 530.

who wandered away into the mountains, weeping and mourning over this earthly existence. The eleventh, twelfth, and thirteenth loves are also conceived as forms of abstinence, namely the *exclusive* quest of knowledge, the *exclusive* love of worship, and the longing for rest as an euphemistic term for laziness. Apparently, the whole treatise is aimed against abstinence, and the question arises: What abstinence does Saadia have in mind? What group practised it at that time? All descriptions of the abstainers, both at the beginning when he speaks about abstinence directly and at the end when he deals with it under three different names, point to Sufism. It was this movement that Saadia aimed in these chapters to show was one-sided and destructive; except that, as was his custom in other discussions, he included in his condemnation other theories of conduct that too were narrow and one-sided.

The name "Sufi" is, as is now accepted, derived from the Arabic word for wool. Indeed Baḥya, in a description that parallels that of Saadia, explicitly refers to the Sufis as dressing in worn garments and wool.[21] The movement attained its highest development both in practice and in doctrine, both as asceticism and as mysticism, in the very place and time in which Saadia lived. Hallaj shook the Mohammedan world to its foundations with his mystic utterance *ana 'l-haqq*, I am the Truth, meaning God, the only reality, and he was publicly executed for this belief. It would be strange indeed therefore if Saadia, who joyfully tackled every opponent and many religious and philosophical doctrines that were not to his taste, remained silent on this movement that raged around him in his own city.

The Arabic term for abstinence, *zuhd*, was indeed synonymous with Sufism in the first period of this movement. The Sufis saw only evil in this world, and longed for the world to come. They withdrew from human settlements, abandoned all their possessions, relying only on God, gave up all will and striving, and refused human gifts or charity, even

כאישים הרוחניים... וברחו מן היישוב אל המדברות והישימון וההרים הגבוהים... ולובשים הבלויים והצמר (ער׳: וילבסון אלכלקאן ואלצוף). Cf. *ibid.*, IX, 6, where Baḥya seems to identify the Sufi garb with the "hairy mantle and maintains that it was always the dress of the saints (כי הוא לבוש החסידים מקדם). This is, in keeping with his idea in IX, 2, 6, that the prophets were ascetics—a Sufi idea. See A. J. Arberry, *Sufism* (London and New York, 1951), 35.

21 See Baḥya, *Hobot ha-Lebabot*, IX, 3: אנשים שהלכו בגדר הפרישות העליון להדמות

medical treatment.[22] One sect among them was called "weepers" (Ar. אלבכאון),[23] and Saadia apparently referred to this group in his statement: "There are some who maintain that it is proper for man to lead a life of abstinence, to wander out into the mountains and *to weep and lament and mourn over this world.*" And Saadia concludes his criticism of this movement by pointing to the idea of place: "Abstinence is good for man when he practices it in its proper place, namely when he is confronted with forbidden food or forbidden sexual intercourse or forbidden money." But this is indeed what the Sufis argued against, for they maintained that with reference to the forbidden (חראם), *zuhd* applies to all Moslems, whereas they took upon themselves this practice with reference to what is permitted (חלאל) likewise.

Saadia's discussion of the twelfth theory of conduct, the love of worship, speaks even more clearly about this movement. "There are many who maintain that the good life is only that of worshipping God, that man should fast by day and arise at night to praise and give thanks, to abandon all affairs of this world, for his God will supply him with food and medicine and his other needs." This is a clear description of Sufism, extending even to their abandonment of medical care. By the statement "arise at night to praise and give thanks," Saadia probably hints at the Sufi-ceremony of *dhikr*, "remembrance," performed by the Sufi sometimes at night alone in his house.[24] It is interesting that in his criticism, Saadia attacks especially the element of trust, the Sufic complete trust in God (Ar. *tawakkul*), which indeed exposed the Sufists to attack among the Moslems themselves, and because of which they were called *mutawakkilun*, trusters, and were debating the question whether a *mutawakkil* may avail himself of medicine or not.[25]

The Sufi doctrine of trust would naturally include that of "rest" (אלראחה), which Saadia elsewhere regards as a high state, as the quest

[22] See Duncan B. Macdonald, *Muslim Theology*, 174–80. It is true that also among the Karaites in Jerusalem of the tenth century there were abstainers and ascetics, namely, the אבלי ציון. See H. Graetz, *Geschichte der Juden* V (Leipzig, 1909), note 17, 6. But it is not these ascetics that Saadia means, for their asceticism aimed at the hastening of redemption, and no such national motive is mentioned here.

[23] See Reynold A. Nicholson in *Hastings Encyclopedia for Religion and Ethics*, II, 100.

[24] *Ibid.*, 102.

[25] See I. Goldziher, *Vienna Orient. Journal*, XIII, 52.

of the righteous in order to reach the light of God,[26] but which as a way of life he here condemns. He devotes, however, a special chapter to the idea of rest, treating it separately as the thirteenth love, because it was embraced also by other sects and movements, such as the Stoics and the Skeptics, which latter group Saadia particularly opposed.

All this proves that the last treatise was aimed against the Sufis. Its place in the general pattern of the book is now clear. Throughout the book Saadia emphasized the world to come as the purpose of creation and the aim of man. The question then faced Saadia: What attitude should man take toward the world he lives in? Is not Sufism the clear answer—abstinence, turning away from all that is sweet and pleasant, escape from life? Our author's reply is: Man must satisfy his natural inclinations, provided he limits himself as to place, time, and measure, and he actively participates in human society. And Saadia is consistent. If the future world is the highest goal, and if it is an assertion of reason

26 See *Tafsīr Mishlei*, 31, 31: וכדלך אלצדיק אדא אנאל נפסה מא תתמנאה מן אלראחה ואלוצול אלי נור אלבארי. The concept of the Light of God is certainly not foreign to the Bible. It is also Neoplatonic, as we find it in Plotinus, *Enneads*, V, 3, 8; VI, 7, 21, 22. But the Sufis gave it further development. In Sufism it is a pre-existent light that is the medium of prophecy. It is the divine spirit that God breathed into Adam, identified with the Neoplatonic νοῦς,, which is the first emanation from the One, and with the Gnostic Logos, which becomes incarnate in the prophets. See R. A. Nicholson, *The Idea of Personality in Sufism* (Cambridge University Press, 1923), pp. 43, 59, 61. One can see how this Sufi speculation might have helped to shape Saadia's important theory of אור נברא, a created Light, also called Glory—a theory that exerted great influence on later Jewish thought, particularly that of Yehudah Halevi and Maimonides. See particularly Saadia, *Emunot*, II, 11; Yehudah Halevi, *Kuzari*, IV, 3; Maimonides, *Moreh Nebukim*, I, 5, 10, 64.

Incidentally, Yehudah Halevi's expression in *Kuzari*, IV, 13: פיציר הו הו (Heb. וישוב הוא הוא), where the first הו is generally taken to refer to man and the second הו to the Active Intellect, may be a Sufic expression in which הו הו refers to God, but applied here to the Active Intellect. See Hallaj, *Kitab al-Tawāsīn*, ed. Louis Massignon (Paris, 1913), 130; Louis Massignon, *La passion d'al-Hosayn-ibn-Mansour al-Hallaj*, I, 254 and its index of terms. Comp. *Kuzari*, I, 1, where the supposed meaning is expressed clearly אד קד צאר [הו] ודלך שיא ואחדא.

In Saadia's versions of the Bible, the term נור אללה is sometimes used to remove anthropomorphism (as on Gen. 17, 22, Ex. 24, 10; 33, 19, 22, 23; Num. 11, 10. See also on Lev., 26, 12; Isa. 66, 1); and sometimes it is used in translating the term כבוד or Glory, that is, Saadia's concept of the Second Air, the medium of prophecy (as on Ex., 29, 45, 46; 33, 14, 15; Num., 17, 7), or the term רוח, that is, the prophetic spirit, which too is the Second Air (e.g., on Num., 11, 29 and in *Emunot*, III, 10, 123).

that reward for work done is better than a gracious gift, and work means fulfilling the commandments, rational as well as religious,[27] then escape from life and social duties is no way to reward.

But there was some Sufism in Saadia's own philosophy, in spite of his defense of the human body in IV, 2 and VI, 4. Thus he wondered why the love for this world was implanted in the human heart, and tried various answers: "This love was placed in the human heart only that he may not kill himself in time of stress," or to serve as an aid in the study of the Torah, or as a step to the hereafter (X, 11, 208; 14, 210; 17, 212). Thus also he maintained that love of high office and eminence was implanted in us only to stir the longings for the eminent reward in the hereafter (X, 12, 209); that laughter and jest are degrading, placing man on a level with beasts (X, 3, 200); that fasting should be encouraged (V, 7, 146); that abstinence is still mostly true (X, 14, 201).[28] But all this was meant only to balance the soul, to provide counter weight to hedonistic inclinations.

Saadia sharply withdrew from doctrinal or mystic Sufism; he never showed signs of the religious intoxication of *tawḥid* in the Sufi sense of union or fusion with God. Saadia the rationalist kept the line tight between the above and the below. Hence we can hear an anti-Hallajian note in the opening of his book: "Blessed be the Lord, God of Israel, who alone is worthy of being designated as Clear Truth."[29] The hint is: Man cannot call himself Truth. Only God is *al-haq*, and not in the Sufi sense of reality, but, as Saadia goes on, as a source of human reason and verification.

CONCLUSIONS

The last treatise, "On Human Conduct," was not meant as a separate work but rather is connected with his general philosophy in which the

[27] *Emunot,* X, 15, 211.

[28] Ibid., X, 11, 208; 14, 210; 17, 212. Concerning Saadia's pessimism, see V, 5, 143; X, 4, 201; 11, 208. Saadia's general position is a theoretical negation of this world together with a practical affirmation thereof as a place for social deeds to constitute provision for the road to the hereafter. In this he is followed by Baḥya in his *Ḥobot ha-Lababot*, IX, 3. Extreme Sufism, which both Saadia and Baḥya oppose, negates this world both conceptually and practically.

[29] *Emunot,* in the beginning of the introduction אשר לו יאות עין (צ״ל: ענין־באבר) האמת הברורה (אלחקיק במעני אלחק אלמבין). Other meanings have been proposed, but only Tibbon's seems possible.

hereafter is the goal of life, thus raising the question of attidude to this world. Saadia believed in an ethical pluralism, affirming all ways of life that flow from Platonic psychology; but his view differs from the Aristotelian "mean" in regarding all inclinations as God-implanted and therefore good, only awaiting their "place" or situation for which they were originally "set". And the treatise is primarily a polemic with Sufism, though Saadia himself was not entirely free from the latter's sombre atmosphere.

Epilogue To Part I

REMARKS IN RESTROSPECT

A HUNDRED AND FIFTY years before the Arab al-Baghdadi, Saadia delved into the problems of epistemology and classification of the sources of knowledge. Indeed, the points of contact between Saadia's introduction to his *Emunot* and theories eleven to thirteen in the first treatise, on the one hand, and the first chapter of al-Baghdadi's *Uṣūl ad-Dīn*, on the other, invite special investigation. In this classification of sources Saadia granted first authority to the intellect, which according to him can ascend the pyramid of knowledge, which begins with a broad empirical base and ends with the sharp peak of subtlest truths. There are, to be sure, hidden spots to which the intellect has no access. Saadia, unlike Yehudah Halevi, makes no attempt to complete the ways of reason with paths of faith, for faith in his view strives to be fortified *with* reason. And with all the limitations of the intellect, it is still our only power to know what can be known about the world and its Creator. The importance of faith is to protect man with true ideas while on the road, in the interim, until the intellect reaches its destination.

Through this rationalistic approach we arrive at a concept of a timeless and transcendent deity, above all categories, above will. It is noteworthy that it is through reason that we attain transcendence. The mind itself posits something above itself, a non-mind. And all those who aimed to introduce intermediators into a world view in order to bring creation nearer to the human reason really followed roads other than reason and drank from springs of mysticism. Hence angels and prophets occupy little place in Saadia's system, in order not to blur the border line. And the world was created wholly and suddenly, not by degrees, nor through combinations of letters and numbers, because this too involves intermediation and association. Here again it is sudden creation that is more in harmony with reason than evolution. And it is because of this transcendence that Saadia denies any other kind of eternity, such as that of the soul, since this would constitute a likeness of the divine and impair the transcendence. And it is also because of this transcendence that he refrains from positing as a goal and ideal the Sufic idea of *tawḥid* or union with God. Thus Saadia's system is a complete dualism without any bridges: just God and the world.

And epistemological rationalism tends toward cosmological rationalism or teleology. Saadia's frequent appellation for God is *ḥakam*, the Wise. The world came into being not by chance nor by necessity but by intention and design—and all for the sake of man. Also the Torah, not only in its rational commands but also in its primarily revealed laws, is all rational, and here Saadia is more rationalistic than Maimonides, who identifies morals with conventions, that is, with the nonrational. Saadia endeavors to base on reason even such conventional laws as "Thou shalt not steal." Evil is harmful, and the good is useful. This is absolute utilitarianism. And we must add that essentially there are not two separate domains, morals and religion, since reason rules in both. Ethics is absorbed in wisdom and religion.

And this reason that fills the universe is also beneficent, and teleology and theodicy are identical. The world came into being only to confer benefits on man, to make him worthy of the goodness of the hereafter. One of the proofs of redemption and the coming of Messiah is that reason requires extra reward for a people of extra suffering. And if the world is good, then the body is not a grave for the soul, not a source of evil and defilement; and the thirteen "loves" or instincts implanted in man are all good, and no single instinct need be built up on the destruction of another instinct. Morals are not monistic but pluralistic in their motivation.

Such is the system erected by Saadia, the pioneer of medieval Jewish thought, mostly under the influence of Muʿtazilite rationalism. Still, the word "system" may not exactly apply. For this term connotes a certain strain, a tying together of ideas that tend in opposite directions, like a system of stars each one pulling away and yet so balanced in their opposite tensions that they are held together by their very pulling apart. The two Talmudic paths of snow and fire are each a continuity, a linear consistency; whereas he who walks between them and carves out of the two attractions a path of his own creates a system. Saadia's philosophy is in general a coordination of principles, an idyllic line, but perhaps not a system because it lacks the sort of strain that we find, for example, in Maimonides and Yehudah Halevi and in other great personalities in the history of thought. There is no inner conflict or wrestling of forces· Thought was not yet split between Aristotelianism and the Kalām. It was the same thought that was enlisted in support of faith, and faith on its part showed as yet no signs of fear of thought. Saadia, it is true, presents many opponents in every treatise, but he strikes them down with comparative ease. There are many opponents but not one main contester.

And yet here and there we feel the presence of one opponent whom he combats with particular zest, since at first he was himself on his opponent's side. I refer to the advocate of the mystic or Neoplatonic viewpoint with its ideas of intermediation and the soul's pre-existence and the body as evil from which the soul longs to leave for a better world. It is mysticism and not reason that he opposes, though he yields to the former occasionally. He thinks, for example, that in spite of the fact that "all of our knowledge is built upon what we perceive with our senses," knowledge is not all absorbed from the outside, but lies hidden in the soul prior to experience, which only discovers it, just as the ear discovers tunes—an idea that comes close to Platonic "recollection" in the garb of Plotinus, that is, the idea of knowledge coming at birth and enduring in a potential state. And we find this yielding in his theory of morals. Foı in spite of his moral, as well as physiological, vindication of the body, Saadia knows also the soul's longing for another world; he finds much truth in asceticism and upholds the intelligent man who "leads nature with his reason," for nature is sluggish in the doing of the good and alert in violence and transgression. But the main mystic idea, that of mediation, originating in Neoplatonism and assuming various formulations, to which he submitted in his commentary on *Sefer Yeṣirah*, he now combats consistently, and against it he powerfully locks the doors of his intellectual structure. And it is this combat that imparts to Saadia's philosophy the strain and character of a "system."

Part II

THREE ESSAYS

SOME ASPECTS OF YEHUDAH HALEVI'S MYSTICISM

THERE WAS a vein of mysticism running through all of medieval Arabic philosophy. Even the great Aristotelians, al-Farabi and Avicenna, devoted much thought to the nature and conditions of prophecy.[1] But this gift, they believed, resulted from a union with a supernal being of pure reason, and the way to union lay through reason. It is the philosopher in whom, according to the summary of that viewpoint given at the beginning of the *Kuzari*, hereditary and environmental factors developed intellectual, moral, and practical capacities, which, when perfected through instruction and training, cause a divine light to dwell with him so that he and the Active Intellect become one.[2] Indeed reason was not only a condition but also, in itself, a reliable source of physical and metaphysical knowledge, even though it was through a slow, gradual, syllogistic process, as compared with prophecy, which gives truth in a timeless flash.[3] It is this rationalism, both as metaphysics and epistemology, to which Yehudah Halevi is opposed.

[1] See M. Horten, *Texte zu dem Streite zwischen Glauben und Wissen im Islam*, pp. 3, 4, 7. See also quotation from Avicenna in note 4 and al-Farabi's *Hatḥalot ha-Nimṣaīm* in Filipowski's *Ha-Asif* (1849), p. 41 וזאת ההשפעה המתהוה מן השכל הפועל אל השכל המתפעל כאשר יתמצע ביניהם השכל הנקנה היא הנבואה.

[2] See *Das Buch Al-Chazari des Abū-l-Ḥasan Jehuda Hallewi*, ed. by Hartwig Hirschfeld (Leipzig, 1887), I, 1, p. 5. This edition will be the basis of reference throughout this essay. See also I, 87, p. 39 שלא תהיה הנבואה כאשר חשבו הפילוסופים מנפש יזדככו מחשבותיה and al-Farabi's statement in note 1.

[3] V, 12, p. 319 וכבר יצליח הכח הדברי בקצת האנשים מהתדבקו בשכל הכללי במה שירוממהו מהשתמש בהקשה והעיון ויסיר מעליו הטורח בלמוד בנבואה ותקרא סגולתו זאת קדושה ותקרא רוח הקדש. This agrees literally with the view of Avicenna as quoted by Palqera and cited by Cassel in his edition of the *Kuzari*, p. 27, note 3. See Kaufmann's *Attributenlehre*, p. 204, note 181. Cassel and Kaufmann as well as Moscato misinterpret ויסיר מעליו הטורח בלמוד בנבואה for the meaning is, as Hirschfeld gives it, "escaping such necessity *by inspiration* and revelation." Palqera's התעוררות in his quotation from Avicenna as well as in his *Reshit Ḥokmah*, p. 55, is a better rendering than למוד for the Ar. אלהאם. See also V, 14, p. 327 ולמה יצטרכו אל התבונה

His presentation of the Active Intellect seems to be drawn mainly from the writings of Avicenna. Like al-Farabi and Avicenna, he calls it the Holy Spirit or Ruaḥ ha-Qodesh.[4] Like al-Farabi and Avicenna, he gives it sublunary place and rank, whereas Al-Gazali regards it as the regent of the moon, and Alexander of Aphrodisias as identical with God.[5] However, there is a Neoplatonic view, found in Baḥya's *Kitāb Maʿānī al-Nafs*, that identifies it with the first emanation also called Name, Shekinah, and Glory;[6] and it would seem that Halevi followed this view

---

במושכליהם חלק אחר חלק. In V, 12, p. 319, the author does not contradict himself in saying ואעפ״י שנראה מעשהו בזמן בהרכבת ההקשות בעיון ובמחשבה הנה הבנתו לתולדת איננו נתלית בזמן אך עצם השכל מרומם מהזמן for though the grasping of the conclusion when the two premises are given is timeless, still that part of an intellectual operation involved in obtaining the premises is a gradual and timely process. In this way, Saadia's emphasis in the introduction to his *Emunot we-Deʿot* on the timeliness of thought and his statements כאשר היו צריכים בחלק (رسم = בחוק) הבריאה בכל פעל שיפעלוהו אל מדה מהזמן ישלם בה פעלם חלק אחר חלק... כל הברואים לא יתכן שיהיה מדעם בלא סבה והיא הדרישה והעיון הצריכים למדה מהזמן need not be taken as opposed to the view of Halevi.

4 I, 87, בשכל הפועל הנקרא רוה״ק או בגבריאל. Similarly al-Farabi in *Hathalot*, p. 2. והשכל הפועל הוא אשר ראוי שיאמן בו שהוא הרוח הנאמן ורוח הקדש. By רוח נאמן is meant Gabriel (Kaufmann, *Attributenlehre*, p. 205 note 181). As for Avicenna, see the Palqera quotation cited by Cassel, *Kuzari*,, p. 27 ואפשר שיהיה הכח השכלי מוכן במקצת הנפשות בהקיץ והדבקות בשכל הכללי עד שלא יצטרך להתיגע אלא יספיקהו התעוררות והנבואה וזה יקרא רוח הקדש. ולא הוכן בזה המעלה אלא הנביא. See however Palqera's *Reshit Ḥokmah*, p. 55, where, in an interpolation in his version of al-Farabi's *Iḥṣa al-ʿUlūm* (see *The Jewish Quarterly Review*, N.S., XXV, 227–35 and XXVII, 100), Palqera states from another source והרוח הצדקת מטבע העצמים הרוחניים השניים ורוה״ק מטבע הכרובים thus regarding the Holy Spirit as higher than Gabriel. A. M. Goichon in her *Lexique de la langue philosophique d'ibn Sīnā* (Paris, 1938), p. 145, states that to Avicenna the Holy Spirit was a psychological state, the highest disposition of the human soul when it is in constant contact with the Active Intellect. See notes 12, 15, 50. As for the meaning of the "Universal Intellect," see *ibid.*, p. 231: فاوّل قابل التجلّيه هو الملك الالاهى الموسوم بالعقل الكلّ.

5 I, 1, p. 7 והוא מלאך מדרגתו למטה מן המלאך הממונה בגלגל הירח. See also V, 21 ואחרית מדרגתם והקרוב מהם אצלנו השכל הפועל. See Delmedigo's *Nobelot Ḥokmah*, p. 17 קצתם יאמרו שהוא האל ית׳ וזו דעת אלכסנדר האפרודיסי ורבים מהאחרונים עמו... ואלגאזיל הערבי יחשוב שהוא מלאך המניע גלגל הירח ובן סינה יחשוב שהוא שכל למטה מגלגל הירח... ואבונצר וב״ר יחשבו שהוא שכל נבדל תחת גלגל הירח.

6 *Kitāb Maʿānī al-Nafs* ed. by I. Goldziher in *Abhandlungen der Königlichen Gesellschaft der Wissenschaften zu Göttingen. Philologisch-Historische Klasse, N.S. IX, Nro. 1* (Berlin, 1907), pp. 53–54 פאול הדה אלמבדעאת ואבסטהא ואשרפהא ואקרבהא נסבה מן מבדעהא גל ועלא הו אלדי יסמונהא אלעבראניון שכינה... ואדלהא עליה הו אלמסמי שם ושכינה וכבוד... והו אלספיר אלאול ואלתרגמאן אלאעטם ואלחאגב אלאקרב והו אלדי

in V, 10, where he says that philosophers regarded it below, that is, next to God (Ar. מלכא דון אללה, Tibbon: מלאך אחרי האלהים). But in the face of Halevi's other utterances, the word *allah* should be taken here technically as a name for a species of angels. Thus in V, 21, Halevi states: "And they called those Intelligences *allah* and secondary causes[7] as well as other names; and the last of their rank and nearest to us is the Active Intellect."[8] Maimonides also in his *Yesodei ha-Torah*, II, 7, places the Active Intellect or אישים at the end of a hierarchy of angels the last four grades of which he designates as *elohim*, *bnei elohim*, *cherubim* and *'ishīm*.[9]

On the other hand, Halevi's presentation of the function of the Active Intellect seems to agree with that of Avicenna and al-Gazali, that the influences of the Active Intellect extends to all sublunar things including minerals, as against al-Farabi, followed by Averroes, who limits it to man, that is, to the translation of human thought from potentiality to actuality.[10] There is an intermediate view, that the influence of the Active

---

יסמّיה שלמה בן דוד חכמה... ויסמונה חכמא אליונאניין אלעקל אלפעאל. According to Shahrastani, top of p. 44 this Neoplatonic view was also held by the later Mutazilites: اوية العقل الاول الذى هو اول مبدع وهو العقل الفعّال الذى منه يفيض الصور على الموجودات. al-Gazali too in one place identifies the highest angel, the Obeyed One, who moves the all-surrounding sphere, with the Active Intellect, according to A. J. Wensinck, "On the Relation between Ghazali's Cosmology and his Mysticism," in *Mededeelingen der Koninklijke Akademie van Wetenschappen, Afdeeling letterkunde deel 75, Serie A*. No. 6, p. 19.

7 This term is also used by al-Farabi in *Hatḥalot*, p. 2 והשניים הם אשר ראוי שיאמר בהם הרוחניים והמלאכים והדומים להם.

8 See also IV, 1 אלהים תאר למושל בדבר מן הדברים ויש שיהיה בכל... ויש שיהיה בחלק כשהוא רוצה בו כח מכחות הגלגל. Halevi frequently joins the word אלהי with מלאכי. Thus in I, 42, המעלה הזאת אלהית מלאכותית and in IV, 3, p. 243 הסוג האלהי המלאכי. Indeed in V, 10, 21 it is called just המדרגה האלהית.

9 Cf. Meir Aldabi, *Shebilei Emunah*, 26: והמעלה העשירית שהיא מעלת הצורה הנקראת אישים הם המלאכים המדברים עם הנביאים ונראים להם במראה הנבואה ולפיכך נקראו אישים שמעלתם קרובה ממעלת האדם.

10 V, 10 p. 307, על דעת אנשי ההקשה כי היסודות כאשר ימזגו מזגים מתחלפים כפי התחלף המקומות והאוירים והערכים הגלגלים והיו ראויות לצורות מתחלפות מאצל נותן הצורות והיו כל המוצאים מה שיש להם מכחות וטבעים המיוחדים להם. Similarly in V, 4, p. 299. As for the Arabian thinkers, see Delmedigo, *Nobelot Ḥokmah*, ובן סינה יחשוב שהוא שכל למטה מגלגל הירח הממונה על כללות העולם היסודי והוא נקרא בל׳ ערבי קולכודיאה (?) ר״ל הנותן הצורות הן בהיולי שמפשיט ומלביש הצורות הן בשכל ההיולני שהן צורות מושכלות וכן דעת הרמב״ם ז״ל ח״ב פ״ד ואבונצר וב״ר יחשבו שהוא שכל נבדל תחת גלגל הירח אבל אין ממשלתו בכללות העולם היסודי כ״א על כללות המין האנושי ר״ל

Intellect embraces animals and plants but not minerals, which are what they are by virtue of their composition and require no "divine forms." This view too as held by *some* thinkers is mentioned by Halevi.[11]

But Halevi opposes the entire emanation system of which the Active Intellect is a part. "People accepted it and were beguiled by it to such an extent that they thought it conclusive because they ascribed it to Greek philosophers. But it is only an assertion, carrying no conviction, and is open to various objections."[12] Instead of the Active Intellect, he posits what he terms *al-amr al-ilāhī* (Tibbon: *ha-ʿinyan ha-elohi*) as the goal for human striving. What does this term mean? It can be taken in the general sense of divine nature or being, in which case Tibbon's rendering is correct, or else in the technical sense of the Neo-platonic

---

על הנפש המשכלת לבדה. See also al-Farabi. *Hatḥalot,* p. 2: והשכל הפועל פעולתו ההשגחה בחי המדבר. Tibbon in his Glossary on Maimonides calls it an Aristotelian view. Shem Tob in his commentary on the *Moreh,* I, 72, joins the name of al-Gazali to that of Avicenna. See also quotation from Shahrastani in Emil Berger's *Das Problem der Erkenntnis in der Religionsphilosophie Jehuda Hallewis* (Berlin, 1916), p. 67.

11 See V, 10, p. 307. Shem Tob, in his commentary on the *Moreh,* I, 72 and II, 12, maintains that this view was held by Maimonides. See also Moscato on *Kuzari* (Wilna, 1904), V, 10 p. 28. Delmedigo however (see above note 10) infers from *Moreh,* II, 4 that Maimonides followed Avicenna. Delmedigo probably referred to the passage עד שיהיה יחס השכל הפועל ליסודות ומה שהורכב מהם יחס כל שכל נבדל המיוחד לגלגל ההוא, but see Shem Tob, ad. loc.

12 See IV, 25, p. 283 and V, 14, p. 329 and pp. 355–57 where he regards that theory as heresy. In IV, 3, p. 245, Halevi says concerning the eternal angels ושמא הם הרוחניים שאומרים הפילוסופיים ואין לנו לדחות דבריהם ולא לקבל אותם. This would seem to be out of keeping with his emphatic opposition to the assumption of Separate Intellects. But Halevi opposes only the view that there are agencies other than God that move the spheres and therefore interfere with divine sovereignty but not to the idea of the existence of pure Intellects. To this philosophical notion, he is completely indifferent. Both Avicenna and al-Gazali maintained that there were such spiritual beings higher than the movers (see quotations in Steinschneider's *Alfarabi* p. 115, note 49). See also Palqera's *Reshit Ḥokmah* p. 55 in a quotation from an older source: העצמים הרוחניים אשר מקצתם עושים מניעים ומקצתם מצוים והם המגיעים מאדון הכל ית׳ הנבואה. The word מצויים is probably a rendering of امر. Similarly Avicenna in Goichon, *Lexique de la langue philosophique d'ibn Sīnā,* p. 145 الجواهر الروحانية التى تودّى الوحى and p. 384 فاوّل ذلك درجه الملايكة الروحانية المجرّدة التى تسمّى عقولاً ثم مراتب الملايكة الروحانية التى تسمّى نفوساً وهى الملايكة الفعلية. See notes 4, 45, 50. Neumark in his *Toledot ha-Pilosofiah be-Israel,* II, 286, takes the word רוחניים in the *Kuzari* passage to mean Platonic Ideas,

Logos, in which case teh Hebrew rendering is inadequate. The latter is the view of Goldziher who does however admit that Halevi did not use the term in this sense with systematic precision.[13] Now, it is true that, as A. J. Wensinck has shown, through the channel of the Syrians who were acquainted with the terminology of the fourth Gospel as well as with the works of Philo, the notion of Logos reached the Arab thinkers, and that sometimes in the writings of al-Farabi and al-Gazali the word *amr* has this meaning.[14] But it seems very unlikely that this is the sense of the term anywhere in the *Kuzari*, for the following reasons.

1. If the term *amr* is used technically, to denote Logos, it is strange that nowhere in the *Kuzari* is it used alone but is always accompanied, and occasionally several times in the same paragraph, by the word *ilāhī*. This shows that Halevi used the word *amr* only in the general sense of nature or being.

2. The term is first presented in I, 42 as parallel to the three lower grades of being: *amr ṭabīʿyī* or nature, *amr nifsānī* or soul, and *amr ʿaqlī* or intellect, in all of which the word *amr* can only have the general sense, so that the expression *amr ilāhī* to denote the fourth and highest grade can only mean divine nature or divinity. Indeed in the next paragraph he calls it *al-ilāhūt*, divinity.

3. In III, 17, p. 165, reference is made to the *amr ilāhī* as the giver of the Torah, as the one who arranged Israel in the wilderness under four standards, and who rested upon Israel in order to be a God unto them. If a deutero-deity is herein intended, Halevi becomes the champion of the very doctrine attributed to the philosopher at the beginning of the book, of the aloofness and unconcernedness of the First Cause, a doctrine that he repudiates, as for example, in the beginning of IV, 3.

4. Parallel passages indicate the meaning. Thus the saying: "There is no niggardliness with *al-amr al-ilāhī*" in V, 10 p. 309, is repeated on the same page in the words: "There is no niggardliness with Him, blessed be He." The statement in V, 20, p. 345: "The speech of the prophets when they are enwrapped by the Holy Spirit is dictated verbatim by

[13] See *Revue des Études juives,* L, 32–41 and Emil Berger, *Das Problem der Erkenntnis in der Religionsphilosophie Jehuda Hallewis,* pp. 69–72.

[14] See Wensinck, "On the Relation between Ghazali's Cosmology and his Mysticism," pp. 5, 6, 13, 15, 17, 20. See also *Risālat Fuṣūṣ,* ed. Dieterici, in his *Alfarabi's Philosophische Abhandlungen,* §9 وعالم علمه بعد ذاته هو الكل الثانى لا نهاية له ولا حدّ وهناك الام.

al-amr al-ilāhī and the prophet cannot change[15] a single word" is parallel to the passage in I, 87, p. 39: "The speech addressed to Moses had its origin in the Creator and was not due to any thought or counsel on the part of Moses."

5. Halevi combats the theory of emanation in IV, 25 and V, 14, and he emphasizes in many places God's unremitting administration of the universe.[16] In V, 21, he warns: "Let us take no heed of the words of the philosophers who divide the divine world into degrees, since we reject anthropomorphism.[17] It is God alone who leads all things corporeal." The assumption of Goldziher and Berger that Halevi opposed only that emanational doctrine that grew out of Aristotle's cosmology and that was polytheistic but not the Neoplatonic form, which was "rich in religious motives," is disproven by the fact that Halevi voices his dissatisfaction even with the emanationism of the *Sefer Yeṣirah*. "Where is the need of the letters *hē*, *waw* and *yod* or an angel or a sphere or other things when we affirm the divine Will and creation and that God created the multitudinous things in one moment... and sustains them each moment by his divine power" (IV, 26). Even to the philosophical assumption of spiritual realities in which Halevi saw no interference with the belief in God's sovereignty, he maintains an attitude of cold indifference: "we need not accept them nor reject them."

It is union with this *amr ilāhī*, therefore, the divine essence itself, and not with any intermediary, that constitutes the highest attaintment of man; and in his expressions for this ecstatic state, Halevi goes even beyond al-Gazali. The latter condemned the use of the terms *ittiḥād* (identification), *ḥulūl* (fusion), and *wusūl* (union), as inconsistent with true unity,[18] whereas Halevi, either because the word *amr* muffles the anthropomorphic ring or because biblical and Talmudic literature paved the way for such utterances, uses *ittiṣāl* most commonly, and does not hesitate to employ the term *ḥulul*, though he avoids the term *ittiḥād*

15 Ar. וליס אלי אלנבי תגייר כלאמה מן כלאמתה. Tibbon renders: ואין לנביא דבר בבחירה מדבריו evidently reading תכייר instead of תגייר.

16 See, for example, III, 17, p. 167 כי לאלהים בעולם הזה ממשלה מתמדת ואינו כאשר חושבים הטבעיים שהוא על הטבעים אשר נסום. See also V, 10, p. 307 ועל האמת שהבורא יתברך ינהיגם בתכונה מהתכונות קרא אתה התכונה ההיא אם תחפוץ טבע או נפש או כח. The Arabic has in addition או מלכא but as the context shows we should read מלכה disposition, quality. See also V, 21.

17 Hirschfeld's rendering "as soon as we are free from our bodies" is incorrect.

18 See Duncan B. Macdonald, *The Religious Attitude and Life in Islam*, p. 187.

except in the exposition of the philosopher's idea of the Active Intellect.[19]

But how can this union be effected? Not through *qiās* or reasoning. Great, it is true, are the achievements of the philosophers in the realm of logic and mathematics. "They established the demonstrable sciences on an unlimited basis and excelled in them and there is no conflict of opinionin those sciences."[20] But they lose all their reliability and unanimity when they enter the realm of physics and particularly that of metaphysics. Halevi examines in detail their theory of emanation (IV, 25, 26; V, 14, 21), their cosmogony (V, 2–8, 14), their psychology (V, 14), and shows their unconvincingness. The difficulty is not entirely due to their reasoning. "There are things which it is not in the nature of man to conceive by means of reason" (V, 14; I, 64). "There is a curtain of bright light conquering human vision" (V, 21). "A rationalistic faith is open to many doubts" (I, 13). "Proofs are deceiving, leading man to heresy and false thoughts" (IV, 3; V, 16). "The masses do not follow the philosophers because the soul feels the truth" (IV, 17). "There is much in heaven, earth, and sea not known to the philosopher" (V, 14).

In place of reason, Halevi offers the direct, mystic experience and the certitude of prophecy. He calls it דוק (Tibbon טעם), a term that he uses sometimes in a literal sense, as personal taste and opinion, and therefore synonymous with *qiās*,[21] but mainly as a sufi-term for mystic intuition and therefore antynomous with *qiās*. Indeed he finds the difference between the God of Aristotle and the God of Abraham to result from the fact that the former is proven through *qiās* and the latter is experienced through *ḍawq*. The term is defined in Arabic literature

[19] אתצאל (Tibbon: התחברות, חבור, התדבקות, הדבקות, דביקה). See, for example I, p. 4, 19; I, 27, p. 17; I, 68, p. 31; I, 109, p. 59; II, 2, p. 73; V, 12, p. 323. As for חלול (Tibbon: חול), see for example, I, 95, pp. 42, 46; I, 103, p. 54; III, 23, p. 179. As far as I have noted Halevi used אתחאד (Tibbon: התאחדות) only once and not in connection with *amr ilāhī* but with the Active Intellect in the exposition of the philosopher's viewpoint in I, 1, p. 5. Similarly in V, 12 p. 321, in the summary of Avicenna's psychology, he uses the verb אחדת (Tibbon תתאחד).

[20] V, 14, p. 328 ואנפרדוא לדלך ולא כלאף בין שכצין פי תל אלעלום. Hirschfeld gives here a meaningless rendering because he takes ואנפרדוא in the sense of "and they separated," whereas the word can only mean here "and they excelled," "they were unique." Thus in IV, 15 ואנפראדה means "and His uniqueness." On the other hand, the Hebrew commentators and Buxtorf and Cassel mistook Tibbon's correct rendering והתיחדו in the sense of being united instead of "and they were distinguished."

[21] See III, 49, where Tibbon rightly סברא, opinion.

as a mystic light projected by God into the heart of His chosen and as the beginning of the appearance of divinity.[22] Other terms used by Halevi are משאהדה̈, the general experience of beholding God, of which *ḍawq* is the first taste,[23] בצר, בצירה̈, and עיאן, all of which mean mystic visions of God.[24] In IV, 15 and III, 53, the prophetic sight is described as that state where man almost ceases to be man, joining the company of angels; and a new spirit, the Holy Spirit, enters into him, showing him true dreams and wonders. He sees the God of revelation and laughs at his former doubts and at *qiās* through which he sought God and is ready to undergo martyrdom because of the sweetness of union. He becomes so much at one with *al-amr al-ilāhī* that he no longer cares if he dies. It is a new plane of being, Halevi emphasizes in I, 41, as high above that of men as the latter is above that of the animals. Compare al-Gazali's outcry:

> Why should it be impossible that beyond reason there should be a further plane on which appear things which do not appear on the plane of intelligence, just as it is possible for the intelligence itself to be a plane above the discriminating faculty and the senses; and for revelations of wonders and marvels to be made to it beyond the reach of senses and the discriminating faculty? Beware of making the ultimate perfection stop at thyself! Consider the intuitive faculty of poetry, if thou wilt have an example of everyday experience taken from those special gifts which particularize some men.[25]

Halevi too likens faith, in general, to the poetic gift in V, 16 p. 331.

Halevi's discussion of prophetic experiences follows so closely Arabic patterns that his Hebrew translator occasionally finds only vague equi-

[22] See IV, 16, 17 and Kaufmann, *Attributenlehre*, pp. 121, 234. See Jurjānī, *Definitiones*, ed. G. Flügel (Leipzig, 1845), p. 112 والذوق فی معرفة الله عبارة عن نور عرفانیّ یقدفه الحقّ بتجلیه فی قلوب اولیائه یفرقون به بین الحق والباطل من غیر ان ینقلوا ذلك من كتاب او غیره. See also p. 288 الذوق اوّل مبادی الجلتیات الالهیّة. See also 'Abdur-r-Razzaq's *Dictionary of the Technical Terms of the Sufies*, ed. by Aloys Sprenger (Calcutta, 1845), p. 162 الذوق هو اول درجات شهود الحق بالحق فی اثناء البوارق المتوالیه عند ادنى لبث من التجلى البرقى. al-Gazali in his *Mishkāt al-Anwār* p. 41, bottom, speaks of اهل الذوق.

[23] משאהדה, Tibbon: ראיה, I, 10; IV, 15, 16. In IV, 3 באלמשאהדה̈, Tibbon באלאשארה̈ = ברמיזה (Goldziher in *Zeitschrift der morgenländischen Gesellschaft*, vol, 41, p. 693). See quotation from 'Abdu-r-Razzaq in note 22.

[24] בצר, בצירה (Tibbon ראות, ראיה), IV, 3, 15, 17. See Jurjani, *Definitiones*, p. 47, البصیرة قوة القلب المنوّرة بنور القدس یرى بها حقائق الاشیاء وبواطنها. For עיאן Tibbon has ראות עיניהם in I, 19, 25.

valents for his terminology and is sometimes inconsistent and even contradictory. He recognizes two states of prophecy. One he calls *ilhām* or illumination (Tibbon: למוד, but also עזר, דעת, הודעה),[26] which implants the primary ideas in the human mind as distinguished from the inferred or acquired ideas,[27] and which imparted to the *synhedrin* their scientific knowledge and inspired the composition of the Mishna.[28] It is the state of the saint (ולי״, כרי״, Tibbon: חסיד)[29] who is constantly aware of the presence of God and sees the Shekinah, the heavenly forms and the angels, and hears the Echo.[30] It can be acquired also by one who was not born an Israelite.[31]

Higher than *ilhām*[32] is the degree of *waḥī*, inspiration,[33] which is limited to Israelites and to the land of Israel,[34] and consists of specially created images and forms, such as an outstretched hand, a drawn sword, fire and lightning—all of which convey in one flash and symbolically the greatness, power, and love of God—and also of hearing a divine message, warning, announcing, or predicting.[35] Halevi repeatedly emphasizes the utter passivity of the prophet's mind when it receives a divine message, for therein lies the triumph of prophecy over *qiās*.

25 Al-Ghazali's *Mishkāt al-Anwār*, translated by W. H. T. Gairdner (London 1924), pp. 82–83.

26 See V, 12, 20. In I, 87, עזר ואומץ = אלהאם ותאייד. In III, 39, p. 189, תאייד ואלהאם = אומץ והודעה. In II, 26, דעת. Comp. expression in I, 109, בענין האלהי בנבואה ומה שהוא קרוב לה.

27 V, 12, p. 315, ויהיו בו הצורות המושכלות אם בלמוד אלהי ואם בקנין ואשר הם בלמוד (באלהאם) הם המושכלות הראשונות אשר ישתתפו בהם כל בני אדם אשר על המנהג הטבעי ואשר הם בקנין (באלאכתסאב) הם בהקשה ובחדוש המופתי. Here we see the inconsistency of Tibbon, for in V, 20, p. 349 we read כי התורה שהיא מאת האלהים מקנה הנפשות מנהג המלאכים ותכונתם וזה מה שאין משיגים אותו בלמוד where בלמוד stands of course not for באלהאם but for its opposite באלאכתסאב.

28 I, 97; III, 39, p. 189; III, 41, p. 193. See also "The Confession of Al-Ghazzali" translated by Claud Field (London, 1909), p. 53: "He who studies the medical science and astronomy is obliged to recognize that they are derived from the revelation and special grace of God."

29 See II, 14, p. 81; II, 23, p. 91; III, 11, pp. 153, 157; III, 19, p. 173.

30 III, 11, 19.

31 I, 115.

32 III, 1, היא מדרגת החסידים ולמעלה ממנה מדרגת הנביאים. Similarly III, 11, p. 157.

33 Tibbon: נבואה but also חזון. II, 28; III, 41; IV, 27; V, 12.

34 I, 115, p. 65 כי האזרחים לבדם הם ראויים לנבואה וזולתם תכלית ענינם שיקבלו מהם ושיהיו חכמים וחסידים אך לא נביאים. See also II, 12–14.

35 IV, 5.

Prophecy is not due to thought and counsel. It does not spring from a soul of purified thoughts, as the philosophers maintained. It does not rise from investigation and research.[36] "For the speech of the prophets when they are enwrapped by the Holy Spirit is in all its words directed by the divine essence, and the prophet exercizes no freedom of choice even in a single word."[37]

All these distinctions between *ilhām* and *waḥī* (the former internal, the source of Talmudic traditions, found in the *walīs* but open to all mankind, and the latter entirely external and literal, the source of the Bible and limited to Israel) are standard Mohammedan doctrine except for the necessary change of the "Talmud" to the "Sunna," the "Bible" to the "Bible and the Koran," and "Israel" to the "prophets culminating in Mohammed."[38]

Halevi however differs from the general Mohammedan belief that while the power of *muʿjizāt* or miracles is vested only in the prophets, there are *karāmāt*, that is, wonders, spontaneous miracles, extraordinary phenomena appearing of themselves and for the glorification and protection of that somewhat larger class called *walis* or saints.[39] This tended to give rise to a cult of saints, who according to some Sufis stood even higher than the prophets.[40] Halevi insists on the superiority of the prophetic level,[41] and ignores the difference between wonders and

36 I, 87. שלא תהיה התחלת התורה מעצה ומחשבה מחמת אדם ואחר יחברהו עזר ואומץ מאת האלהים... שלא תהיה הנבואה כאשר חשבו הפילוסופים מנפש יזדככו מחשבותיה ותדבק בשכל הפועל הנקרא רוה״ק או בגבריאל וישכילהו. See also III, 53, חשבו כי ההתחלה אמנם היא מהמחקר והחפוש ושהנביאים אמנם היו חכמים גדולים. Al-Farabi and Avicenna took a different stand and it is against them that Halevi levels his criticism. For Al-Farabi, see note 1; and for Avicenna see particularly Goichon, *Lexique*, p. 375 فيمكن ان يكون شخص من الناس مويد النفس بشدّة الصفاء اشدّة الاتّصال بالمبادى العقليه الى ان يشتعل حدسا اعبى قبالاً الهام العقل الفعّال. It is al-Gazali who taught Halevi not only the essential uniqueness of the plane of prophecy but also that it is independent of learning. See his *Mishkāt al-Anwār* (Cairo, 1904), p. 14: والانبياء كلهم سرج وكذلك العلماء ولكن التفاوت بينهم لا يحصى. Similarly on p. 26: فالاول صاحب مشاهدة والثانى صاحب اشتدلال بآياته والاولى درجة الصدقين والثانى درجة العلماء.

37 V, 20, p. 345.

38 See Edward Sell, *The Faith of Islam* (London, 1880), pp. 37–38.

39 See Duncan B. Macdonald, *Muslim Theology, Jurisprudence and Constitutional Theory*, p. 313.

40 *Ibid.*, pp. 263, 282.

41 V, 10, אם יהיה ראוי לנבואה או למודי אם מדרגתו למטה מזאת ויהיה חסיד לא נביא.

miracles, denying both kinds to the saints.[42] In this position Halevi sided with the rationalistic Muʿtazilites.[43]

A source of confusion and contradiction in Tibbon's version is his use of the Hebrew word *kavod* or *karāmāt*, wonders, even in places where the Arabic original has *kavod* or *kevod Adonai.* These are two different concepts; for whereas wonders distinguish prophets from saints, *kavod* or glory may be revealed to both classes and to all Israel. It is a manifestation of divinity and is of the same order as Shekinah, מלכות, Fire, Cloud, Image, Form, Rainbow—all attesting to the divine word.[44] It consists of spiritual forms fashioned out of the fine spiritual substance called the Holy Spirit.[45] It is that fine substance that, following the divine will, assumes form when God desires to appear to the prophet, or else it is the totality of angels and spiritual vessels, the Throne, the Chariot, the Firmament, the Wheels, and other imperishable things; that is to say, it is either temporary in its form or permanent but in either case the same essence—the *Ruaḥ ha-Qodesh* in a glorious epiphany.[46] "And this is the meaning," Halevi says at the end of IV, 3, "of the Glory of God, the Angelhood (מלאכות) of God, and the Shekinah of God in religious terminology. Sometimes they are applied to natural phenomena, even as it is said: The whole earth is full of His Glory and His Kingdom reigneth in all; but in truth the Glory and the Kingdom (מלכות) are revealed only to the saints, the pure and the prophets."

The term מלכות, Kingdom, is used in this passage as synonymous with *kavod*, but geneologically they differ. Goldziher in his introduction to his edition of the *Kitāb Maʿānī al-Nafs*, ascribed to Baḥya, states

42 V, 20, p. 343 ומבקש למוד (אלהאמאת) אם הוא חסיד או אותות וכבוד (מעג̇זאת וכראמאת). See also V, 20, p. 347 הכבוד = אלכראמאת ואלמעג̇זאת אם הוא נביא או המון נרצה והאותות. However in I, 4, p. 9, מעג̇זאת = כבוד. In III, 53, p. 207, Tibbon translates כראמאת by גדולות, in I, 4, p. 9, by גדולה. In I, 109, מעג̇זאת = מופתים. Comp. Palqera's *Reshit Ḥokmah*, p. 55: והכבודים דומם למופתים, where כבודים probably stands for כראמאת.

43 See Macdonald, *The Religious Attitude and Life in Islam*, p. 50.

44 IV, 3, p. 231, עד שהיו רואים אותו במצוע מה נקרא כבוד ושכינה ומלכות ואש וענן וצלם ותמונה ומראה וקשת וזולת זה ממה שהיה ראיה להם שהדבור עמם מאצלו וקוראים אותו כבוד ה׳.

45 II, 4, וכן מצטייר מן הגשם הדק הרוחני הנקרא רוה״ק הצורות הרוחניות הנקראות כבוד ה׳. How different this concept of the *Ruaḥ ha-Qodesh* is from that of Avicenna! See notes 4, 12, 50.

46 IV, 3, p. 245. See *Qol Yehudah*, a.l. See also IV, 25, p. 279 והקדים רוח אלהים והוא רוה״ק ממנה נבראים המלאכים הרוחניים ובה מתחברות הנפשות הרוחניות.

that the word כבודים in the expression אלמלאיכה̈ ואלכבודים in the *Maʿānī* means angels and should be vocalized כְּבוּדִים, and that it has its origin in the Koranic مكرمون and كرام for angels.[47] But the expression in the *Maʿānī* and the statements of Halevi show that it denotes more than angels, and its fuller form כבוד ה׳ as given both in the *Maʿānī* and in the *Kuzari* as well as the use of the Hebraic form in the Arabic text reveal a consciousness of a Hebraic concept. Biblical in origin, in a theophanic sense,[48] the term was early developed under the influence of Neoplatonism to convey the sense of a metaphysical entity, so that Benjamin Nahawendi stated that before creation God created the Glory and His throne,[49] and Saadia amplified it further by assuming a Second Air, a fine all-pervasive substance that was created before all things, and that carried the divine words to the prophets and was the instrument of demonstrations and visions and was designated in the Bible by the terms Glory, Holy Spirit, Throne, and Shekinah.[50] In this Saadianic sense, it became the Hebraic parallel to Avicenna's "spiritual substances which convey prophecy," and to which Halevi, in his distrust of the metaphysical assumptions of the philosophers, registers an attitude of indifference.[51] On the other hand, the term *malekut*, Kingdom, the terminological synonym of *Kavod*, owes its origin to the Arabic conception of an *ʿālam almalakūt*, the supernal changeless world of angels, in distinction from *ʿālam almulk*, the lower world of sense and perception. Al-Farab

47 *Kitāb Maʿānī al-Nafs,* ed. by Goldziher, p. 37.

48 See for example, Ex., 16, 10 והנה כבוד ה׳ נראה בענן, Ex., 24, 17 ומראה כבוד ה׳ כאש אוכלת, Ezek., 3, 23 ואקום ואצא אל הבקעה והנה שם כבוד ה׳. See also *Mekilta* on *Beshallaḥ*, 2, 4: עד שנגלה הקב״ה עליו בכבודו.

49 See Yehudah Hadassi, *Eshkol ha-Kofer* (Eupatoria, 1836), 47: ובנימין הנהאונדי משכילי נ״ע אמר כי קודם כל בריה ברא אלהים הכבוד וכסאו.

50 *Commentaire sur le Séfer Yesira,* par le Gaon Saadya de Fayyoum, publé et traduit par Mayer Lambert (Paris, 1891), p. 72: فالكتب المقدسة تسمّى الهواء الثانى اللطيف כבוד كما قال מלא כל הארץ כבודו... تسميه والامّة שכינה... وبهذا الهواء اللطيف الثانى يتادّى كلام النبوّة . . . وبه تظهر خميع البراهين للانبياء المرئية . . . الهواء الخاص اللطيف الثانى هو لله عزّ وجلّ على التمثيل كالكرسى للملك . . . وهذا الشى ايضا هو الذى تسميه ال חכמים רוח הקדש. See also *Maʿānī al-Nafs,* p. 10. This corresponds to Halevi's first view of Glory; Halevi's second view is expressed by ibn Ezra on Ex., 3, 15, quoted in *Qol Yehudah*, ...והעולם העליון הוא עולם המלאכים הקדושים שאינם גופות ולא כח בגופות וכל זה העולם כבוד וכלו עומד. See notes 4, 12, 45. See also Neumark, *Toledot ha-Pilosofiah be-Israel,* I, 172.

51 See note 12.

says concerning the Active Intellect that "it is necessary to believe that he is the faithful spirit (i.e., Gabriel) and the Holy Spirit and that his rank is called *malakūt*."[52] "The world of *malakūt*," says al-Gazali, "is the Perserved Table and the angelic world."[53] This will explain why in that passage from the end of IV, 3 it is used interchangeably with מלאכות angelhood (Ar מלך = angel).[54] Indeed in V, 10, p. 304, Halevi uses the full phrase עאלם אלמלכות (Tibbon: עולם המלאכות) describing it as the world of rest and timeless perception symbolized by the Sabbath.

Both al-Farabi and al-Gazali identify *malakūt* with *amr*,[55] and it is tempting to take it also as the meaning of Halevi's *al-amr al-ilāhī*; but considerations, already mentioned, make us forbear. And there is a difference. The vision of the Kingdom and the Glory is granted to those whom the Divine Essence leads. One is the cause, the other the effect.[56] Furthermore, al-Farabi, followed by Albo,[57] identifies it with the Active Intellect. Indeed in this light we discern more clearly the meaning of the philosopher in the opening of the *Kuzari* concerning the soul of the perfect man that "it becomes an angel and reaches the nethermost rung of the kingdom which is pure from matter and which is the degree of

[52] See quotation from al-Farabi in Wensinck, "On the Relation Between Ghazali's Cosmology and his Mysticism," p. 6: العقل الفعال هو الذى ينبغى ان يقال انه هو الروح الامين وروح القدس ورتبته ويسمى الملكوت and *Haṭhalot* p. 2 והשכל הפועל הוא אשר ראוי שיאמן בו שהוא הרוח הנאמן ורוח הקדש ויקרא בדומה לשני אלה השמות מן השמות ומדרגתו הנקרא אישים ר״ל מלכות שמים. A rendering of *malakut* by מלכות שמים is also found in *Kuzari*, III, 1, p. 141. Comp. Albo's *'Iqqarim*, II, 11 השכל הפועל שהוא מלכות שהוא הספירה העשירית.

[53] See Wensinck, "On the Relation Between Ghazali's Cosmology and his Mysticism," p. 19: عالم الملكوت وهو اللوح المحفوظ وعالم الملايكة.

[54] Similarly in II, 7, כבוד ה׳ ומלאכות ה׳ ושכינה = כבוד ושכינה ומלכות. In view of this fact, Tibbon should not be criticized (Comp. Hirschfeld on I, 107, p. 57) for translating אלמלכותיה by המלאכותיים, since Halevi himself regards them as equivalent. See also Tibbon's rendering of this term in I, 1, p. 7; I, 42; I, 103, p. 57. However, in I, 103, מלאכותי = מלאכ֗י angelic.

[55] See Wensinck, "On the Relation Between Ghazali's Cosmology and his Mysticism," pp. 6, 13, 15, 17.

[56] See IV, 3, p. 231 בעבור שהיה דברו והנהגתו דבק בבני אדם והיו דבקים הסגלה מבני אדם בו עד שהיו רואים אותו במצוע מה נקרא כבוד ושכינה ומלכות וכו׳. See IV, 3, p. 233, כנוי לענין האלהי הדבק בו ואחריו בהמון זרעו דבקת מחשבה והנהגה. Ar. תדביר וסיאסה. Perhaps Tibbon read תפכיר. See, I, 109, והתחבר הענין האלהי בנו בגדולה ובכבוד ובמופתים. See also II, 4, p. 75.

[57] See note 51.

the Active Intellect." Halevi however does not accept this identification. The Active Intellect with its rationalistic and somewhat polytheistic connotations he rejects; but he accepts the *ʿālam almalakūt*, as well as *ittiṣāl ḍawq*, *ilhām*, *waḥī* and *karāmāt*, all of which are terms and distinctions taken from the very warp and woof of Mohammedan doctrine. Escaping from Arabic rationalism, he found refuge in Muslim mysticism, which was more congenial to his Jewish teaching.

POSTSCRIPT[58]

קולכודיאה

In note 10, I quoted, from Delmedigo's *Nobelot Ḥokmah*, a passage discussing the Active Intellect and designating it as קולכודיאה; and, not knowing the meaning of this term, I put a question-mark after it. Later I found this term, spelled קולקודיאה and קולקודיא in the *Minḥat Ḳenaot*, by Yehiel b. Samuel of Pisa, edited by David Kaufmann, on pp. 30, 67; and in the earlier mention, Kaufmann also adds a question mark. I shall now explain this term.

At first, one is tempted to regard it as two words: קול "word of," or, as in Turkish, "the servant of," and כּדִי which in Persian means "God." But this rendering lacks authority. The word is a corruption from كدخدا, "master of a family, magistrate, ruler"; for the Active Intellect is the master and ruler of the sublunar world. This is indeed the very term applied to the Active Intellect by the Sufi, Shihāb al-dīn al-Suhrawardī, as quoted by I. Goldziher in the introduction to his edition of Baḥya's *Kitāb Maʿānī al-Nafs*, p. 42. Baḥya, in the *Maʿānī al-Nafs*, ch. 16, calls the Active Intellect אלחאגב אלאקרב "the nearest," or "the first Chamberlain"; and Maimonides in *Moreh Neubkim*, II, 6, followed by Albo in *ʿIḳḳarīm*, II, 11, identifies it with the rabbinic שרו של עולם. P. Dozy, in his *Supplément aux Dictionnaires Arabes*, gives the form كدخدائية, "menage, gouvernment domestique."

Both Yehiel of Pisa and Delmedigo no longer knew the meaning of the term and explained it as נותן הצורות.

[58] This note, which appeared in *The Jewish Quarterly Review*, vol. 36, p. 79, called forth a learned comment by Professor H. A. Wolfson in *The Jewish Quarterly Review*, vol. 36, 179–82.

SOME TEXTUAL NOTES ON YEHUDA HALEVI'S *KUZARI*

TWO SCHOLARS, I. Goldziher and S. Horovitz, have examined the Arabic and Hebrew texts, respectively, of the *Kuzari*, the former in his article entitled "Hirschfeld's Buch Al-Chazari" in *Zeitschrift der morgenländischen Gesellschaft*, XLI, and the latter in his article entitled "Zur Textkritik des Kuzari" in the *Monatsschrift*, XLI, in which he discusses the Hebrew translation by Yehudah ibn Tibbon. The following are some additional notes on these texts.

The references to the *Kuzari* (designated by K) are made according to part, chapter, and page of H. Hirschfeld's edition (Leipzig, 1887) of the Arabic and Hebrew texts.

1

K, III, 49, 201 דברי הטבעים והגלגלים. The Arabic original reads אקואל אלטביעיין ואלפלכיין, "the words of the physicists and astronomers." We should therefore read in the Hebrew דברי הטבעיים והגלגליים. The word טבעיים for טביעיון, physicists, occurs in K, I, 5, 11, and also in *Moreh Nebukim*, II, 15, where Ḥarizi renders: חכמי הטבע. The unusual word would be גלגליים for astronomers.

2

K, IV, 25, 281 ואיך יאצל הדבור וההברה ממנו על המדברים. The word דבור, Arabic אלנטק, should not be taken as "speech," which does not suit the context, but as "reason." The word הברה, which Cassel translates *Laut*, we should read as הכרה, discernment, understanding, which is the usual Hebrew translation of the Arabic original תמייז. Thus in K, IV, 25, 271 תמייזהא is rendered הכרתם. Saadia's ספר ההכרה is in Arabic כתאב אלתמייז. In *Moreh*, III, 51, Samuel ibn Tibbon translates תמייז by הכרה, and Abraham bar Ḥiyya in *Hegyon ha-nefesh*, p. 5, uses הכר for "discernment."

3

K, IV, 31, 290 ומן גריב קולהם ולפטֿהם פי סמום בעץ̇ דֿואת אלמכאלב קולהם דריסת חתול. The expression קולהם ולפטֿהם, "speech and utterance," is too redundant, and the Hebrew translation, חכמתם ודקותם, does not correspond to it at all. It is possible that קולהם may, under the influence of the second קולהם, be a misreading for עלמהם or עקלהם. As for ולפטֿהם, we should read ולטפהם, as the Hebrew translation shows. Yehudah ibn Tibbon translates לטף by דק in several places. Thus he translates וליס ידרך מתֿל הדֿא אלפסאד ללטאפתה אלא דֿוי אלארואח אללטיפה̈ (K, II, 60, 119) by ואיננו משיג בהפסד הזה (read כהפסד) לרב דקותו אלא בעלי הרוחות הדקות.

Samuel ibn Tibbon also has דקות in *Moreh*, I, 54 for the Arabic לטף. Horovitz ("Zur Textkritik des Kuzari") makes a similar emendation in K, I, 5, where, instead of בלפטֿה... תלפטֿוא, he reads בלטפה... תלטפוא, in order to bring out the sense of Tibbon's יתחכם... מתחכמים.

4

K, V, 2, 296. The term אלקצ̇א means providence, predetermination. Thus in K, V, 20, 347, the Hebrew rendering is גזירה. The term אלקדר has the same meaning, and in K, V, 19, 337 it is similarly translated. Sometimes the two Arabic terms are used together, אלקצ̇א ואלקדר, for the single idea of providence or predetermination, and they are usually translated by the one word גזירה. Thus in *Moreh*, III, 17, 337 (Arabic text, Jerusalem, 1931) בל כל ורקה̈ סקטת בקצ̇א וקדר מן אללה, and Samuel ibn Tibbon translates אבל כל עלה נופל בגזרה מן השם.

So also *Iqqarim*, ʿI, 13 כי כל הדברים הם בגזרה הנקרא אלקצא ואלקדר. Accordingly, in K, V, 2, 296 אלקצ̇א ואלקדר should be taken to mean one idea, that is, predetermination, and Yehudah ibn Tibbon's translation גזירה וחפץ ויכלת, explained by Moscato as "providence and human freewill and power," rests on a confusion with another sense of the term *qadar*.

5

K, V, 12, 316 נתאיג̇ צ̇רוריה̈ ברהאניה̈ או כ̇טאביה̈ סופסטאניה̈ או שעריה̈. We should insert או between כטאביה and סופסטאניה. Thus the Hebrew reads הלציות או הטעיות. The inclusion of Aristotle's *Rhetoric* and *Poetics* among his logical treatises or the *Organon*—so also in Maimonides' *Treatise on Logic*, ch. 6, and in Shem Tob ibn Palqera's *Reshit Ḥokmah*, pp. 37–38—

occurs in al-Farabi's *Iḥṣa al-ʿUlūm*, ed. Angel Gonzales Palencia (2nd edition, Madrid, 1953), pp. 46–50, and constitutes a Neoplatonic view, as opposed to the Peripatetic classification, such as that of Andronicus and Alexander of Aphrodisias. See Ibrahim Madkour, *L'Organon d'Aristotle dans le monde Arabe* (Paris, 1934), p. 13, and Ingemar Düring, *Aristotle in the Ancient Biographical Tradition* (Göteborg, 1957), p. 243.

I have already shown that Palqera's *Reshit Ḥokmah*, in its second part, is a literal translation of al-Farabi's *Iḥṣa al-ʿUlūm*. See my "Palqera's *Reshit Ḥokmah*" in *The Jewish Quarterly Review*, XXV, pp. 227–35, and "Note" in *The Jewish Quarterly Review*, XXVII, p. 100.

6

K, V, 14, 328 ושיעה̈ ארסטוטאליס ושיעה̈ אפלאטון וגירהם ואצחאב אלמט̋לה̈ ואלמיטאן והם מן שיעה̈ ארסטוטאליס. The word ואלמיטאן, which ibn Tibbon translates by וההולכים the Peripatetics, is difficult. Goldziher ("Hirschfeld's Buch Al-Chazari") emends ואלמשאיין. But perhaps the word ואצחאב fell out before ואלמיטאן, and the expression means "those that withdraw." The term "Peripatetics" was understood by some as meaning goers or walkers for the sake of health, but to others it meant those who go away or *withdraw* to solitary places conducive to meditation. Steinschneider in *Heb. Ueb.*, p. 74 quotes Narboni's statement: ונקראו כך לפי שהיו מתעמלים בהליכה להנהגת הבריאות ואחשוב שהיו עושים זה ג״כ לבקשת התבודדות מן הצבועים.

He quotes other authors to the same effect, particularly Joseph ben Shem Tob, who expressly calls the Peripatetics כת המתבודדים.

Thus Halevi mentions here four philosophical schools: Aristotelians, Platonists, Stoics, and Peripatetics. The interesting element is that he lists the Peripatetics in addition to the Aristotelian school and regards them as being an offshoot of the latter with apparently some views of their own. Thus also Shahrastani, II, 253: משאוון ואצחאב אלרואק ואצחאב ארסטוטאליס "Peripatetics, Stoics, and Aristotelians."

7

K, V, 15, 331 חכמי שרשי האמונה. This translation of the Arabic אצוליון, the Mutakallimun, is significant. Maimonides in *Moreh*, I, 73, also uses the word אצוליון, and the various translations and commentaries bring out four different meanings of this Arabic term derived from a word meaning "root," or "origin." (1) Samuel ibn Tibbon, in translating it by

קדמוני המדברים שהיו עיקר חכמת הדברים, seems to take it in the sense of "the fathers of the Kalam." (2) Harizi, in rendering it by המדברים בעיקרים and בעלי העיקרים, evidently takes it to mean those who deal with the fundamentals, principles, or dogmas of religion. (3) Narboni and Efodi understand it to mean atomists. (4) Joseph Caspi defines it as dogmatists, that is, those who advance views without proof. Yehudah ibn Tibbon's translation of the Arabic אצוליון by חכמי שרשי האמונה seems to favor the second view, which is that of Munk on *Moreh*, I, 73.

8

K, V, 18, 334 לכן ליס כחיאתנא אלמחדתֿה ואלחרכה̈ לאכן חיאה̈ מענאהא אלעקל אלמחץ̇. The word אלמחדתֿה̈, "which is created," is not well connected with the following. The Hebrew rendering הנגדרת shows that we should read אלמחדדה̈, "which is defined."

The use of the term הנגדרת by Yehudah ibn Tibbon is interesting in view of the fact that Samuel ibn Tibbon states in his *Perush meha-Millot Zarot* that he coined the verbal forms of the term גדר, forgetting that his father had used the word נגדר before him. So also in *Ḥobot ha-Lebabot* (ed. Zifroni), I, 7, p. 128. Similarly, he thought he had coined the term מקצר, "imperfect," and regretted this coinage, but he was preceded therein by his father, who had used it in *Emunot we-De*ʿ*ot*, V, 2, 138 (edition Yozefov) and in Baḥya's *Ḥobot ha-Lebabot* (ed. Zifroni), pp. 80, 87, 94, etc. and further back by Abraham bar Ḥiyya. See the preface to "The Philosophical Terminology of Abraham bar Ḥiyya."

NATURE AND SPIRIT IN MAIMONIDEDES' PHILOSOPHY

I

THE ARISTOTELIAN fundamental concept of nature as a network of immutable laws is deeply implanted in Maimonides' philosophical system. The Arabic Mutakallimūn denied the existence of such laws, or the existence of any causal connection between phenomena, and affirmed an atomism of space and time together; so that at each atom of time the world comes to nought and is created anew by God, and there is therefore no relationship or continuity between one moment and another. Maimonides submits the Mutakallimūn to sharp and lengthy criticism, because according to them there is no nature and hence no knowledge, and there is furthermore no room for ethics and freedom because all acts are God's. But, on the other hand, Aristotle posits too much nature, and Maimonides cannot go all the way with him either.

He makes a sharp differentiation between nature and chance. Nature is constant, like the heat of the fire, like the falling of the stone, whereas chance is not constant. But even what is not constant but only "frequent," that is, what happens in most cases, he admits into the realm of nature,[1] and in this respect Maimonides may be said to approach the new concept in physics, the statistical view on natural law. He identifies biblical angels with the laws of nature and scoffs at those who take a less naturalistic view.

> How bad and injurious is the blindness of ignorance! Say to a person who is believed to belong to the wise men of Israel that the Almighty sends His angel to enter the womb of a woman and to form there the foetus, he will be

A lecture delivered on November 14, 1955 in Tel-Aviv on the inauguration of the Institute for Humanities (in Hebrew, "for the sciences of the spirit"), which, together with the Institute for Natural Sciences, was to form the Tel-Aviv University.

[1] *Moreh,* I, 20, 45. References to Maimonides' *Moreh Nebukim* are made to part, chapter, and page in the Warsaw edition, 1872. Quotations follow the translation of M. Friedlander.

satisfied with the account; he will believe it, and even find in it a description of the greatness of God's might and wisdom; although he believes that the angel consists of a burning fire, and is as big as a third part of the universe, yet he considers it possible as a divine miracle. But tell him that God gave the seed a formative power which produces and shapes the limbs, and that this power is called "angel"... and he will turn away.[2]

For the sake of clarification, let us compare this statement with the position of a work known as *Kitāb Maʿānī al-Nafs*, attributed to Baḥya, where likewise nature is identified with angel. But there the identification stems from the Neoplatonic view that nature is one of the three emanations—reason, soul, and nature—that intermediate between God and matter. Maimonides' conception on the other hand is not transcendent. Nature is a system of immanent physical laws.

The idea of nature contradicts miracles. But Maimonides defends them as temporary occurrences and not as permanent changes in nature. He is inclined to accept the Talmudic idea that "God made an agreement with the sea that it should divide before the Israelites," indeed, "not only with the sea but with all that has been created in the six days of creation." In other words, when God created the natural law, he also created the miracle, so that "miracles belong to the realm of nature; for... when God created the universe, with its present physical properties, He made it part of these properties, that they should produce miracles at certain times."[3] All this means that sometimes nature temporarily deviates from its path, and yet remains nature: its very deviation is nature, being an original endowment.

Thus Maimonides, as against the Arab thinkers, stands firmly on the Aristotelian ground of natural law, interpreting also some biblical accounts of angels naturalistically, but widening the concept of nature to include one-time violations of it. Now what are the borders of nature? Is it confined to the material world? No, for if by nature we mean a certain law of sequence, a certain causal connection or *necessity*, then it includes also the upper worlds, for "the heavens and all that is in them are constant, never changing."[4] It must also include the movers of the spheres, those "separate intellects," that is, that which is separated from matter, since these too act, according to Aristotle, by way of

2 *Moreh*, II, 6, 23.
3 *Moreh*, II, 29, 56.
4 *Moreh*, II, 20, 45.

necessity. Hence nature is a wider concept than the material universe. Indeed, again according to Aristotle, since nature and law are the same, all is nature, and there is no supernatural at all, for even the Causa Prima acts not by way of choice or free will but by way of necessity. Hence, in spite of the expression "a primal cause apart from nature,"[5] in connection with Aristotelianism, from the standpoint of the system as a whole, God too is nature. The whole cosmos is one compulsion of which God is a part, and all is law and necessity and causality.

II

Maimonides was aware of the profound difference between the Aristotelian standpoint and that of Judaism. Thus he says: "When the philosopher, in his way of expressing himself, contends, 'Reality is my evidence; by its guidance I examine whether a thing is necessary, possible, or impossible,' the religionist replies, 'This is exactly the difference between us; that which actually exists has, according to my view, been produced by the will of the Creator, not by necessity.'"[6] "Everything is according to [Aristotle] the result of a law of nature and not the result of design.... For all this he endeavors to state the reason, so as to show that the whole order is the necessary result of the laws of nature. He has not attained his object."[7] "For we all mean the same, only with this difference, that, according to Aristotle, everything besides that Being is the necessary result of the latter... while, according to our opinion, that Being created the whole universe with design and will."[8] "If we were to accept the eternity of the universe as taught by Aristotle, that everything in the universe is the result of fixed laws, that nature does not change, and there is nothing supernatural, we should necessarily be in opposition to the foundation of our religion."[9] "We agree with Aristotle in one half of his theory. For we believe that this universe remains perpetually with the same properties with which the Creator has endowed it.... The universe had however a beginning.... This is our opinion and

[5] *Moreh,* III, 13, 17. Comp. also *teba'* versus *nefesh* in II, 4, 18. Yet, in II, 19, 40–41, he regards the spherical movements as nature, calling them חיוב טבעי and סידור טבעי.

[6] *Moreh,* I, 73, end of the tenth proposition.

[7] *Moreh,* II, 19, 40–41.

[8] *Moreh,* II, 21, end.

[9] *Moreh,* II, 25, 51.

the basis of our religion. The opinion of Aristotle is that the universe being permanent and indestructible is also eternal and without beginning ....We have already shown that this theory is based on the hypothesis that the universe is the result of causal relation, and this hypothesis includes a certain amount of blasphemy."[10]

In this declaration, positing the divine will in opposition to Aristotle's view, in which the objectionable element is not only the theory that the world is without a beginning but also, what is connected with it, that all is necessity, reaching upward even to the Causa Prima itself, Maimonides touched on the main difference between paganism and Judaism. For the pagan world, as I tried to show elsewhere,[11] is monistic —all matter, or, as in this case, all nature; whereas Judaism introduced two worlds—nature and spirit—and throughout the generations tried to define and sharpen the borderline between them. We can now understand Maimonides' statement in I, 69, that although he designates God as the ultimate form of the universe, he does not mean the ultimate form that Aristotle describes in his *Metaphysics* as being without beginning and without end, "for that is a physical form and not a purely intellectual one."[12] Here Narboni wonders: "Where does Aristotle assume an absolute, eternal form and yet physical?" And really one may ask: Did not Maimonides know of a pure form in Aristotle's system, pure of all matter, namely God? But Maimonides clearly saw that in a system where law and necessity are supreme, God too becomes nature, *physics*, or in Hebrew *teba*ʿ, pure of matter but not free from necessity, and there is no upper world.

Thus Maimonides wrestled on the one hand with the Arabic Mutakallimūn, who assumed an everlasting creationism so that there is no nature at all, and on the other hand with Aristotle, according to whom there is no supernatural, since all is law and necessity, even the First Cause. He tries to establish natural law together with divine freedom or the Will, which is "the spirit of the living creature in the wheels."[13]

There was some hesitation at the beginning about this conception of God as Will, which the orthodox Arabs made their primary tenet, as

10 *Moreh*, II, 29, 57.

11 See my *Ancient Jewish Philosophy* (Wayne State University Press, 1964), pp. 7–17.

12 *Moreh*, I, 69, 103: כי הצורה ההיא הנזכרת שם טבעי לא שכל נפרד.

13 *Moreh*, III 2, 4: והרוח הנה אינו הרוח המנשבת אבל היא כונה כמו שבארנו (א׳,מ׳) בשתוף שם רוח.

against the rationalistic concept of a God bound by reason and justice. Saadia Gaon, in his *Emunot we-De*ʿ*ot*, in contradistinction to his earlier writings, eliminated the Will from his description of the Deity, probably because of anti-Christological reasons, since the hypostatization of the Will was connected with the doctrine of an intermediary Logos. We have discussed it earlier in our "Philosophy of Saadia." Solomon ibn Gabirol, indeed, both in his philosophy and in his poetry, made the divine Will when in action a separate entity, an intermediary between the Creator and creation. Maimonides however found it necessary to introduce the Will in order to assert freedom as opposed to Aristotelian necessity, to bring out the cleavage between Judaism and paganism. But it was probably as a direct reference to ibn Gabirol that he emphasized that God's Will is not outside of His essence but constitutes His very essence.[14]

Yet will alone does not fully define the spirit, for if the spirit is only an arbitrary will and has no reference to values, why is it spirit? Wherein is it superior to any force or nature? Is not every force a spirit, if the latter term implies no values? And is this the meaning of spirit in Judaism, which Maimonides posits so sharply against Aristotelianism? We must introduce something more into the meaning of the term "will." Indeed, Maimonides himself also uses an alternative. In I, 69, he says that when we seek the ultimate reason for the existence of the universe as a whole, we arrive at the final purpose "which is the execution of the will of God, according to one of the opinions... and the final answer will be, 'It is the will of God.' According to the view of others... the final purpose is the execution of the decree of His wisdom, and the final answer will be, 'It has been decreed by His wisdom.'" Thus apparently there are two opinions on the cause of creation: one is will, the other is wisdom, though inscrutable. The same alternative is stated in III, 17 and in III, 25. In II, 17, we learn that it was the rationalistic group among the Arab thinkers, that is, the Muʿtazilites, that defined that cause as wisdom. But do we have here an alternative, or are the two terms rather in apposition?

Maimonides learned the idea of wisdom not from the liberal Arabs whom he frequently censures, as he criticized in general all circles in Islam that did not follow Aristotle. Rather, this view of the world as

14 ושאין רצונו וחפצו או חכמתו דברים יוצאים חוץ לעצמו ר״ל שיהיו זולת עצמו (א,סט, 104); רצונו שהוא עצמו (ג,יג, 19

being a necessary outflow from divine wisdom is originally Aristotelian. Indeed, it is from the Greek master that he learned the all-intellectualistic approach to God, the idea that in God "the thinker and the thinking and the thought are one,"[15] that He is one eternal Thinking in which the subject and the object are the same. Maimonides was therefore compelled to conceive of God as Wisdom, not because of apologetic reasons or theodicies that motivated the Arab liberals, but because of consistent Aristotelian metaphysics. But here he was confronted with the aforementioned religious Jewish difficulties: how can we speak of divine will and creative freedom, indeed, of creation at all, if God is only a narcissistic thought?

For the difficulty is not only that thinking is logical necessity and therefore contradicts free creation; it lies also in the fact that wisdom in itself is a cognitive, not an active, concept. If God is cosmic logic, we still need a connecting link in order to explain the transition to creation. In the Aristotelian system this presents no problem, because God is essentially no efficient cause, first because the world is not created and all is co-eternal with God Himself, and second because all moves not according to a will above but according to a will below, the infinitely unattainable will to rise toward Him, to attain His perfection. But according to the religionists it is difficult to see how we can pass from God as pure thinking to creation, from cognition to action. Greek thought did not attribute action to God. It was as if the Greeks were ashamed of thinking of God in action. But Judaism is entirely permeated with divine activism. Accordingly, wisdom alone is not enough either as a concept of the Deity; we must introduce will, yet not as an exclusive element, as in the Arab-orthodox concept, but mated with wisdom. But then the difficulty is: How do we reconcile the two—reason, which is all necessity, and will, which is all freedom? In fact, Maimonides is sometimes receptive to both views, as if they were different expressions of the same idea.

This is an important question, and we must therefore clarify the two concepts.

The idea that God is either Will or Wisdom is used by Maimonides

[15] *Moreh,* I, 68, 101. Cf. Aristotle, *Metaphysics,* L9, 1075a: "Since, then, thought and the object of thought are not different in the case of things that have not matter, the divine thought and its object will be the same, that is, the thinking will be one with the object of its thought."

in connection with two subjects: namely, the purpose of creation and the purpose of the Torah, in which he finds some common features. As to the first subject, he tries, in III, 13, to refute the view that creation has a purpose, namely, man. In place of this monistic, anthropocentric teleology, he posits a mundane plurality of purposes. After every part in creation God saw that "it was good," and "the Lord hath made all things for Himself" (Pr., 16, 4), meaning rather, in Maimonides' interpretation, for *itself*, for the work itself; although there are things that are only means to other things, as the sense-organs to the mind and the plants to the animals. He ends his criticism of teleology with these words: "This must be our belief... we must be content and not trouble our mind with seeking a certain final cause for things that have none, or have no other final cause but their own existence, which depends on the Will of God, or, if you prefer, on the divine wisdom."[16] Here we see that this wisdom is not a wisdom of purpose, of "something for the sake of something else,"[17] but of recognizing the intrinsic value of a thing. It is not rational wisdom but aesthetic, like that of a creator or a painter. Consequently, the God of Maimonides is freed from the rigidity of the static Aristotelian concept of God as ultimate form, or as the logic of the cosmos, and He becomes a Maker or an Artist, τὸ ποιοῦν, as in Plato's *Philebus*, 26E–28D. And in art the will and the aesthetic necessity, or the will and the creative wisdom, come together. When the wisdom lies in seeking means to a willed end, the will and the wisdom are separate. But when there are no ulterior purposes, and the thing is its own end, then the wisdom and the will are identical. Creative necessity and freedom are one. Similarly in III, 25, Maimonides combines the two origins of creation, that is, not only the will but also wisdom, which "made the actual existence of the universe necessary,"[18] so that we have here again will, wisdom, and necessity as one.

And this concept of God as artistic, that is, unteleological, wisdom, follows also from Maimonides' discussion of the second subject: What is the purpose of the Torah? He begins his chapters on the "reasons of the commandments" (III, 2b) by positing a parallel between creation

16 *Moreh*, III, 13, 20.

17 *Moreh*, III, 25, 38.

18 *Moreh*, III 25, 39: רוב חכמינו ויודעינו לא יאמינו שזה ברצון לבד לא בזולתו אבל יאמרו שחכמתו ית׳ אשר תבצר ממנו השגתה חייבה מציאות זה העולם בכללו בהכרח כאשר נמצא.

and the giving of the Torah. On both subjects, one opinion finds the origin in will and the other in wisdom. Now here Maimonides seems inconsistent. For in his *Eight Chapters*, ch. 6, he opposes "some of our later sages [a veiled reference to Saadia Gaon] who were infected with the sickness of the Mutakallimun," speaking of "rational laws." Why does he scoff there at Saadia, when he does the same thing here in explaining the "reasons of the laws"? We cannot enter upon a full discussion of this difficulty here.[19] Suffice it to say that here toc relative reasons, "something for the sake of something else," may be found, but teleological wisdom is one thing and intrinsic wisdom is another. There is a use or purpose for every command. But this is the logical fate of everyone who seeks a purpose—whether in law or in creation—that ultimately he finds himself standing before a mist that defies his quest. We seek and find the benefit of every moral law in particular, but what is the reason of morals as a whole? Morals have no rational authority; only agreement, convention, general assent. Hence Maimonides opposes Saadia, who followed the Arabic Muʿtazilites in speaking of rational laws. Thus indeed he says, in *Moreh*, I, 2, that the laws are not rational, like syllogisms in logic or proofs of theorems, but only conventional (*meforsamot*). What then is the meaning here, from the standpoint of the Lawgiver, of the motive of wisdom, which Maimonides accepts? And why does he say in II, 25 that the answer to all questions of creation and the Torah is "He willed it so; or, His wisdom decided so... we do not understand His will or the necessity of His wisdom"?[20] And the answer again is that it is not rational, teleological wisdom, for all such wisdom comes to a point at which it fails. It is intrinsic, immediate, aesthetic, wisdom.

III

To summarize, nature is law, necessity, and causality; and what is not law is not nature, only accident. And spirit, "the living spirit of the wheels," is free, creative wisdom. Now the Arabs left no room for nature, and Aristotle saw no need for spirit, which is supernatural, free. Then came Maimonides, and in opposition to the Arabs he affirmed nature, for otherwise there is no knowledge; and in opposition to

19 See *supra*, "The Philosophy of Saadia" ch. 5, Sec. 2.

20 *Moreh*, II, 25 (end).

Aristotle he asserted the supernatural, for otherwise there is no nature. This supernatural Maimonides was willing to describe in Aristotelian, somewhat logico-pantheistic terms as *forma formarum*, as the highest category in cosmic logic, as thinking-thinker-thought. But here we find ourselves in a closed alley. Indeed, Aristotelian philosophy knows no road from God to the world, no road to creation or providence. In the light of Judaism, Maimonides discovered in the supernatural wisdom and will one quality, that of the artist and architect.

This is the supernatural spirit. And the human spirit partakes of both, of the necessity of nature and of freedom of will; and in the creative moment the two coincide.

Part III ❧

STUDIES IN PRE-TIBBONIAN PHILOSOPHICAL TERMINOLOGY

THE PHILOSOPHICAL TERMS AND IDEAS OF ABRAHAM BAR ḤIYYA (THE PRINCE)

1. ABRAHAM BAR ḤIYYA, THE PRINCE

THIS STUDY aims to present the various philosophical, mathematical, astronomical and calendrical terms—ancient and medieval philosophy drew no sharp line of demarcation between any of the above sciences, as is also shown by the variety of meaning of the term *pilosofim* (q.v.)—that Abraham the son of Ḥiyya, a pioneer in the use of the sacred tongue for his meditations and investigations, employed in his chiefly ethical work *Hegyon ha-Nefesh*, in his geometrical work *Sefer ha-Meshiḥah weha-Tishboret* (at the end of which Guttmann has an inadequate list of terms), and in his calendrical work *Sefer ha-ʿIbbur*, in his astrological and eschatological work *Megillat ha-Megalleh*, and in his astronomical work *Ṣurat ha-Areṣ*. It will aid us, together with subsequent studies in pre-Tibbonian terminology, in determining with some exactness the debit and credit accounts of the great translators. Interesting is the fact that Samuel ibn Tibbon himself did not seem to be fully aware of the whole extent of his debt, for he claims to have been the first to use the terms גדר as a verb, to define or be defined, ציור in the sense of understanding the "true form" or the essence of a thing, and מקצר in the sense of doing something partly, (see his *Perush Millot Zarot*); while as a matter of fact all these terms had been used before him by our author. See also *supra*, "Some Textual notes on Yehudah Halevi's *Kuzari*," note 8.

Little is the Nasi's philosophical bequest; but whatever its dimensions in surface and in depth, it occupies a conspicuous niche because of his theory of emanation and ascetic tendencies, representing the thin small stream of Neoplatonism that flowed gently during the first period in Medieval Jewish thought before the broad tide of Aristotelianism arrived. Moreover the Nasi, unlike Gabirol, attempts by a process of Philonic exegesis an identification of the law of Moses with the teachings of

Plotinus, even as a later thinker attempted, in more thoroughgoing a manner, a reconciliation of Mosaism with Aristotelianism.

As in my previous work entitled *Philosophical Terms in the Moreh Nebukim*, I shall here also describe the philosophical ideas under the various terms, which are generally arranged here according to their grammatical roots.

As a rule I have not included any term that is biblical or Talmudic unless it is a pivotal point in our author's thinking, or when it has a different meaning.

Among the linguistic peculiarities that I could hardly regard as terminological to warrant their inclusion, mention may be made here of the following:

אחר *since*, *because*. HMT, 18. In Talmud: **מאחר**.

אמר ב... *believe in*. MM, 138. See PT.

הן... או *either... or*. HN, 39.

הנה *here*. HMT, 11: Ar. هنا. See PT. In Bible, generally "hither"; but see Gen., 21, 23.

הצעיר *to afflict*. HN, 27.

ואם *even if*, *although*. HN, 3, 20b. Ar. **ואן**. See PT.

וכגון (1) *and others like*. HN, 26b, 33; HMT, 80; MM, 48. In Talmud: *for example*.

(2) *about*. MM, 98.

טוב ומוטב *good and evil*. MM, 126.

יכול *it may be* (Mod. Heb. **יוכל היות**). HN, 20, 26b; HMT, 24, 58.

יכול... יכול *either... or*. HN, 20b; HMT, 91; SI, 63.

ל... *because*. HN, 41 **לאשר הוא לשון בינה**, Arabic influence.

לאלתר *above*. HN, 24b, 27b; HMT, 28, 110. In Talmud: *forthwith*, *soon*.

מאפיס *annihilates*. MM, 27.

מרגיש *stormy*. HN, 22b.

הרגשות *storms*. MM, 146.

צדיה *desolation*. HN, 34.

רהב *fear*, **מרהיבים** *fearing*. HN, 28, 30b, 40b. Cf. Ar. رهب *feared*, *dreaded*, and رهبة *fear*, *fright*.

ומשם *hence*. SA, 4. **יוצא על** *agrees with*. SA, 13.

The book *Hegyon ha-Nefesh* abounds in misprints. In addition to those corrected in the introduction by Rapoport, the following may be recorded:

p. 2, l. 29 **יצירת** read **יציאת**
p. 2b l. 9 **ואמת** read **ואמרו**

p. 4b l. 12 להמציא read להמצא
p. 4b l. 19 להחתימן read להתחימן?
p. 6b l. 4 תמונה read תמורה
p. 9 l. 17 לא אשר read הלא אשר
p. 12 l. 32 זמון read דמיון
p. 13b l. 17 ומעלו read מועלו
p. 18b l. 3 אמורים read אסורים
p. 19b l. 18 פועל read פעול
p. 20 l. 31 כימי read בימי
p. 20b l. 17 בראשון read כראשון
p. 24b l. 33 וכגון read וכיון
p. 30 l. 28 ונשתקק read ונשתתק
p. 33b l. 29 מקוה read המקום
p. 33b l. 26 מופרשים read מפורשים. שונים read שנויים
p. 37 l. 25 פירושים read פרושים

I have permitted myself the use of the following abbreviations:

HN—*Hegyon ha-Nefesh*, ed. Freimann, Leipzig, 1860.
HMT—*Hibbur ha-Meshiḥah weha-Tishboret*, ed. Guttmann, Berlin, 1913.
SI—*Sefer ha'Ibbur*, ed. Filipowski, London, 1851.
MM—*Megillat ha-Megalleh*, ed. Poznanski-Guttmann, Berlin, 1924.
SA—*Ṣurat ha-Areṣ*, Offenbach, 1720.
PT—*Philosophical Terms in the Moreh Nebukim*, by I. Efros, N.Y. 1924.
A.—Abraham bar Ḥiyya.

א

אברכוס (= אברכש q.v.). SA, 39.

אברכ״ש *Hipparchus* (fl. 146–126 B.C.E.), whom A. praises as the discoverer of the extent of a lunar month but as having probably borrowed his knowledge from Jewish sources. Rather curious is the chronological statement, put into the mouth of Ptolemy, that Hipparchus lived 80 years after the death of Alexander the Great and 126 years after the building of the second Temple, (3410 A.M.) which—see מנין שטרות — yields the year 3,536 in the mundane era, or 225 B.C.E. See SI, 37–38, 40, 78.

אדם *man*, king of the animal world, crown of creation (*sof ha-nibraot*), a rational animal, possessing also the distinguishing powers of plants and animals, namely growth and movement (HN, 1a, 1b). Three differences are discernible in the creation of man, marking his superiority. First, all other animals were created through the medium of something else, such as earth or water, while man was formed directly by God. Second, in the account of the making of man, all three expressions occur ("and He created," "and He made," "and He formed") that are used in the story of the genesis of all other living things combined. Third, man was appointed ruler over all animals (HN, 7a). Men, from the religio-ethical standpoint, fall into five classes: (1) the *shefal ruaḥ* whose rational soul naturally rules over his evil instincts from his childhood to the end of his days so that he never has to repent; (2) the *nidkeh leb* who early conquers his evil inclinations and is the *ba'al teshubah, par excellence*; (3) the repentant that never returns to sin; (4) the repentant that slides back to sin; (5) the one that never repents. The first two are the perfectly righteous or *Ṣaddiqim gemurim*, the last is the absolute sinner, and only the middle two classes constitute the category of "men of repentance" (HN, 21a). From another standpoint, men—A. speaks particularly of "believers" —may be grouped as follows: (1) those that devote themselves completely to the service of God and hold themselves totally aloof from mundane affairs; (2) those who, while following the divine precepts, form nevertheless an *economico-social* group, without jealousy, or hate, so as to supply their bare physical needs; (3) those united as a *political* entity with a ruler to maintain social order within and to fight with the enemies without. The Ten Commandments suffice for the first individualistic group, and are addressed to man in the singular—*thou* shalt not—because they are the law for the man that stands alone. All other laws, in Exodus, Leviticus, and Numbers, implicitly included in the Ten Words, are meant for the economic group, such as the community of Israelites during the forty years of the wilderness. Deuteronomy is designed to meet the needs of the third or political group (HN, 35–39). Comp. our author's preference for the first group with the Stoic extolling of ἀπάθεια or indifference to all external circumstance and with the ideas of Plotinus, who teaches that in the ethical ladder civil virtues are the lowest rung because they do not touch the soul, and that ascetic virtues are the intermediary rungs leading to divine virtues or the contemplation of God—the highest stage. See *Israel*.

און גליון *Evangel, the New Testament*, SI, 109, 110.

אור *Light*, corresponding in the phraseology of the Biblical cosmogony, to pure form. HN, 3b. See *ṣurah* and *nefesh*.

For the five lights, see *'olamot*.

אות *proof*. See SI, X; HMT, 119; and MM, 4.

(אזן) מאזנים *Libra*, the seventh sign of the zodiac, when the sun touches the celestial equator and the days and nights are equal. SI, 10. See *galgal ha-mazzalot*.

אחדות *unity*, the basis of number, thought it is not a number *per se*, just as letters are the basis of language, though they themselves are not language. This latter idea is shown by the fact that every number is one half the sum of the two numbers immediately coming before and after it (e.g. 10=[9+11] ÷ 2), but this cannot be said of unity. See HMT, introd., XI. The whole passage is found almost verbatim in a quotation from Dunash ben Tamim in Barzillais Comm. on the *Book of Creation*, p. 144. See also *ibid*., 111, 338.

אחדות, אחדים *units*, HMT, 11. See also MM, 8.

באחר *later*. SA, 3.

מאוחר *mentioned after its logical place*. See *muqdam u-me'uḥar*. See also MM, 8.

מתאחר (1) = *me'uḥar*. See *mitqaddem*.
(2) *later*, SI, 49, MM, 9.

איכיות *qualities*, MM, 5.

אין *nothing*, MM, 1. מאין אל יש *creatio e nihilo*, MM, 49.

איתן *root*, *essence*, SI, 74, 79. This sense is derived from its primary meaning of permanence. Comp. Ar. واتن.

אלהית *divine*, MM, 55. See פילוסופים.

אמהות *elements*, for example, water, air, etc. HN, 4b. Comp. Talmudic *yesh 'em lemiqra*, where our word means—like the Ar. امة—*authority*, *law*. See PT and Ginzberg's note.

אמידה *guess*. HMT, 81. See HN, 2a, note 2.

אומנות *science*. SI, VIII, 15. MM, 50. See, however, Barzillai, Comm. on *Book of Creation*, p. 65, in a quotation from David ha-Babli, where our term is explained as "art" in distinction from "science." See also *ibid*., 106.

אמונה *faith*, *belief*, "Those people of the law who do not uphold the faith are not helped much by their learning" (HN, 17a). Belief and *yir'ah* are related in the sense that the former alone is common among fools, while the latter alone is nothing but a vague fear or dread and therefore presupposes the former for its full value. HN, 26a.

אמצעי see מהלך.

מאמרות, מאמר (1) *expressions*, *statements*. HN, 6b.
(2) *categories*. See *yesodot*.

(3) *treatise, part of a book.* SI, 5.

נאמרות, נאמר *words, expressions.* HN, 3b: כי רוב נאמרות כן בלה״ק. Perhaps we should read **רוב המלים נאמרות**. See *Perush millot zarot* s.v. *ekut*, where our term is suggested to express the idea of categories or predicables. See also Palqera's *Meqor Ḥayyim*, II, 11 (end).

אמת See על.

אמתה *truthfulness.* HN, 37b.

אמתי See גובה, דביקה, מהלך.

אסף *to add.* HMT, 57: **אסיפה** *addition.* See also *ibid.*, 58.

אופן (1) *orbit*, hence different from *galgal* (q.v.), which denotes a sphere. SI, 10.

(2) *horizon.* MM, 119.

אופן הגובה (1) *sphere of altitude*, that is, the arc describing zenith-distance (the distance of a point from the zenith, measured on the vertical circle of the point) and altitude, which is the distance from the astronomical horizon on the vertical circle. SA, 26.

(2) *a circle*, governing the movement of an epicycle, the center of which is on the same line with the centers of the deferent and the earth, but as distant from the deferential center as the deferential center is from the earth. The radius of this center determines the place and velocity of the five planets. SA, 29, 30.

אופן גדול *a primary circle*, that is, dividing the sphere into two equal parts, for example, celestial equator, astronomic horizon. SA, 6.

אופן גלגל הגובה (= **א׳ הגובה** q.v.) SA, 29.

אופן דומה, א׳ ד׳ לאופן המזלות *zodiac-like orbit*, geocentric and hence similar to the zodiacal belt. SA, 13, 17.

אופן חצי היום *meridian.* SA, 8.

אופן יוצא, א׳ י׳ המרכז *eccentric circle.* SA, 13, 18.

אופן ישר *equatorial horizon*, the plane of which passes through the north and south poles and is perpendicular to gravity. SA, 9.

אופן המזלות (SI, 17) see *galgal.*

אופן המישור *celestial equator*, dividing the sphere into two equal parts, moving itself, and other spheres beneath it, from east to west. SA, 5; SI, 18. See *galgal.*

אופן המפרש *astronomical horizon* or the great circle of the celestial sphere, midway between the zenith and the nadir, passing through the point of observation and perpendicular to the vertical line. SI, 10.

See SA, 5, where א׳ מפריש is explained as *separating* and hiding the lower half sphere.

אופנים מתמוטטים *inclined horizons*, the planes of which do not pass through the north and south poles .SA, 9.

אופן נוטה *lunar ecliptic*, geocentric but inclined to the north and to the south about 5°, intersecting the אופן הדומה at two points forming the dragon. SA, 17, 18, 20, 33.

אופן סובל *deferent*, a circle upon the circumference of which another circle, the epicycle, is moving and carrying a dlanet. SA, 12, 17.

אפס *non-being*, as opposed to *yesh*. HMT, 1; MM, 5. Ḥarizi sometimes uses this term in his translation of the *Guide* where Tibbon uses נעדר. See PT. When the whole universe was still lodged in Pure Thought, it consisted of three elements: matter, form, and nonbeing. Creation meant the elimination of the last element and the combination of the first two. MM, 5. PT s.v.

אפיסה *absence*. SI, 26, MM, 5.

איפרכוש, אפרכש (= אברכש q·v.). SA, 13, 15.

אוק׳, אקלידס *Euclid*, Greek mathematician of the 3rd century B.C.E. HMT, 66, 83.

אקלים *climate*, *climatic zone*. The 66 degrees above the equator that are inhabited (see *yishshub*) are divided into 7 zones. The further the zone is from the equator the longer is its longest day at the summer solstice and the shorter is its shortest day at the winter solstice. The longest day and the shortest day at any point are equal to 24 hours, so that at the end of 66 degrees N. Lat. the longest day is 24 hours and the shortest is zero. SI, 7, 27. In SA, 7 and 36: אקלימה and איקלים.

אריה see *galgal*.

אריסטו Aristotle, "the head of the sages of Greece." SI, X. אריסטוטאליס MM, 50.

א׳ הארץ, ארך (1) *longitude*, so called because the inhabited part from east to west is longer than that extending from south to north. SI, 6, 14, 15. See ישוב.

(2) *astronomic longitude*, that is, east or west of the meridian. SA, 26

מאורע *accident*, *quality*, MM, 8, 18.

אריתמאטיקא, ארתמטיקא *arithmetic*. HMT, 81.

ב

בדיקה *astronomic observation*. MM, 12.

בהו *void*, used in the biblical account of creation to express that (הו + בו = בהו) through which *tohu* or matter becomes being, or that which is self-subsistent, and therefore corresponds to the Aristotelian form. HN, 3a. Yehoudah Halevi, however, speaks of both *tohu* and *bohu* as referring to the *hyle* (*Kuzari*, V, 2). See Naḥmanides on Gen., 1, 1, who seems to agree with our author in his interpretation of *bohu* and gives a midrashic source. So also Baḥya on Gen., 1, 2, and Ḥayim Vital's *Eṣ Ḥayyim* קיצור אבי״ע ch. 10. See *ṣurah*.

בהמית see *nefesh*.

ביאה (1) *connection*. MM, 68.

(2) *entrance* of the sun into Aries: hence, the *vernal equinox*. MM, 122.

בחן *demonstrate*. HMT, 14: והנה מה שרצינו לבחון *quod erat demonstrandum*.

בחירה *choice*, *selection*. MM, 60.

בטול *cessation*, *negation*. HN, 31b.

בטילה *negation*. HN, 39.

בטלנים *false thinkers*. MM, 48, 51. Comp. Ar. באטל

בטלמיוס ,בתל׳ Ptolemy, the celebrated astronomer of Alexandria (fl. 127–151 C.E.) whose astrological work *Liber quadripartitus*, A. quotes under the name *Arbaʿ ha-Maʾamarot*. See *Heb. Ueb.*, 525. SI, VIII, 36, 37. See also SA, 13, 15, 31, 32, 39; MM, 119.

בי״ת (1) *with*.

(2) *in*. The idea of "inness" can be taken in nine senses: (1) the particular in the general, (2) the general in the particular, (3) the species in the genus, (4) the genus in the species, (5) form in matter, (6) accident in matter or in accident, (7) accident in place, (8) accident in a vessel or container, (9) accident in time. MM, 7. For the Aristotelian origin of this classification, see Guttmann, introd. XV.

בית *House*, a zodiacal sign as an abode of a certain planet, one of the twelve equal divisions into which the zodiac is astrologically divided. Six of them are above the horizon, and six are below. They are numbered from the east immediately below the horizon, then under the earth to the west, and thence through the zenith to the east again. Each House has its own astrological significance. Thus the eighth House is that of death; the ninth, religious law and prophecy; the tenth, royalty. When planets exchange their Houses they act as if they were in conjunction, which is a good omen in the case of benign planets and vice versa. Each planet rules over a certain House and is especially powerful if found therein. Thus the Sun rules Leo; the Moon, Cancer; Saturn, Aquarius by day and Capricornus by night; Jupiter, Pisces by day and Sagittarius by night; Mars, Aries, and Scorpio; Venus, Taurus and Libra; Mercury, Gemini, and Virgo. Furthermore, the Sun is strong in Aries, the Moon in Taurus; Saturn in Libra; Jupiter in Cancer; Mars in Capricornus, Venus in Pisces; Mercury in Virgo. On the other hand, each planet is weak if located in the seventh sign after the one of its strength, that is, the Sun is not very effectual in Libra, the Moon in Scorpio, Saturn in Aries, Jupiter in Capricornus, Mars in Cancer, Venus in Virgo. MM, 120, 123, 124, 126, 132, 135, 137.

בית גבהות "*House of dignity*" or powerful influence. There is such a House in the zodiac for every planet, for example, Aries for the Sun, Libra for Saturn, etc. See בית. The seventh sign from the "House of dignity" of a planet constitutes his "House of detriment" or weakness (בית שפלות), for example, Libra for the Sun, Aries for Saturn, etc. MM, 129, 130, 132. See also ברייתא דמזלות 14. ב׳ היופי MM, 123, 140.

בית מגורה "*House of fear*," inimical to, or seventh from, the one that a planet rules, for example, Taurus from Mars, which rules over Scorpio. MM, 130.

בית שפלות see ב׳ גבהות.

בלוי *finite*, *perishing*. HN, 6a.

בלימה *matter*, *hyle*. HN, 3a, MM, 1, 5. See *tohu*.

בן רשד SA, 11. See this name in "more About Abrahom bar Hiyya's Philosophical Terminology." *Infra*, p. 235.

בנוי *composed*, *constructed*. HN, 3a.

תבנית *Aristotelian form*. HMT, XI. Maimonides, however, takes pains to show that this word denotes only outward or physical form and therefore cannot be applied to God (*Moṛeh*, I, 3). See *ṣurah*.

בעל מעון (1) *sharer of House* (see *bait*). MM, 120.
(2) *ruler of a House*. MM, 123.

בעלי הענין *specialists*. HMT, 7. Comp. Dunash פירוש ס׳ יצירה, p. 23.

בקר על *examine*, *look into*. HN, 38, 39.

ברא *creation* of potentiality or matter, whereas *yaṣar* and *asah* refer to actuality. MM, 8, 16. So also Baḥya on Gen., 1. 1. See *meṣiut*.

בריח *diameter*. HN, 24; SI, 9.

בירור (1) *proof*. HN 38. See ה״א הידיעה והב׳.

(2) *choice*. MM, 60.

התברר *to be proved*. HN, 38.

אלבתאני, אלבאתאני *Battani*, famous Arabian astronomer who died 929 (*Heb. Ueb*., 549). SA, 39, 40.

בתולה see *galgal*.

בתלמיוס see בטלמיוס.

ג

גאולה *redemption* of Israel and Judea from exile, conjoined with a transformation of the heart from a state of ability to choose between right and wrong to a state of moving instinctively and inevitably to the right. Then the Jews—peoples of any other faith will be no more—will constitute a community of men who have attained the degree of indifference to all mundane affairs and of unremitting service of God. This last idea is Stoic and Neoplatonic. See *Adam* and *Israel*. HN, 41. In MM, our author attempts to find through exegetic and astrological computations the year of redemption and arrives at the following possibilities: 4790, 4896, 5118, 5163, 5208, A. M. Wars lasting 45 years will mark the beginning of the Messianic era, then will come the restoration of the Davidic dynasty, and then—the resurrection of the dead. MM, 46, 83, 107, 151.

גאלינוס *Galen*, celebrated ancient medical writer (c. 130–200). MM, 50

גובה (1) *altitude* or distance from astronomical horizon. SA, 26. See *'ofan*.
(2) *apogee*. SA, 11, 20.

גובה אמיתי *true apogee* of an epicycle, that is, when looked at from the center of the earth. Thus *AOE* is the deferent of which *C* is the center and *D* the earth-center. Then *F*, the point on the epicycle made by

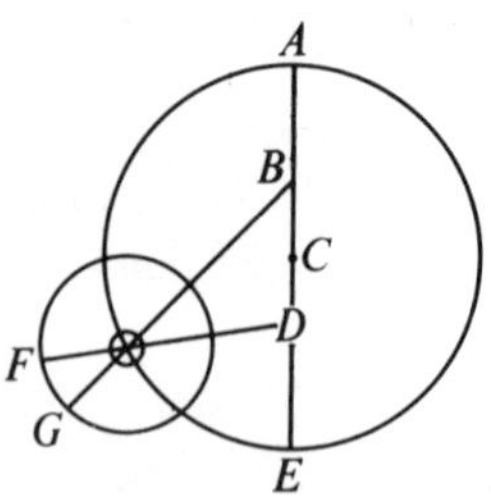

the geocentric line is the true apogee; while *G* looked at from *B* (a point on the diameter equidistant with *D* from *C*) is the גובה בינוני or mean apogee. This is one of the irregularities of the moon. SA, 22. See *ḥilluf* and *petilut*.

גובה בינוני (1) *the intermediary point* between perigee and apogee, when the sun or the moon appears to be at its uniform velocity. SI, 16, 20, 79. Also called מרחק בינוני.
(2) see *gobah amitti* and *niftal.*

גבה גדול *apogee* or the point at which the sun or the moon is furthest from the earth and appears to be at its slowest rate of motion. SI, 16, 20. Also called מרחק ארוך.

גוֹבה קטן *perigee* or the point at which the sun or the moon is nearest to the earth and appears to be at its highest speed. SI, 16, 20, 80. Also called מרחק קצר and גובה קרוב.

גובה רום *apogee*. SA, 11. ג׳ אמיתי = גובה רום אמיתי SA, 32.

גובל *intercepts* (an arc). SA, 12. נגבל (1) *intercepted*. SA, 13, 20.
(2) *determined, described, delineated.* SA, 29.
(3) *limited, completed.* MM, 69.
מגביל (1) *describing, intercepting* a circle or an arc. SA, 18,13, 29.
(2) *determining, tracing*. SA, 11.

גבול *orb*, the space on the celestial sphere within which the influence of a planet, star, or House is supposed to act. Thus the orbs of Saturn are 5° in Aries, 5° in Taurus, 6° in Gemini, 4° in Cancer, 7° in Leo, 2° in Virgo, 6° in Libra, 6° in Scorpio, 5° in Sagittarius, 4° in Capricornus, 5° in Aquarius, 2° in Pisces: so that all the territories of Saturn amount to 57°, which number has an astrological significance. MM, 29. See ברייתא דמזלות 14. See also *sha'ar*.

גבול מעמד העמוד *the foot* or the point where the perpendicular touches the base of a triangle. HMT, 42, 54, 55.

גדודי מעלה *heavenly bodies*. SA, 5.

גדל היפי MM, 120, 123, 124, 125, 140.

מתגדל *grows*. HN, 2b.

גדר (1) *definition*. HN, 1; HMT, XI; MM, 4, 59. See PT.
(2) *scope, domain*, HN, 38.
(3) *square root*. HMT, 41. A. here borrowed the Ar. word جذر.

גדיש *cone* or umbra of an eclipse. SA, 23.

גו *body*, anything tridimensional. HMT, 8.

גוונים see *mazzalot*.

גוף (1) *body, matter* (what the Tibbons call *geshem*). "Matter, embracing all beings, is breadth and depth and length adhering to something having magnitude" (HN, 2). Similarly A. defines גו and גולם in HMT, 8. See also HN, 1b, 2b, 5. Matter then is tridimensionality plus something susceptible of extension, the first part constituting the Aristotelian form and the second, the "something"—the *hyle*. A. then does not seem to share the view of Saadia and Maimonides, who maintain the accidentality of space, but prefers to align himself with Gabirol, who thinks that extensity is the form, the very essence, which combines with the original undefined *hyle*. See *supra*, "Problem of space in Jewish Med. Phil.," pp. 32–46. Immovable matter falls into three classes: (1) immutable in form, like the firmament; (2) mutable in form and lacking the power of growth, like minerals; (3) endowed with the power to grow but immutable. HN, 4.

(2) the *hyle*, in distinction to form. HN, 4, 5.

(3) *volume*. SA, 2.

גוף העולם *universal matter*, the result of the elimination of non-being and the combination of matter with form. MM, 5.

גופי הרקיעים *the heavenly bodies*. HN, 2b.

גוזר *assert*, *affirm*. HN, 6, MM, 9, 13.

גזרה *conjugation*, *derivation*, *stem* (what grammarians call *binyan*). HN, 20.

גזורים *decreed*, *allotted*. HN, 28; MM, 50, 111.

גיאומטריא see *ḥokmah*.

גלגל *to move*. SI, 20. גילגול *motion*. HN, 1b. MM, 8. מתגלגל *moving*. HN, 1b, 11; HMT, 81. MM, 7.

גלגל *sphere*, hence different from *ofan* (q.v.), which means orbit. SI, 10. But see *Keter Malkut* (in Zangwill-Davidson's *Gabirol*), lines 118, 171.

גלגל הגובה See *ofan*.

גלגל יוצא המרכז *eccentric sphere*. MM, 113.

גלגל המזלות *the zodiac*, marked by twelve constellations: טלה Aries, שור Taurus, תאומים Gemini, סרטן Cancer, אריה Leo, בתולה Virgo, מאזנים Libra, עקרב Scorpio, קשת Sagittarius, גדי Capricornus, דלי Aquarius, דגים Pisces. The first six are northern constellations, while the last six are south of the celestial equator. SI, 10. It is an inclined sphere in which the seven planets move from west to east. Also called *ofan ha-mazzalot*. SI, 17; SA, 5, 13.

גלגל דומה לגלגל המזלות *the all-embracing sphere*, the center of which is the earth and which is the deferent (רקיע סובל q.v.) of the lunar epicycle. Also called דומה לגלגל המזלות and גלגל הדומה. SI, 19, 20.

גלגל המישור *celestial equator*. SI, 9; MM, 112.

גלגל הסובל *the deferent of an epicycle*. SI, 20. See רקיע הסובל.

גלגל ההקפה *epicycle* or a circle whose center moves around a longer circle called the deferent. SI, 20; MM, 113. The moon moves in such an epicycle.

גלגל רום *apogee*. MM, 132.

גלגל השוה *celestial equator*. SI, 78.

גלח *Christian clergyman*. SI, 45, 109, 110.

גולם *body*, a tridimensional being. HMT, 8. MM, 53, 55. See Barzillai, Comm. on *Book of Creation*, 14. See *guf*.

גורמים *charging*, *accusing* (Ar. جرم V, VIII). See HN, 33: היו מאשימין את איוב וגורמים שהיסורים הבאים עליו הם באים מפני רוע מעשיו. I do not know of any other place in Hebrew literature where the word is used in this sense. It may therefore be a misprint for ואומרים.

גרמא *cause*. MM, 9. Talmudical.

על גררא *in connection*, MM, 5.

גשם *matter*, *body*. MM, 52. See also ibn Ezra in the introduction to his commentary on the Pentateuch.

ד

דבוק (1) *intimacy*, *attachment*, *union*. HN, 2b.

(2) *conjunction*, a meeting of Saturn and Jupiter in the same sign. It is called minor conjunction (*qdibbu qaton*) with reference to its recurrence in $19^{7}/_{8}$ years in the ninth sign from the previous conjunction. It is called an intermediate conjunction (ד׳ אמצעי) with reference to its returning in 60 years to the same sign. Its recurrence in 238 years but in the next trigon is called major conjunction or *dibbuq gadol*. Its return in $953^{1}/_{3}$ years in the same trigon is called great conjunction (*dibbuq rab*). Its recurrence in 2859 years after 154 minor conjunctions to the beginning of the sign of the same trigon is called grand conjunction (ד׳ עצום). MM, 117. See *ḥibbur*.

דבוקים see *shemot*.

דביקה *the ecliptical conjunction* or the meeting of the moon with the sun in the same longitude or right ascension. The moment of conjunction is the *molad* in the stricter sense of the word. SI, 35. See *ḥodesh*. It is a "true conjunction" (עת דביקה אמתי) when regarded from the center of the earth, and only apparent (נראה) when observed from the earth-surface. SA, 28. MM, 119.

הדבק *to be in ecliptical conjunction*. SI, 35. See *debibah*. See Gabirol, *Keter Malkut* lines 135, 212.

נדבק *adjacent* (e.g., lines of a triangle). HMT, 18. See *shemot*.

(דבר) על דרך הדבור *loosely speaking*. Opposed to *be'iqqar*. SI, 76.

דברן *rational.* HN, 1b.

דברנית *rational.* See *nefesh.*

דגים see *galgal.*

דוגמא *analogy*; hence, *inexactness.* SI, 22. על ד׳ *loosely speaking.* HMT, 100; SI, 22, 33, 94. MM, 7, 16. Comp. על דרך הדמיון "so to speak" in *Kuzari*, IV, 25.

דומה *similar* (e.g., triangles) HMT, 120. See *galgal, ofan.*

דיוק *precision, exactness.* MM, 5, 13.

דמות לקותה *a quasi-eclipse*, when a star is furthest from the sun and is invisible on the earth. SA, 38.

דמיון *example, illustration.* HMT, 25, 42; SI, 32.

דמיון הדבר *loose speech, analogy.* Opposed to *be'iqqar.* SI, 76. See *dugma.*

מדמה *illustrate, give example.* HMT, 85.

דעתן *rational, intelligent.* MM, 5.

דקדוק *exactness, precision.* SI, 120. מדוקדק *precise, correct.* SI, 74.

מדקדקים (1) *careful investigators.* HN, 10, 24b; HMT, 62; SI, 81. (2) *grammarians* (?). HN, 10b.

דרך הדבור see *dibbur.*

דרך הסבה לכתחלה *demonstratio a priori*, reasoning from cause to effect HN, 6b. I do not know of any other author who uses this expression

ה

ה״א הבירור *declarative he* (comp. the *he* in the Talmudical expression והתניא, which sometimes means "and *so* it has been taught"). HN, 30.

ה״א הידיעה והבירור *the definite article.* HN, 6b.

ה״א המודיעה והמפרסמת *declarative he.* HN, 29.

ה״א התימה והשאלה *interrogative he.* HN, 30.

האיי *Hai Gaon.* SI, 97.

הוגה see *nefesh.*

הגרים *Arabs.* MM, 96.

הוים (1) *created.* MM, 51.
(2) *existing.* MM, 23. See PT. נהיה *being created.* MM, 17.

הוויות *formations, creations.* SI, X. MM, 17.

היולי The traditional pronunciation of the Heb. is *hiyyuli*; the proper vocalization, however, of the Ar. term that the Heb. language incorporated is هَيولى as found in Dozy's *Supplément aux dictionnaires*

Arabes. The change of the Gr. "upsilon" to the Ar. "ya" and "waw," not sustained in some other cases, may to my mind be explained by the influence of the Ar. هيولى *the hyle* (ὕλη) the primordal matter, corresponding to the word *tohu* in biblical phraseology, non-existent by itself, realized only when wedded to form or *bohu*, which does have reality *per se*, only it is not perceptible. HN, 2, 3. This concept of the absolute negativity of the *hyle*, its immateriality, indeterminateness and in fact non-existence, is not Aristotelian but Neoplatonic. Matter is an absence, a στέρησις, just a ὑποκείμενον for the existence of bodies. See Plotinus, *Ennead*, III, 6, 18. There are two kinds of *hyle*: the pure and the coarse; out of the first kind were made the heavenly bodies and out of the second, all subluner beings (HN, 2). Halevi also speaks of the matter of the spheres as being **חומר זך וקיים** (*Kuzari*, IV, 25). Comp. the Aristotelian or rather Pythagorean ether or quintessence. According to A., the heavenly bodies are also composed of matter and form—which is not the view of Avicenna and Maimonides, who maintain the simplicity of the spheres. See PT.

הולך על *in conformity with, according to.* HN, 4. MM, 21. See PT. **הולכת על סדר אחד** *is constant.* HMT, 68.

מהלך, מהלכות (1) *movements.* HN, 4b. There are three rectilinear movements, according to the element in which the movement takes place, that is, walking on the earth, floating on the water, and flying in the air (fire tolerates no moving object), and one circular movement, that is, that of the spheres. Astronomically, there are two main movements: (1) that of the eighth diurnal sphere from east to west, (2) that of the zodiac from west to east. SA, 5.
(2) *celestial equator.* SA, 8, 16.

מהלך אמצעי *mean velocity*, for example, of the sun in her eccentric circle, as opposed to *maqom amitti*, true velocity, which varies with reference to her geocentric orbit. The difference between the two movements is the arc (*qeshet ha-shinnui*) on the zodiac intercepted between the geocentric and the eccentric radii, both crossing the center of the sun's circle. SA, 13. **מהלך מחובר** *complex lunar movement*, composed of (1) the moon's movement on an epicycle, (2) the movement of the epicyclical center on the deferent, (3) that of the center of the deferent moving in a small circle round the center of the earth at a radius of the distance between the centers of the earth and the deferent, (4) that of the nodes. SA, 21. The result of the third element is that the deferential apogee moves eastward; that the eplcyclieal center, moving east, completes its revolution around the deferent in a half-month; and that as the epicyclical center moves away from the apogee, the distance between it and the center of the earth is decreased, so that the "angle of correction" becomes greater, reaching a maximum of $7°\frac{2}{3}$. SA, 20. See *tiqqun.* מ׳ מריץ *acceleration* (e.g., at perigee). SA, 29. מ׳ מתון *retardation* (e.g., at apogee). SA, 25, 29. מ׳ מתחלף *varied velocity.* MM, 117. מ׳ נחוץ *acceleration.* SA, 25. מ׳ פשוט *simple movement* (of the moon). This is based on the view that the geocentric radius moves the epicyclical center on the deferential circumference from west to east, so that the epicycle moves east at the rate of 13°14′ and the inclined sphere moves the line of nodes in the zodiac-like sphere (*ofan domeh* q.v.) westward on the zodical poles at the rate of 3′. This lunar movement is found at new moon and full moon, though many of the former thinkers ascribed such a movement to the moon all the time. SA, 17, 18. Later observation, however, discovered some irregularities, and concluded that at all other times the moon has a complex movement. See *mahalak meḥubbar*. SA, 19, 21. מ׳ שוה *mean velocity*. SA, 13, 18. SI, 16; MM, 117.

הפוך *change*. HN, 2b.

התהפך *be reflected* (as light). SA, 22.

ו

ותיק *constant, permanent, firm* (Ar. وثيق). HN, 2b, 3b, 5. Comp. Talmudical *talmid watiq*.

ז

זהיר *luminous, shining*. HN, 2b; MM, 22, 56.

זיהור *brilliance, light*. MM, 120.

זוית חדה *acute angle*. ז׳ נצבה *right angle*. HMT, 8. ז׳ הראש *apex of a cone*. HMT, 116. ז׳ נרוחת *obtuse angle*. ז׳ שטוחה *plane angle*. HMT, 8.

זוית התקון see תקון.

נזור *receding, deviating*. MM, 113. Particularly, receding like the apogee of the lunar deferent to the west. SA, 20, 23.

זכות *future reward* (as opposed to ʿ*onesh*) HN, 20. It is an act of divine mercy rather than justice, for the physical betterment resulting from right deeds should be sufficient recompense. This distinguishes man from other animals to whom such grace is not shown. Viewing it as a mark of distinction, we can understand why A. regards future punishment as an equal act of grace (*ibid.*, 9). See *Torah.* A detailed analysis is given elsewhere (*ibid.*, 32). God's dealings with men assume the form of *ḥesed, ṣedaqah, or mishpaṭ. Ḥesed* represents the creation of the world, which was due to His loving-kindness, guided by wisdom, since the cosmic change from potentiality to actuality was not necessary *per se.* Such is the view of Joseph al-Baṣir, the Karaite, but it deviates from that of Plotinus, who taught that the creation of the world was a necessary consequence of God's absoluteness. It should be observed, however, that the author's admission of the guidance of wisdom in the realization of cosmic potentialities makes creation at least logically necessary. *Ṣedaqah* means the reward of the righteous in the world to come, which is an act of charity, for only "one of a thousand is worthy of it." *Mishpaṭ* signifies the distribution of joy and sorrow, on scales of justice, in this world. Justice here and loving-kindness in the hereafter mark the divine dispensation of good and evil. The affliction of the righteous, however, is meant as a test of moral strength and is amply rewarded. See *raʿ*.

זמן *time.* Prof. Wolfson (*The Jewish Quarterly Review*, X, 1–17) calls attention to two definitions of time: (1) the Aristotelian definition, that it is the number of spherical movements; (2) the un-Aristotelian definition, that it is duration. The first view gives time a partly real and partly ideal aspect, while the latter makes it entirely ideal, independent of reality and even pre-existent. Averroes represents the first view, and Avicenna and al-Gazali, the second view. Our author, Prof. Wolfson maintains, takes the un-Aristotelian attitude because in HN, 2 he says: ואינו כ״א אמירה מעמדת הנמצאות. It seems to me, however, that our author did not draw so sharp a line between the two concepts, for he immediately concludes; ואם אין שם נמצאות אין שם אמירה שהזמן תלוי wherein the dependence of time is emphatically stated. Indeed in MM, 10, we have the exact Aristotelian definition: אין הזמן אלא מנין החלוף בנקדם ומאוחר. See also SI, 3 and MM, 8 אין הזמן אלא מנין גלגל החלוף על הנמצאות בנקדם ובמאוחר. Similarly Avicenna الحركة من جهة التقدم والتاخر (see J. Forget's: ibn Sina, *Le Livre des théorèmes*, 150). See also M. Worms, *Die Lehre von der Anfangslosigkeit der Welt* (Baeumker's *Beiträge*, III, 4), pp. 23, 34, 59, who shows that both Avicenna and Gazali define time as measure of motion and that it is al-Farabi who attacks this Aristotelian definition, maintaining that الحركة قتصلة بهه اشيا تشمى زمان. From both definitions, A. concludes that time per se has no reality—which does not deviate from Aristotle—and is subjective, and that it has had a beginning (i.e., at Creation). HN, 1; MM, 5, 6, 10. However, it has a potential existence before (not temporally but essentially or logically speaking), just as potentiality logically preceded creation. MM, 8, 10.

זנובים see כוכבים ז׳.

זקיק *transparent*. SA, 22.

זקנות המולד, זקן (SI, 65). See *molad*.

מזרחיים see מערביים.

ח

חבל *chord*, a measure. SA, 35.

חבור (1) *treatise*, *book*. SI, 3. MM, 1. The word occurs frequently, which disproves Kaufmann's assumption that the term was not common in the days of Barzillai. See Barzillai's commentary on *Book of Creation*, p. 335.

(2) *conjunction* of two planets, particularly that of Saturn and Jupiter—the highest and slowest of all planets and also the largest, except for the Sun. This conjunction of Saturn and Jupiter occurs once in $19^{7}/_{3}$ years and 12 times in each trigon. Beginning, for example, with Aries, of the fiery trigon, it takes 48 conjunctions in 953 years until it returns to the same trigon to Leo. Then again 953 years or 48 conjunctions, and it comes to Sagittarius; and after the same stretch of time, to Aries again. Thus it takes 2859 years of 144 conjunctions to the beginning of a sign of a given trigon. MM, 116, 117. 119. See *dibbuq*.

מחדד הזויות *having acute angles*. HMT, 42.

חדה see זוית ח׳.

החדל *cease*, *perish*. HN, 1b. נחדל; *ibid.*, 13.

חדוש (1) *creation*. HN, 42b. MM, 28, 56. Ar. חדת̇.

(2) *event*, *happening*. HN, 31.

(3) See *ḥodesh*.

מחדש *creates*. HN, 31b.

חודש *a month*, extending from one moment of the moon's conjunction or *debiqah* with the sun to the next such moment. Hence one can speak only loosely of a solar month. The term denotes the synodic month, which is longer than the sideral month of 27 days, 27 hours,

43′ 11″, because at the second conjunction the earth is at the distance of about 29° 6′ 20″ from the point of the former conjunction. SI, 33. The new moon shows itself in its first *phasis*, which is called חדוש שני, while the moment of conjunction is called חדוש ראשון (SI, 34). The length of a synodic month is 29 days and 12+793/1080 hours. SI, 37. See *lebanah*.

חדשים ארוכים *long months*, that is, when the moon retards and the sun accelerates. SA, 25.

חדשים קצרים *short months*, that is, when the moon accelerates and the sun retards. SA, 28.

מְחַוֵּג *drawing a circle*. HMT, 76.

מחוגה *circle, sphere*. SA, 2.

חוש *take into consideration*. SA, 25.

חושי הגוף *bodily senses*. HN, 2b. Is this earliest source for this use of the word *ḥush*? In MM, 5: חוששי הגוף q.v.

חזיון *astronomy*. SA, 1, 11.

חוזים *astronomers, astrologers*. MM, 4, 146.

חזיונות הכוכבים *astronomic observations*. MM, 12.

חוזק *volume, solid-contents*. HMT, 117.

החזקה *volume, solid-contents*. HMT, 117.

חזוקים *proofs*, MM, 36.

מוחזק *confirmed, proven*. MM, 39; SA, 1.

חוזר *depends, refers*. SI, 36.

חזרה *circular motion*. SI, 76.

מחזור *a cycle*, especially the metonic cycle or one of 19 years, the following seven of which are embolismic: 3rd, 6th, 8th, 11th, 14th, 17th, 19th (the mnemonic sign being גו״ח אדז״ט). The purpose of this cycle—realized according to the astronomic system of Ada but not according to that of Samuel—is to equalize the solar with the lunar year. It is also called *maḥazor ha-lebanah* or lunar cycle. SI, 40, 41, 46, 86, 91.

מחזור גדול ,מ׳ ג׳ לחמה *a major solar cycle*, consisting of 28 years, at the end of which the vernal equinox is again at the first hour of the eve of Wednesday, even as it was at creation. SI, 40, 82. See מחזור כפול.

מחזור גדול ללבנה *a major lunar cycle*, consisting of 21 years, according to the astronomic system of Samuel. SI, 40.

מחזור חמה *a solar* or *four-year cycle*, the first three years of which consist of 365 days each, the last being a leap year of 366 days. At the end of this cycle the vernal equinox is again at the first hour of the eve of Wednesday even as it was at creation. Also called *maḥazor qatan* or minor cycle. SI, 39, 40.

מחזור כפול *a multiple cycle* or one consisting of 15 Metonic cycles. Also called *maḥazor gadol*. SI, 40, 50, 51.

מחזור הלבנה see *maḥazor*.

מחזור פשוט *a simple* or *Metonic cycle*. See *maḥazor*. SI, 51.

מחזור קטן = *maḥazor ḥammah* (q.v.).

חטא *sin* or *wrong action*; hence different from *pesha'*, which is wrong speech, and from *'avon* denoting wrong thinking, which is the worst sin. HN, 13b. This recalls Kant's doctrine that it is the motive that determines the morality or the immorality of an act. Elsewhere (*ibid.*, 24b), the author states that the order of increasing gravity is *ḥet'*, *'avon*, *pesha'*, but there the term *'avon* means wrong thinking not translated into action. Sins of thought alone or cf action alone or of speech alone require no confession or penitence; only a combination of two of these types needs atonement. There is, however, a difference of opinion as to sins of intentional speech, for some think that these cannot be atoned for except by punishment in the hereafter (*ibid.*).

חייב *requires, necessitates*. MM, 9. Ar. אוגב.

חיוני *vital*. MM, 64.

חיות *life, vitality*. MM, 53.

חיה see *nefesh ḥayyah*.

חיל *degree*, 1/360 of the sphere, 1/30 of a sign. SA, 5.

חכם *wise*, one who has a "healthy soul." HN, 5.

חכמה *physical health* (*ibid.*). Wisdom is identical with the soul of man. HN, 15, 17. Our author manifests implicit faith in the mind, for he accords objective reality to what the mind postulates in order to round out a scheme of classification. "Any potentiality the actualization of which wisdom affirms must have already changed to actuality" (HN, 5). He also maintains that *ḥaqirah* or speculation leads to faith, since an understanding of the physical architecture of the universe or the physiological structure of man makes for a belief in the wisdom and unity of the Creator (HN, 1b). His idea that the order of the world points to the existence of God is Philonic. Wisdom is one of the attributes of God and is therefore pre-existent. MM 24.

(2) *science*. MM, 115. It is to be differentiated from מלאכה or *art*, for example, astrology, which is not based on strict scientific proofs. SA, 1. See *ḥizzayon*. So Palqera, *Reshit Ḥokmah*, p. 45.

חכמה חיצונה *secular science, philosophy*. SI, 6. MM, 4, 27, 111. Comp. Talm. **ספרים חיצונים**. See *Heb. Ueb.*, p. 375.

חכמה יצירית *physics* (the term is unusual). *Yeṣirah* (q.v.) = ṭeba'. SA, 23. Comp. **יצרית**. Baḥya in his introduction to the **חובות הלבבות**: **חכמת היצירות שקורין לה בלשון ערב אלעלם אלטבעי**.

חכמי המדע see *madda'*.

חכמי המחקר *philosophers*. HN, 3 (where the reference is to Plato and Aristotle), 3b, 4b (where the Neoplatonists are meant), 5b, 6b, 10. MM, 5. See Steinschneider's *Jewish Lit.*, pp. 296, 310 and PT. s.v. **בעלי העיון**. Barzillai in his comm. on *Book of Creation* (173, et al.) uses *ba'alei ha-meḥqar*.

חכמי מלאכת הככבים *astronomers*. HMT, 69. MM, 113.

חכמה מופלאה *Wondrous Wisdom*, God. MM, 8.

חכמים קדמונים *former sages*. See HN, 2, where A. refers by this phrase to Plato and Aristotle, who maintained that matter is composed of form and *hyle*.

חכמת החשבון that part of *arithmetic* that deals with numbers in the concrete and hence different from *ḥoqmat ha-mispar* (q.v.), which deals with numbers in the abstract. The former is practical arithmetic, while the latter is abstract arithmetic (HMT, XI). Guttmann (SI, 120) is therefore wrong in translating the term by mathematics.

חכמת הכוכבים *astronomy*, SI, 21. This is divided into **ח׳ החזיון** or *astronomy* and **מלאכת הנסיון** or *astrology*. SA, 1. Comp. Palqera, *Reshit Ḥokmah*.

חכמת המנין *arithmetic*, divided into abstract and practicai arithmetic. HMT, XI.

חכמת המספר *abstract arithmetic*. HMT, XI. Comp. however, Rieti's *Mikdash me'at*, ed. Goldenthal, 13b. See *ḥoḳmat ha-ḥeshbon*.

חכמת הניגון *music*. HMT, XI.

חכמת הרופאים *medical science*. MM, 50.

חכמת השיעור *geometry*. HMT, XI. SA, 5.

חלוטה *absolute, not conditional*. HN, 31.

חלולה see *ṣurah*.

חילוף (1) *opposite, reverse*. HMT, 73. See HN, 10 **בחילוף** on the contrary. (2) *change, variance*. HMT, 68. MM, 5, 8. See HN, 5 **חלופין** and 9, 6, **חליפין** (which occurs also in SI, X).

(3) *irregularity, inequality*. Ptolemy called attention to the following irregularities: (1) acceleration and retardation (this is called **ח׳ פשוט**

and is explained by the view that the center of the sphere of the irregular planet is not that of the zodiac, that is, is not geocentric but eccentric or epicyclical. (2) "evection" coming to its maximum value at quadratures and disappearing at conjunctions and oppositions (this is explained by a recession of the apogee of the lunar difference to the west at the uniform rate of 11° 2′ per diem together with the progression of the center of the lunar epicycle to the east at the rate of 13° 11′. (3) a discrepancy between the true place (מקום אמתי, מהלך אמתי) of the moon in its epicycle and its apparent place, which, however, does not occur at conjunction, opposition, and quadratures—this is explained by the view that the line of apsides of the lunar epicycle revolves not around the center of the zodiac but some other point on the diameter. This together with the principle of the "angle of correction," זוית התקון (q.v.) enables us to identify the place of the moon more correctly. SA, 22, 32. See *Yesod Olam*, III, 3, 16. See also *maḥaloqet*.

חלופה as opposed to שוה. See קטומה.

מתחלף *varies*, *varied*, *different*. HN, 19b; HMT, 40, 42, 68.

חליצות *vigor*, *strength*. HN, 17b. Cf. Is., 58, 11.

חלק (1) *party*, *division*, *category*. HN, 28; MM, 41.
(2) *1/88 of a circumference*. HMT, 69.
(3) *a degree* or 1/360 of a circumference. SI, 7, 16, 26.
(4) *1/1080 of an hour*. SI, 37.
(5) *degree*, 1/30 of a Sign; hence, corresponding to a day. MM, 119.

חלק המעבר zodiacal accompaniment of a star across the meridan. This is not the "place of the star" (מקום הכוכב); for the latter is found on an arc from the ecliptical pole, while the former is found on an arc from the equatorial pole through the star to the ecliptic. SA, 35. See *maʿalah*.

חולקים זה לזה *intersect each other*. HMT, 34.

חילוק *difference*. SA, 35.

חלוקה *quotient*. HMT, 65.

מחלוקת *difference*. מ׳ המראה *parallax*, of the difference between the true place (v. מקום אמתי) and the apparent place of a star. SA, 25.

מתחלק *divisible*. HMT, XI.

חומר *matter*, as opposed to *form*. SI, X, MM, 5, 66. See *guf* and *meṣi'ut*.

חומר ראשון *materia prima* (ὕλη πρώτη), the common substrate of all things. SI, X. See היולי.

חמה see *shenat ḥammah* and *maḥazor ḥammah.*

מחומש,—ים,—ות *pentagon.* HMT, 76. 99. See Barzillai's comm. on *Book of Creation*, 111.

חנות *mercy.* HN, 9, 21b. Comp. *Ḥobot ha-lebabot, sha'ar ha-yiḥud*, 10.

מחנות הלבנה *mansiones lunae*, constellations not far from the ecliptic. SA, 38. Comp. *Neḥmad we-na'im*, 299.

חסאן בן מר חסאן SI, 54, 94.

חסד see *zekut.*

חסיד one, according to A., whose soul is "alive." HN, 5.

חסר *defective, imperfect.* HN, 36. See PT.

חוסר מן *less than.* HMT, 8, 62. In HMT, 64: מחסר.

חסרון *defectiveness* of a month consisting of only 29 days. As applied to a year, it means that the months of *Ḥeshwan* and *Kislev* during the year in question consist of 29 days each. SI, 59, 62.

חופפת *one of the sides forming an angle.* HMT, 98.

חץ *a perpendicular line* on the middle of a chord drawn from the circumference. HMT, 64.

חצוב *etymologically derived.* HN, 3b, 19b; SI, 33; MM, 61.

חצי קטומה *a trapezoid*, the top and the base of which are parallel and unequal and one side is perpendicular. HMT, 56.

חצוייה see *maṣebah.*

חקירה see *ḥokmah.*

מחקר *philosophical investigation.* HN, 21b, 35b. See *ḥakme ha-meḥqar.*

חשבון *computation, calculation.* SI, 120. See *ḥokmat ha-ḥeshbon.* חשבון הכוכבים *astronomy.* SI, 15.

חשבון המזלות *order of Houses* (v. *bait*). or Signs counting from the Ascendant Sign (מזל הצומח) q.v.; while מעלות המזלות denotes the order beginning with Cancer inhabited by the nearest planet, the moon. MM, 120, 121, 137.

חושב *compute, calculate.* SI, 120.

חשבן *mathematician.* SI, 15, 98, 100; MM, 111, 119, 122.

מחשב *compares.* HN, 9b, מדרך המחשבו אל דבר אחר.

מחשבה טהורה *Pure Thought, God.* HN, 2, 2b. MM, 5. In both references, the expression is used to designate that which moves form to combine with matter, so that it strongly reminds one of the Logos of Philo and of the *nous* of Plotinus. See *Ṣurah.*

נחשבים *imaginary, assumed.* HN, 24. See PT. s.v. מחשבי.

חושש *to be impressed, affected, moved.* See HN, 31 והטוב הוא דבר שאדם

חושש בו... והרע הוא תמורת הטוב יהיה דבר שאין אדם חושש בו. See also *ibid.*, 39. It is connected with the word חוש (q.v.). Comp. Ar. حسّ. See *Kuzari*, IV, 25 (ed. Hirschfeld, p. 271). ושהמלאכים יותר חוששים לה ומרגישים for the Arabic ואן אלמלאכים אשדّ אנפעאלא להא. It has a different meaning in the Talmud. See also MM, 6, 61. In MM, 5 חושׁשי הגוף means *senses*. See *ḥush*. Kaufmann in a note on Barzillai's Comm. on ס״י wrongly explains חושׁשי הגוף as meaning *accidents*.

חששא (see previous word) *impression*, *perceptibility*. HN, 2b. התהו הוא דבר שאין לו שום ערך ולא חששא. See also HMT, 62. אין בין שני החשבונים האלה אלא דבר שאין בו חששא. The word is unusual and has a different meaning in the Talmud. See also MM, 5, 61; SA, 25, 26.

חתוכי המצבה *conic sections*. HMT, 68.

חתם *decide*. SA, 24.

חתומה See *ṣurah*.

ט

טבע *nature*. HN, 9. ט׳ יצירת הגוף. MM, 50: טבע יצירתו. HN, 42 טבע הלב. See also MM, 9 and Ginzberg's note in PT.

טבעית v. *nefesh*.

(2) *substance*, *material*. SA, 23 שהם ברואים מט׳ אחד but read perhaps *matbeʿa*. Comp. SA, 24 שהן דומים לה במטבע אחד.

טובות *the pleasures of this world*, which are counterbalanced by pains and misfortunes. Pleasure is merely negative, the absence of pain. Eating and drinking only break the hunger and quench the thirst; and if indulged in for their own sake they spell disease. Salvation lies in hate for mundane life. HN, 43. These psychological and ethical ideas have a distinctly Schopenhauerian ring.

טלה *Aries*, the first sign of the Zodiac. SI, 10. See *galgal*.

(טעה) מוטעה *faulty*. SI, 52.

טעם (1) *meaning*, *sense*. HN, 9b; HMT, 7. MM, 49.

(2) *proposition*, *theorem*. HMT, 11, 18, 24; SI, 5.

(3) *argument*. SI, 75; MM, 16, 29, 74, 75.

טעמים מקובלים *accepted propositions*. HMT, 34.

טענה (1) *difficulty*, *objection*. HN, 31. טוען על *finds fault in*. Comp. Ar. طعن على inveight against. HN, 32.

(2) *argument*, *proof*. SI, 24.

טריגון *trigon* or the junction of 3 signs. The zodiac is divided into four trigons: (1) the watery trigon: Cancer, Scorpio and Pisces: (2) the earthy trigon: Taurus, Virgo and Capricornus: (3) the airy trigon: Gemini, Libra and Aquarius: (4) and the fiery trigon: Aries, Leo and Sagittarius. MM, 116.

ט׳ האש, ט׳ המים, ט׳ העפר, ט׳ הרוח, ט׳, v. טריגון.

ידיעה See ה״א הידיעה והבירור

מיודע v. *lashon*, *shem*.

מדע *thought*, *reason* (Comp., Ec., 10, 12). See HN, 1b, 5, 32, 36. Philosophers are called *ḥakme ha-madda*ʿ (HN, 15b) or *anshe ha-madda*ʿ (HN, 32), but more often *ḥakme meḥqar*.

מודיעה see ה״א המודיעה והמפרסמת.

יום שוה *uniform day* or 360° 59′ +. This is also the uniform movement of the sun. SA, 16. See also קדוש החדש Ch. 12.

יום מלאות האורים *full moon*. SA, 19.

מיוחד *particular*. MM, 8.

מיוחדת *distinguished*, *singled out*. HN, 3b.

מתיחד *distinguished*. HN, 11; HMT, 47, 74.

מיוחסות *relegated*, *referred*, *ascribed*. HN, 2b, 5.

מתייחס *referred*, *ascribed*. HN, 3.

מולד (ילד) *the moment of ecliptical conjunction*; the moon's first phasis. See *ḥodesh*. The first conjunction or *molad* of Nisan, in the history of the world, took place on Wednesday at the end of 9 642/1080 hours, but since we begin to count years from Tishri we take the pre-creational *molad* of Tishri, preceding the *molad* of Nisan, which was on Monday at the end of 5 204/1080 hours. In terms of week days, the difference between one and the next *molad* is one day, 12 793/1080 hours; that between one and the next Tishri *molad* of a common year is 4 days and 8 876/1080 hours. If it is a leap year, the difference is 5 days and 21 589/1080 hours. The difference between one and the next *molad* of the beginning of a cycle is 2 days and 16 595/1080 hours (SI, 46). It is only after 14,669 years and 8 months that the *molad* becomes exactly equal to the original one (SI, 48). If the *molad* is at the very end of 18 hours of the day or later, it is called *molad zaqen* and the new moon is declared on the next day, or, if the next day is unsuitable, for example, Sunday for Rosh-ha-Shanah, on the third day, SI, 54. This, however, applies only to Tishri. See also SI, 69.

יסודות *elements*. HN, 2b. See PT and Ginzberg's note.

מוספת (יסף) *greater*. SI, 11. MM, 79.

תוספת *addition, increase*. MM, 20.

יוצאים אל המעשה *move from potentiality to actuality*. HN, 6. See *ma'aseh*.

הוציא *to actualize, to change the potential into actuality*. HN, 2.

מוציאה אל *yield, result in*. MM, 111.

יצחק ב״ר ברוך SI, 52, 54, 55, 62, 93.

יצר v. *bara*. יתיצרו *are formed, created*. MM, 65.

יצירה (1) *created object*. HN, 5. ראויה אחרו הוצרה להפסד מן היצירה. In a similar passage, p. 5b, the word *yaṣur* is used.

(2) *composition, essence, nature*. HN, 1b. שרשי יצירתו. See also p. 3: עיקר הדבר ושרש יצירתו אשר הוא מתקיים בה... לא ידעו תקון יצירתו, and p. 9: טבע יצירת הגוף; MM, 50. See *Moreh*, II, 36, p. 78 where Tibbon uses the word *yeṣirah* for the Ar. גבלה, while Ḥarizi translates it by בטבע הבריאה. See PT, p. 68. See also SI, 3, 4.

יצור *matter*. HN, 5, ...והוי מבין מן הגוף במקום הזה הדבר אשר היה שמו תהו ואנו קוראים עתה יצור או נוצר.

See also *ibid*., 5b. תהיה נשמתו... נצלת מן היצור.

יצירית v. *ḥokmah*.

יצרית v. *nefesh*.

נוצר *matter*. See *yaṣur*.

יראה see *emunah*.

יש *substance*, as opposed to *efes*. HMT, 1. See *'ain*.

ישוב *inhabited part of the world*, the dimensions of which according to A. as well as according to general ancient geography were much greater measured from east to west than from north to south. Indeed, according to A. this part extends all over the longitude, as far as the Atlantic Ocean which "no man can pass;" but latitudinally it extends 66° north and 16° south of the equator. SI, 7, 14. See רוחב, אורך, אקלים.

מיושבים see כוכבים מ׳.

תושבת *base* (of a geometrical figure). HMT, 8; SA, 39.

ישועה *redemption, messianic era*. MM, 3, 30.

ישר (1) *straight line*. HMT, 61. ששה ישרים. See also *ibid*., 67.

(2) *regular, without recession* (as opposed to נזור). SA, 32, 38. See also *'ofan*.

ביושר *in a straight line*. HMT, 20. מישור see *galgal*. See also נקודות היושר.

תתיישר *will be fitted*. HN, 8.

ישראל Just as God separated man from other animals, so He separated Israel from other nationalities to be consecrated to Him and to be called by His name. Israel in the time of redemption will not fear other nationalities but will be feared by them, its superiority being due to its belief in unity and its acceptance of the Law. Other peoples may also attain to this high eminence, for the gates of penitence are open to all (HN, 7–8, 34). One can see how this viewpoint differs from that of Yehudah Halevi, for while A. seems to regard Israel as a religious and hence a very elastic group, Halevi takes a nationalistic and racial view and hence cannot agree that a change of tenets admits one to the House of Israel. See *Kuzari*, I, 115.

יתירים "*angels*:" the first, the fourth, the seventh, and the tenth Houses (v. *bait*). These, the eastern, western, northern, and southern points, are the main factors in the interpretation of a horoscope. MM, 121, 130, 143, 144, 149, and XXXIV.

מותר *difference*, *margin*. Esp. the length of a given solar period minus the same period according to the lunar reckoning. SI, 40, 46, 48–50, 86.

יתרון *fullness* (of a month that has 30 days). As applied to the year, it means that *Ḥeshwan* and *Kislew* in that year consist of 30 days each. SI, 59, 62.

יתרון, מותר *difference*. SA, 20.

מותירה *grows longer*, *increases*. HMT, 4.

מיתר (1) *chord* (of an arc). HMT, 121.
(2) *subtense* or *a line opposite to a given angle*. HMT, 98.

כ

כבד *any conjugation outside of the Qal*. HN, 19b.

כבד בתוספת ה״א עליו the *hif'il conjugation*. HN, 19b.

כבד מוכפל הלמד the *pi'el conjugation doubling the third radical* (as in verbs with quiescent *vav*). HN, 20.

כיבוש *intercalation*, *embolism*. SI, 78. כבוש *intercalary*, *embolismic*. SI, 113. כבושה *intercalation*. SI, 97.

כבושה (1) *an embolismic year* or one consisting of 13 months. SI, 39.
(2) *a leap year* or every fourth solar year having 366 instead of 365 days. SI, 40.

כידורי לכת, כדורים, כידור (1) *planets*. SA, 11.
(2) *orbit* SA, 13.

(כול) מכילה *capacity, measure of capacity, volume*. HMT, 116. SA, 3. See Talmudical dictionaries.

(כון) תכונה *nature, characteristic*. HN, 2b. See *tekunah*.

כזב *a lie*, as grave a sin in the eyes of God as a murder. HN, 34.

כח (1) *power, capacity, soul*. HN, 11. See *nefesh*.

(2) *potentiality*, as opposed to *ma'aseh* (q.v.) or *actuality*. HN, 2; SI, 26.

כח ההמרה *the animal power* of changing the form of absorbed food, requiring, however, the supplementing כח המצייר to transform it into tissues. MM, 64.

כח הממיר=כח ההמרה q.v. MM, 64.

כח המציר *formative power*, that which changes the food into tissues. Hence different from כח הממיר q.v. MM, 64.

כוכבים *seven planets*, each one serving at one place for one hour, beginning with שבתי, which was the first to function at the first hour on the evening of Wednesday of creation week and then the others in rotation. SI, 29.

כוכב הזנב *comet*. SA, 40.

כוכבים זנובים *comets*. MM, 113, 149.

כוכב חמה *Mercury*. See SI, 29: נסב מנוגה אל כ׳ ח׳... ויהיה כ׳ ח׳. See PT, s.v. "ḥammah" and Ginzberg's note. See also Davidson's note in Zangwill-Davidson's *Gabirol*, p. 180. See also MM, 23; SA, 30, 38, 41.

כוכבים מיושבים *fixed stars*, in the eighth heaven or sphere. SI, 76; MM, 11, 121; SA, 35.

כ׳ ל׳ הנבוכים, כוכבי לכת *planets*. Astronomers disagree as to whether planets move in epicycles or in eccentric circles. MM, 113. Maimonides (see PT s.v. גלגל הקף) denies the existence of the epicycle. Do the planets shine by light reflected by the sun? SA, 23. Are they celestial spots? SA, 24. Order: not שצ״ם נחכ״ל, as some believed, but שצ״ם חנכ״ל SA, 11, 31.

כוכבים מאפילים *nebulous stars*. SA, 39. They are 14 in number.

כוכבים מסובבים *planets*. SA, 2.

כוכבים נבוכים, כוכבי נבוכה, כוכב נבוכי *planets*. MM, 13; SA, 12, 30, 41. Especially the five planets (excluding the sun and the moon) that are so named because they appear to move confusedly, sometimes together with the two luminaries eastward and at other times together with the diurnal sphere westward. SA, 33. Their apogee moves one degree in 100 years. SA, 30.

כוכבים עליונים *the 3 planets above* the sun: Saturn, Jupiter, and Mars. SA, 38.

כוכבים עני̇נים (r. ענונים) *nebulous stars.* See *kokabim ma'afilim.*

כוכב הפסד *destructive star*, for example, Mars. MM, 122.

כוכבי שבת *fixed stars* SA, 4, 10. Is their light acquired from the sun, and are they celestial spots? SA, 23, 24. They have no movement latitudinally, and Indian astronomers deny them any sort of movement. SA, 35. They are of six magnitudes. SA, 39. Greek and Roman thinkers maintained that the fixed stars moved at the rate of 1° in 100 years; Arab astronomers changed it to $1\frac{1}{2}$°; while Indian and Chaldean astronomy ascribes to them a movement of only 8° east and 8° west, because the zodical pole moves in a circle, the diameter of which is 8°, and the pole completes this circle in 1600 years. Hence their Hebrew name and their Greek and Latin names, "return stars." SA, 40.

כוכב שליט *the Ruler*, the planet ruling over a certain sign, particularly the ascendant (see *ṣomeaḥ*). Thus the Sun governs Leo; the Moon, Cancer, Saturn, Aquarius and Capricornus; Jupiter, Picses and Sagittarius; Mars, Aries and Scorpio; Venus, Taurus and Libra; Mercury, Gemini and Virgo. The position of the Ruler in the zodiac is an important factor in the horoscope. MM, 120. Also called *Kokab moshel.*

כוכבים תחתונים *infra-solar planets*, Venus, Mercury, and the moon. SA, 37.

כוכב תלתלי *comet.* SA, 40.

כלה *finite, transitory.* HN, 6.

תכלה *end.* HN, 6, 17b. In Ps., 119, 96, it means perfection. See also SI, x.

כולל *general* (as opposed to particular). MM, 7.

כלל See שכלל.

כללי *totality.* HN, 34.

כללים *categories, classes.* HN, 20b.

כנוי (1) *pronominal suffix.* HN, 13, 22b. MM, 67.

(2) *name.* HN, 26b. ואין שום כ׳ משתתפת עמו בשם וכו׳. The word, however, refers to the thing named rather than to the name. In Talmud it means "surname." Comp. Ar. كنى namesake; homonym. See also MM, 17.

כוננות MM, 50. Read הויות Comp. SI, X.

כנס *to add.* HMT, 120.

כפל (1) *multiplication.* HMT, 11. MM, 71.
(2) *repetition.* SI, 4.
(3) *multiplication, product.* SI, 52.

כפל יתרון, כ׳ מותר *double the distance* between the moon and the sun. SA, 20. This marks the distance between the lunar epicyclinal center and the deferential apogee.

כפרנות *heresy.* MM, 10, 150.

מוכרח *forced.* HN, 41.

ל

לבנה *moon.* It moves uniformly in two spheres: in the all-embracing sphere, the center of which is the earth, and in an epicycle (*galgal ha-hakafah*, q.v.), rolling upon the circumference of that sphere or deferent (*galgal sobel*, *rakiʿa sobel*, q.v.). The center of the lunar epicycle moves from west to east at the rate of about 13°11′ per day, while the moon moves in its epicycle from east to west on the external arc and from west to east on the internal arc at the rate of about 13°3′ of the epicycle. Hence when the moon moves on the internal arc, it seems to move faster because its direction and that of the epicyclical center are the same. SI, 19. It should be observed that this is at variance with the lunar theory of Hipparchus, who maintained that the earth was not in the center of the moon's orbit, which explains the variations in the moon's motion at perigee and apogee.

לב *thoughts, motives, intentions* (as opposed to *maʿaseh* or deeds). In social relations acts count most, while in the relations between man and God motives weigh heaviest. HN, 36b.

לגיון 1/60 of רהט q.v. SA, 5.

ליוה *join, attach.* HN, 26b.

הלוה (1) *join, attach.* HN, 20b, 24b, 26b.
(2) *add.* SI, 47, 53.

לווי *surname* (Comp. Talm. שם לוי). HN, 10b והרוח הוא הל׳ אל הנשמה.

לווים (1) *related.* SI, 3.
(2) two nouns *connected* in construct state. MM, 102.

לוי *relative term.* See quotation under next word.

נלוים *governed* nouns in construct state. MM, 90, 102. מלוה governing noun in construct state. MM, 90, 102.

לויה *relation, comparison.* HN, 9. שהאחד אתה מבין אותו בלא לויה... כי הרוממות הוא לו לבדו... והשני הוא שם לוי וכו׳. See also SI, 33.

לוח *list, table*. See HMT, 81.

למד see *kabed.*

לקות, ליקות *eclipse*. SA, 22, 24; SI, 15; MM, 57. For various stages, see SA, 25.

לשון *sense, meaning*. HN, 18, נאמרת על לשונות רבות HN, 19, לשון חזרה.

לשון מיודע *noun with definite article*. MM, 90. ל׳ מנוכר *noun with the definite article*. MM, 90. ל׳ שעבר *past*. MM, 56, 67. ל׳ עתיד *future*. MM, 56 ל׳ העתיד להיות *future*. MM, 62.

לשון משותף *homonymous expression*, that is, a word of different meanings. HN, 3b. See PT, s.v. שם משותף.

מ

מדה ישרה *standard*. HMT, 8.

מתמוטטת See קטומה מ׳, מצבה מ׳.

מתמוטטים See *ofan*.

תמונה (מון) (1) *geometrical figure*. HMT, 123.
(2) *the inner form* or *the essence*. HN, 41. תמונת הקול וצורתו הפנימית. Maimonides, however, takes pains to show that the term denotes just the accidental and external appearance. See PT.

מופת *proof, demonstration*. HMT, 23, 91.

תמורה (מור) (1) *reverse, opposite, contrary*. HN, 13, 31; MM, 17; SA, 33, 37. See מזלות.
(2) *change*. HN, 2b, 4b; SI, 12. In the Bible and Talmud it means exchange. See 6b התמונה וההילוף where we should read התמורה. See נקודות הת׳. המיר *change, affect*. SI, 57. See also *mazzalot ḥazaqim*.

המרה *changing*. MM, 50. see *koaḥ*. ממיר. See *mazzal, koaḥ*. תמור (1) change. MM, 61. (2) opposite. MM, 5.

מוש *to meet* (prop. to touch). HMT, 9.

מושיקא see *ḥokmat ha-niggun*.

מות *death*, after which man's reward cannot be affected either through his own post-mortem repentance or through the prayers of his children. HN, 32. See HN, LVIII. For five classes of death, see MM, 109.

מזוג *compounded*. MM, 28. See *mazzalot ḥazaqim*.

מזלות see *ḥeshbon, maʿalot, ṣurot mishtanot, galgal, ʾofan*.

מזל אמתי *sign of truth*, that is, Aquarius. MM, 121.

מזלות אפילה *signs underneath the earth*. MM, 149.

מזל הקפה MM, 134, 148.

מזלות חזקים *fixed signs*. Signs are movable (מ׳ תמורה), fixed (חזקים), or flexed (מ׳ משתנים מב׳ גוונים, מ׳ אשר מב׳ גוונים מזלות מזוגים מב׳ גוונים). The fixed signs are: Taurus, Leo, Scorpio, and Aquarius, and they indicate steadfastness and constancy. The so-called movable signs are: Aries, Cancer, Libra and Capricornus; they prophesy lightness and speed. The flexed Signs are: Gemini, Virgo, Sagittarius, and Pisces. MM, 118, 120, 122, 123, 126, 140.

מזל צומח *the ascendant*, the zodiacal sign appearing on the eastern horizon at a certain moment. MM, 120.

מים in the biblical account of creation, another name for form (see *ṣurah*). HN, 3b. See, however, *Kuzari*, IV, 25 (ed. Zifrinowitsch, p. 245): שרצונו במים האלה החומר הראשון בלי איכות אבל תהו ובהו. See also *Kuzari*, V, 2.

מין *genus*, which is a mental creation. MM, 8. Our author evidently subscribes to Abelard's conceptualism. See PT, s.v. *kolelut*. As to its difference from *kolel*, see MM, 7. מ׳ גדול *genus* MM, 7. מ׳ קטן *species*. MM, 7.

מישור See *'ofan*.

מכילה See כול.

מלאכה See *ḥokmah*. מ׳ החזיון *astronomy*. SA, 12.

מלאכת הכוכבים see חכמי מ׳ הכ׳.

מנה *multiply*. HMT, 121. נמנה, מנוי *multiplied*. HMT, 11.

מנין See *ḥokmat ha-minyan*.

מנין שטרות *era of contracts*, Seleucidan era, which dates from the occupation of Babylon by Seleucus Nicator in the autumn of 312 B.C.E. According to A., however, it dates from the beginning of the reign of Alexander the Great, which took place at the close of prophecy, 40 years after the building of the second Temple, or the beginning of the great assembly. SI, 99. See also SI, 101, where A. says: "And the beginning of his kingdom from which we reckon time was on Monday 26 days in Tishri, in the year 3450." This era is also called *malkut Alexander*. SI, 96. See also introd. to HN, note 7. See אברכ״ש, סעדיה. Cf. *Me'or ʿenaim*, ch. 23.

מנועה *impossible*. HN, 8.

מעון *stellar House*. MM, 120. See *bait*.

מציאות *existence*. MM, 16. God first created potential beings, and afterward actual beings. MM, 15. This can only mean the creation of *hyle*. Gutmann (introd., XXVII) refers to a similar view by Abrabanel. See however MM, 8, 10, where it is emphasized that the priority of potentiality is not to be understood temporally but logically or "by nature." Comp. the Cabbalistic view of the priority of the *hyle* in Baḥya on Gen., 1, 1 and in Eṣ Ḥayyim, שער קיצור אבי״ע ch. 10.

מצוא *existing*. MM, 23. **המציא** to exist. SA, 7. But read perhaps **המצא**.

המציא *create*, HN, 42b. **וממציאו אל הטוב**. See also *ibid.*, 4b **אשר יוכל להמציא בארץ**, but read perhaps **להמצא**. See *ibid.*, 32. See also MM, 49.

נמצא, —ים, —ות *existing things, beings*. HN, 1, 2; HMT, XI. MM, 5, 24. All (?) beings are tridimensional. They may be divided into mutables and immutables or into four classes: (1) those that are unchanging in this and in the next world, (2) those unchanging in this but not in the next world, (3) those unchanging neither here nor in the hereafter, (4) those not unchanging here but unchanging in the hereafter. The pure, immaterial form (see *ṣurah*) belongs to the first class, the heavenly bodies to the second, the sublunar beings to the third, and men—the few that are worthy—to the last class. HN, 5–6.

Being consists of three elements: form, negation of form, and time. MM, 16.

ממציע *taking the middle path*, MM, 37.

מקום (1) *space*. See HN, 3b, where A. defines space as "that which envelops the shape of a body all around from the outside," which follows Aristotle's definition of space as the first limit of the containing body. See *Theologie des Arist.* 29. وذلك ان المكان محيط بالشى الذى فيه ويحصره. This view, which takes cognizance of τόπος not of χώρα, of place but not of space, was the traditional view in Jewish medieval philosophy. See my *Problem of Space in Jewish Med. Phil.*, p. 65. The *'or* or the highest self-subsisting form is not in space but is itself the space of the firmament. Comp. Talm. dictum: "The Holy One, blessed be He, is the space of the world." As for pure space or void, we find no express reference, but it seems that A. followed Plotinus in identifying it with the *hyle* or *tohu* (q.v.), which has no qualities, nor substance, nor even existence; which is τὸ μὴ ὄν. "Modern researches," says Windelband, "have made it clear that the Platonic matter is simply space" (*History of Philosophy*, tr. Tufts, p. 129).

(2) *method, standpoint*. HN, 19b **מי הוא הראוי להקרא שב על מקום תשובה נאמנת**. See PT.

מקום אמתי, מ׳ נראה א׳ *true or geocentric place* of a star, that is, that place in the zodiac in which it would be seen by an observer at the center of the earth; while the apparent or observed place (**מקום נראה**)

is that in which it is seen by an observer on the face of the earth. SA, 18, 20.

מקום נראה SA, 27. See *maḳom amitti.*

מרי *irregularity*, as in the moon's orbit. SA, 16, 19.

מריצת *acceleration.* SA, 28.

מושחים *measure.* HMT, 111.

משיחה (1) *measurement, surveying.* HMT, 4. See *ibid.*, XIII, note 3. See also SA, 38, 39.

(2) *area of a surface.* See HMT, 25, 60, 99, 100, 106, 107, et al. The word is often used as parallel to *tishboret* (q.v.), but while the latter sometimes designates volume, I have not found the word *meshiḥah* used definitely in this sense in HMT. It seems therefore probable that the terms *meshiḥah* and *tishboret* in the title of HMT are not a mere redundancy, but are meant to include plane and solid geometry. See *tishboret.* Comp. مساحة measurement, survey, and علم المساحة geometry. The Ar. مساحة is a common word for area.

משך *steadfastness.* MM, 124. נמשך connected. MM, 6.

מושכי חבל הדלי *a constellation in the region of Aquarius.* MM, 121.

מושל v. *kokab.*

ממשלה *comparison.* MM, 54. ממשל *that to which something is compared.* MM, 54. נמשל *something compared.* MM, 54.

משש *to touch, to be contiguous* or *tangential.* HMT, 121.

מושש *touches.* SA, 22. ממשש *tangent.* SA, 30.

מתינות *retardation.* SA, 29.

נ

נבואה *prophecy*, which manifess itself in 3 stages: (1) *amirah* or man's conceiving a thought that he is sure is divinely inspired though he hears no words; (2) *dibbur* or man's hearing a speaking voice but not seeing any form; (3) *raah, ḥazah* or seeing the speaking Form. MM, 42–43. These three stages constitute the key to the Maimonidean classification of prophecy in *Moreh*, II, 45.

מבט *aspect* or a certain angular distance measured on the ecliptic, determining the good or bad effect of the planet, which throws it to the chief points of the horoscope, for example, the Sun. Good aspects are: sextile (60°) and trine (120°), the evil ones are: the semisquare (45°), the square (90°), sesquiquadrate (135°), and opposition (180°). MM, 120, 124. See *qeshet.*

מביט *throwing an aspect*. See *mabbat*. MM, 122.

מבט ששי *sextile aspect*. MM, 120.

מנגדות, מתנגדיות *parallel*. SA, 5, 6.

ניגון See *ḥokmat ha-niggun*.

נוגעים *affect*, *qualify* (in Tibbonian Heb. משיגים). HN, 9b.

נודני v. *ʿolamot*.

נוהג מנהג אחד *resemble each other*, *being alike*. HN, 20b (*ibid*., 27, נהוגים מ׳ א׳), HMT, 100. נוהג המ׳ הזה *acts in such a manner*. HMT, 1; MM, 2. נוהג על סדר אחד *being constant*, *invariable*. HMT, 68.

מנהג *manner*, *way*, *state*. HN, 5; HMT, 1, 88.

הנהגה *manner*, *conduct*, SA, 34.

נזירה, רות *recession*, like that of the five planets, which, when they move in the inner part of their epicycle, recede west, so that, their movement being subtracted from that of the epicyclical center, they appear to retard. This retardation grows until the planet reaches a point where a geocentric line is tangent to the epicycle when it appears to cease moving. Passing this point, moving towards perigee, the planet moves westward so much faster than the epicyclical center moves eastward that it appears to recede and move backwards. Then it reaches the tangential point on the other side of the epicycle, and again apparent cessation of movement. Passing that point, the planet emerges on the external curve of the epicycle and begins to move in the same direction as the epicyclical center, and the irregularity ceases. SA, 31, 32. See also *nazor*, *ḥilluf*.

הזיר, מזיר, מנזיר *cause recession*. See *nezirut*, *nazor*.

נחוץ *swift*, *quick*. SI, 21.

נחמה *repentance*, *contrition*. HN, 19b, 20. In Bible and Talmud it means comfort, consolation.

נחישה *trying*. MM, 66.

נוטה See מצבה נ׳.

נטה *draw a circle* around a center. SA, 18. נטוי *drawn*. SA, 20. הטייה *inclination* of an epicycle from a deferent. SA, 34.

נכוחית, נכוחות *apposition aspect*. See *mabbat*. MM, 124, 126. נכוחי, נוכחיות, נכחיות *parallel*. SA, 2, 6; HMT, 9.

הכר *power of analysis*, *reason*. HN, 5, Comp. *Kuzari*, IV, 25 (ed. Zifrinowitsch, p. 239), ואח״כ זכר הכרת באיכות, where the word means distinction (Ar. תמייז); also the expression יוכרו בכמות ובאיכות "they are distinguished or divided." See also ספר ההכרה, s.v. Saadia.

מנוכר v. *lashon.*

נמיכות v. *ḳeshet.*

נמוס *law, legislative code* (opposite to revealed law). Gr. νόμος. HN, 36, See PT. MM, 118, נימוס.

נסיות *demonstrated, proven* (נס = מופת) ראיות נ׳ HMT, 18. See מופת in PT. Perhaps the word means empirical, being equal to the modern Hebrew term נסיוניות. See next word. Comp. *mofet nisyoni* in Gershom G. Scholem's "Shaarei Zedeq," *Qiryath Sepher* (Jerusalem), I, 136.

נסיון (1) *astrology.* SA, 1. This meaning is derived from the sense of "trying" or "asking for a sign," in Is., 7, 12. Comp. נסיתי, meaning "I divined" in *Targum Onkelos* on Gen., 30, 27 (quoted in Jastrow's *Talm. Dict*).

(2) *research, investigation, experiment*; particularly, *astronomical experiment.* MM, 12, 13, 41, 64, 114; SA, 1.

נפש (1) *soul.* The soul is described in HN, 5, as a form that clothes the body, the meaning being that the soul is not strictly speaking in the body because pure form is not in "space" (see *maqom*), but that it rather surrounds it. See the whole discussion on this subject in Dieterici, *Theologie des Aristoteles*, p. 31. There are three souls or faculties (see *koḥot*) implanted in man: that by which he grows like plants, that by which he moves like all animals, and that by which he thinks (HN, 11). This, of course, is the Aristotelian division into θρεπτικόν, κινητικὸν κατὰ τόπον, νοῦς. Our author states: "some call them powers and others call them souls," alluding perhaps to the controversy between those who believed in a plurality of souls in man and others who maintained psychic unity. See *Eight Chapters of Maimonides*, ch. 1. The first view is Platonic (see *Republic*, 440 A, B, *Timaeus*, 69, 70), while the second view is Aristotelian. See *De Anima*, II, 2. See also *Minḥat Qenaot* by Yehiel of Pisa, p. 68. Our author seems to adhere to the Aristotelian view, as is seen from MM, 58 where A. talks of the "three powers that the human soul possesses." Even in MM, 73, Guttmann (see his introd., XVI) notwithstanding, A. refers to powers and not to souls; though he uses some figurative language. The first soul is called נ׳ המתאוה or appetitive soul, נ׳ מת׳ וצמחה the appetitive and vegetative soul (MM, 55, 58, 73). The second soul is called נ׳ חיה, נ׳ טבעית, נ׳ יצרית, נ׳ בהמית וחיה, רוח חיים (vital soul, animal and vital soul, instinctive soul, natural soul; MM, 55, 58, 73; HN, 10, 12) by virtue of which man is similar to other animals.

The third soul, which makes man similar to celestial beings, is called ב׳ ההוגה, ב׳ דברנית, נשמת חיים, נשמה חכמה, נפש הוגה ודברנית, ב׳ חכמה והוגה. See MM, 55, 58, 59; HN, 10, 11. See also *Ruaḥ Ḥen*, ch. 1. אמרו הראשונים כי האדם יש לו ג׳ נפשות הצומחת והמשכלת והמרגשת וע״ד האמת הוא עצם אחד המקבל אלו הכוחות. There is a state of war between these two souls for supremacy and dominion, and on the degree of relative strength of each power depends the spiritual classification of a man; whether with the wicked, average, or righteous (HN, 11). A. remarks that the majority of philosophers think that the man who struggles with and finally subdues his animal soul, which yearns for mundane pleasures, is greater than the one whose righteous path is not beset with such stumbling blocks, just as the moral degree of the youth who conquers himself is higher than that of the aged; but the more careful thinkers maintain that the thoughts of one who has to struggle and conquer himself are not as pure as those of the person whose life is never ruffled by winds of sin. Hence the saint is superior to the repentant. On p. 2b (*ibid.*) we find *nefashot* together with angels and seraphim and other forms ascribed to the upper world as pure forms that never combine with the *hyle*. This may seem to be a contradiction, for souls do unite with bodies, forming human beings, and belong to the *fourth* kind of form (see *ṣurah*), but see Dieterici's ed. of the so-called *Theology of Aristotle*, p. 83: فنقول ان النفسى لا تهبط باسرها الى هذا العالم السفلى الحسر لا النفس الكلية ولا النفسنا لكنه يبقى منها شى فى العالم العقلى لا يفارقه. See also *ibid.*, 170: وهذا الصورة فى العالم العالى اعنى العقول والانفس. The soul exists before its incarnation and after it is divorced from flesh; that is, it is immortal (*ibid.*, 5). It has four states: health or wisdom, sickness or folly, life or piety, and death or impiety. When the wise and pious man dies, his soul by virtue of its wisdom leaves its body and because of its piety rises and merges forever with the light of the supreme Form. The wise but impious man's soul will leave its body but will rise only as high as the unchanging heavens and will be forever scorched by the sun. The foolish and pious man's soul will be reincarnated until it acquires wisdom wherewith to rise higher than this world. The foolish and impious person's soul will perish like the beast (*ibid.*).

(2) metaphorically: *wisdom*. HN, 17.

נפשיות *psychic*. MM, 55.

נצב (1) *right* (angle). HMT, 3.

(2) *rectangular*. HMT, 117. See זוית נצבה. מוצבי הזוית rectangular, HMT, 58.

מצב, מצב ארוך *prism* (in geom.). HMT, 98.

מצבה חצוייה *triangular prism*. HMT, 99.

מצבה מוצקת *pyramid* (in geom.). HMT, 96, 100.

מצבה מתמוטטת, *frustum*. HMT, 97.

מצבה נוטה *frustum*. HMT, 97.

מצבה עגולה *cylinder*. HMT, 100.

מצבה קטומה *frustum*. HMT, 97.

מצבה קצוצה *frustum*. HMT, 97, note 3.

ניצוץ *ray*. SA, 22. See Kaufmann's note on Barzillai's comm. on *Sefer Yeṣirah* p. 334: "and Bargeloni did not use this term yet."

נקודות היושר = שתי הנקודות. SA, 5, 34.

נקודות היושר *equinoctial points* or the points of intersection of the celestial equator and the ecliptic when the days and nights are equal. These points are at the beginnings of Aries and Libra. SI, 10. MM, 144.

נקודות היתרות *cardinal points of the compass*, quadratures. SA, 21.

נקודת הנכח, נ׳ נ׳ הראש *zenith*. SA, 7, 26.

נקודות התמורה *solstices* or the points of greatest solar declination either north or south. These points are at the beginning of Cancer when the days commence to grow shorter and at the beginning of Capricornus when the day begins to grow longer. SI, 10.

הקף (נקף) *circumference*. HMT, 73.

הקפת העגול *circumference*. HMT, 34.

הקפה (1) *a complete spherical revolution*. Hence different from *sibub* (q.v.), SI, 3, 9, 23, 79.

(2) *surface, circumference*. SA, 4.

(3) *epicycle*. SA, 29.

מקיפים (1) *circumferences*. HMT, 61.

(2) *forming an angle*. HMT, 18.

הקיש *compare*. HN, 2b, 9b, 10b; HMT, 1. In the Talmud it means *to equalize*.

מקשים, מקישים *compare*. SA, 4, 5, 25.

הקש, הקשה *ratio*. HMT, 18, 71.

הקשה ראשונה *first ratio of a proportion*. HMT, 71.

הקשה שניה *second ratio of a proportion*. HMT, 72.

מוקש (1) *related, refer*. HN, 3: שהן מוקשות מדרך אחד.

(2) *analogous*. HMT, 18; SA, 37.

(3) *proportional.* HMT, 19.

(4) *the first or third term of a proportion.* HMT, 71.

נוקש *the second or fourth term of a proportion.* HMT, 71.

נשיאה, —אות *superiority*, which is a relative term compared with *romemut*, which is absolute exaltedness, attributable to God alone. HN, 9b.

נשמה see *nefesh.*

מתנשם *breathing.* MM, 59, 64.

נשמת חיים *the faculty in man whereby he is akin to angels.* This highest soul migrated from Adam to Shet and his descendants, one man for each generation, until it came to Jacob all the sons of whom were privileged to have this soul; so that the Jewish people alone have this highest mental force that justifies resurrection. MM, 59. See *nefesh.* For a comparison with Yehudah Halevi's views, see Ziemlich in *Monatsschrift*, 29, p. 366.

נותנת *meaning*, *denoting*, *signifying.* MM, 28. Usually נ׳ טעם MM, 39, 126.

ס

סבב see קו הסובב. סבוב *circular movement*, SI, 79. See *haqafah.* סביבת הגלגל *rotation of the sphere.* SI, 3.

סבה *cause.* See דרך.

מסב *revolution*, *rotation.* SA, 16.

מסיבה *rotation*, *circular movement.* SI, 20, 76.

סובל (1) *bearing*, *being the substratum of.* HN, 2.

(2) *the deferent of an epicycle.* SI, 20, See רקיע הס׳, גלגל הס׳, אופן ס׳.

סדר see נוהג, הולך. כסדר, על הסדר *regular*, that is, relating to a year in which *Ḥeshwan* is defective (29 days) and *qislew* is full (30 days). SI, 62, 63.

סטרין *columns* (In Talm. Aram. = side), vertical series of figures. HMT, 69.

סך הכל *sum total.* HMT, 65.

הסכמה *agreement.* HN, 36.

סמך *support*, *fulcrum.* SA, 5.

סמן *a mnemonic sign*, esp. that composed of 3 letters, the first letter indicating the day of the week on which New Year's Day will fall; the second, the defectiveness, fullness, or regularity of the year; and the third letter, the first day of Passover (e.g., בח״ה). SI, 65.

מסמנת *denotes.* SA, 5.

מסמרות הרקיע *poles, north and south poles.* SI, 9.

סעדיה ב״ר יוסף ראש ישיבה Saadia Gaon. A. translates a passage from his Arabic work, which A. calls ספר ההכרה (Ar. כתאב אלתמייז. See Malter's *Saadya Gaon*, p. 263). In this passage we have the date of the composition of the book in the following words: השנה הזאת אשר אנו עומדים בה היום היא שנת אלף רל״ח למלכות אלכסנדר והיא שנת ד׳ תרפ״ו לבריאת עולם, which yield the date 926. SI, 96. See *minyan shetarot*. On p. 59 he quotes apparently from a Hebrew work dealing with the fixation of holidays, which is perhaps the ס׳ המועדים. On p. 94, he quotes from a work by Saadia which he describes as ספר אשר חבר להשיב על המינים. Saadia is also mentioned in MM, 2, 48, 98, 104. His *Sefer 'Emunot* is mentioned in MM, 2, 48. His commentary on Daniel, in MM, 2, 98. His ספר הגלוי, in MM, 2.

ספר *number.* MM, 68, 85.

מספר see *ḥokmat ha-mispar.* מ׳ שטוח *a plane number*, that is, the multiplication product of two different numbers. מ׳ מרובע a *square number* or the product of multiplying a number by itself. מ׳ מעוקב a *cubic number*. HMT, 121.

סתומה see *ṣurah.*

סתור *unknown.* HMT, 34; SI, 39.

סתירה, הסתר, מסתור *obscuration of a star* by the light of the sun when in close proximity. SA, 36, 37.

סרטן see *galgal.*

ע

(עבר) מתעבר, (read: פעול) מתעבר אל פועל *transitive verb.* HN, 19b. See PT, s.v. פעל מת׳.

עבור *science of the calendar*. Hence the title of SI. Esp. *intercalation.* See *maḥzor*. SI, 41, 69.

מעוברת (lit. pregnant) *an embolismic year*, one consisting of 13 months. SI, 39.

עגול פגום *segment.* HMT, 64.

עגל *draw a circle.* SA, 20, 18.

נעגל *moving in a circle* SA, 2.

מעגל, מעגיל *draw a circle.* HMT, 76, 77. מעוגל *circular.* HMT, 5, 6, 101. מעגל *circular.* HMT, 102. נעגלות *curving, circular.* HMT 72, 101. מתעגל *revolves, moves in a circle.* SI, 9.

עגול מקיף *circumference.* SA, 2.

עגולה, עיג׳ *circle, sphere*. SA, 2, 5; HMT, 74. See *maṣebah*.

עגולת הגובה v. *'ofan*.

עגלות נוכחיות, עיג׳ נ׳ *latitude circles*, parallels of latitude. SA, 6, 35.

עיגולה קטנה *small circle*, that is, one that does not go through the zenith and the nadir. SA, 6.

עדיפה *increase, margin of difference*. HMT, 60; SI, 11.

עודף *increase*. SI, 11. מעדיף על (1) *more* or *greater than*. HMT, 67. (2) *liberal toward*. HN, 33. See Talm. Dict.

עוון see חטא.

עיון גס *superficial view*. SI, 57, 67. See PT.

מעיינים *investigators*. MM, 2.

על האמת והעיקר *strictly speaking* (as opposed to על הרחבת הלשון). HN, 2.

על דוגמא *loosely speaking*. See דוגמא.

על דרך הדבור see דבור.

על העיקר *chiefly, primarily*. HN, 20; SI, 53. MM, 6, 7, 16. See also *ibid.*, 30b, where it is opposed to למראית העין. See Barzillai, comm. on *Book of Creation.*, p. 56.

העלה *eliminate*. MM, 5.

עלה *cause*. SI, 78. See Barzillai, comm. on *Book of Creation*, p. 92.

מעלה (1) *degree of superiority*. SI, 25.

(2) *degree*, that is, 1/600 of the spherical circle or 1/30 of a sun. SA, 5.

(3) *magnitude of star*. Fixed stars are of six magnitudes. SA, 39.

(4) מ׳ המזלות (Ar. מטאלעה̈) *ascension of a sing* on the equator. Signs are called ארוכות המ׳ of long ascension when they rise slowly carrying along a great part of the celestial equator; those are called קצרות המ׳ that ascend faster and carry along a smaller part of the celestial equator. Comp. אשפירא p. 52 and *Yesod Olam*, II, 15. See also *ḥeshbon ha-mazzalot*, *qedimah*, and *'olamot*.

עלילה *cause*. MM, 9. So Barzillai in his comm. on ס״י p. 31.

עליוני *upper, higher*. HN, 5b.

עולם הבא *the world to come*. One who lives a life devoted to the service of God and holds himself aloof from all wordly relations needs only the Ten Commandments to attain to the life of the hereafter. Indeed the first four Commandments are enough and some think that the first Commandment containing the idea of unity and implying the selection of Israel is sufficient; the rest is calculated to bring happiness in this world for which the above saint has no desire. Hence in the first four Commandments there is mention of the penalty of the hereafter ("He visits the sin of the fathers on the children"), while in the remaining six, mundane happiness such as longevity is offered. One can attain to *ʿolam ha-ba* by believing in God and in the Torah—one can see here the faint traces of a beginning to dogmatize Judaism—and in conduct by "keeping aloof from the affairs of this world and its evil concerns, refraining from any work that is not connected with any *miṣvah*, and by abhorring world possessions and depising wealth and riches" (HN, 37b). "Those separated unto God eat any food they have, not to satisfy a desire for its good taste but to silence the pain of hunger, and they wrap themselves with any garment to protect the body against the cold without being concerned as to whether it is of wool or of flax" (HN, 43). These sombre and ascetic teachings are good Plotinism, which also taught that virtue lies in freedom from matter, in ascetic purification or κάθαρσις, in retirement and απάθεια, that political virtues are a mere stepping stone on the way to a higher life, and that salvation lies not in conduct but in contemplation and in fearing nothing. See *zekut*.

עולמות *worlds*. There are five celestial worlds: (1) העולם הנודני (should we read הנורני = Ar. نيرانى?), which is the light revealed to angels, prophets, and to chosen few at Sinai; (2) ע׳ הרברבנות (other reading: ע׳ הדברנות), which is the divine voice: (3) ע׳ המדע; (4) ע׳ הנפש; and (5) ע׳ היצירה, which is the light hidden for the world to come. These worlds are also called חמשה מעלות and חמשה אורות. MM, 22. Guttmann wonders as to the origin of this strange classification. The idea of five lights is a definite cabbalistic notion. See Baḥya on Gen., 1, 3 Comp. also الانوار الاربعة in Seybold's *Drusenschrift*; *Kitab Alnoqat Waldawair*, 69, 6. Abrabanel on Gen., 1, 5 gives the essence of our author's classification as follows: (1) the emanation on the Pure Intellects, (2) that on the spheres, (3) on the prophets, (4) on the wise, (5) on the souls after death, as reward or punishment.

עמד על *understand*. MM, 2, SA, 41. Ar. وقف على.

עומד (1) *exists*. HN, 2, 2b.
(2) *continues, endures*, HN, 5.

עמוד *perpendicular*. HMT, 8. **עמידה** (1) *rest, stability*. HN, 5; MM, 6. (2) *existence*. HN, 6b. MM, 9. **העמיד** (1) *bring into existence*. HN, 2; MM, 9. (2) *maintain, keep up*. HN, 9. (3) *constitutes* מעמיד את ענינה. SI, 76.

מעמד (1) *position, place.* HN, 2, 4b, SI, 64.
(2) *one of the two parts of a line divided at the foot of a perpendicular*, the longer part being called **מעמד ארוך** or **מעמד גדול**, the other **מעמד קטן** or **מעמד קצר**. HMT, 42, 54.
(3) *crossectional area, thickness.* HMT, 116, **ראוי להציק את מעמדו**.
(4) *starting-point, basis.* SI, 97 (in a quotation from Hai Gaon).
(5) *stellar position.* MM, 116.

(עין) **מעוין** see **מרובע**.

עינוג *pleasure* (HN, 18), which should consist of abstaining from mundane affairs and desires. The word is Talmudical.

מענה *assent, sanction.* MM, 149.

עינוי *self-affliction.* It is meritorious for the wicked who repent to torment themselves with hunger and thirst in order to redeem the soul from carnal bondage, but the righteous whose souls are always free need not afflict themselves (HN, 16).

ענין (1) *manner.* SI, 19, 23. **בענין** *in such a manner as.* HN, 3; HMT, 14.
(2) *essence, characteristic.* SI, 76. See **בעלי הע׳**.
(3) *meaning.* MM, 4.

עצם *substance, essence.* HN, 8, MM, 9, 27.

עקב *cube*, **מעוקב** *cube.* HMT, 97.

עקום (1) *arc.* HMT, 74.
(2) *segment.* HMT, 67.

עיקום *curve.* SA, 4. **עקימה** *curve.* SA, 12. **עקמימה** *curve.* SA, 29.

עקומה *ellipse.* HMT, 68.

עוקם *curve.* HMT, 66. SA, 2, 6, 12. **עקום** *curve.* HMT, 67.

עקמימות (1) *segment.* HMT, 67.
(2) *curve.* SI, 17.

עיקר *principle of religion, dogma.* HN, 37b. As to our author's first efforts at dogmatizing Judaism, see **עולם הבא**. See **על האמת והעיקר, על העיקר**.

עריבה *setting, sinking.* SA, 38.

מערביים *westerners*, planets while "hidden" in the west after sunset because of the close proximity of the sun. When the sun moves beyond this proximity, these planets appear in the east and are called **מזרחיים**. SA, 37.

ערך (1) *magnitude, amount, weight.* HN, 2, 2b; HMT, 7.
(2) *rate of motion.* SA, 18. See *tiqqun.*

נערכים *terms of a proportion.* HMT, 71.

(עשה) מעשה *actuality* (what the Tibbons call פועל as opposed to *koaḥ* or potentiality). See לב. Comp. *Kuzari*, IV, 25 (ed. Zifrinowitsch, p. 239) יציאת הנמצאות אל מעשה. See also SI, 26. MM, 5. See *Monatsschrift*, 1902, p. 195.

עשה see *bara*.

מעושר *decagon*. HMT, 10.

מעתיקים *adherents of the theory of metempsychosis*. A. regards this theory as sheer folly. MM, 51. Guttman (*Monatsschrift*, 1903, p. 549) calls attention to NH, 5 where the notion of the return of the soul to the same *human* body is affirmed. It is the transmigration of the soul through beasts that is repudiated. See *Minḥat Ḳenaot*, by Yehiel of Pisa, 90.

נעתקות *transmigrate* (of souls). MM, 51.

פ

(פוץ) מפיץ, הפיץ *emanates*. HN, 4b; MM, 22. When immovable matter composed of form and *hyle* had come into being, there took place a second emanation of light from the self-subsisting form, which spread over the firmament and moved from point to point until it gave rise to the movable spheres, which do not change their form, and finally to the three classes of animate beings floating in the water, moving on the earth, and flying in the air, which constitute the three primary (אמהות q.v.) species of motion added to the circular movement of the heavenly bodies. See *ṣurah*.

פילוסופיא, פילוסופי *philosophy*. SA, 10, 11.

פילוסופים *geometricians*. HMT, 20. See SI, 37 where it means astronomers. No sharp line of demarcation was drawn between philosphy and mathematics.

פילוסופים אלהיים *metaphysicians*. MM, 10. See PT.

פנות, פינה *boundary*, *limit*. פינה וגבול HN, 8, 13.

הפסד *destruction*, *decay* (as opposed to הוויות). SI, X. See PT. See *kokab*.

נפסד *perishable*, *destructible*. See SI, IX, However. in our text of HN, 3b we have *nifrad*. See MM, 58.

פועל *verb*. HN, 19b. MM, 62. See פעלים MM, 42.

פעול *object* הפועל הזה אינו מתעבר אל פועל (*ibid.*), where the last word is evidently a corruption for פעול.

פעולה *verb*. HN, 10b, 19b. MM, 62; SA, 1.

נפרד *unlike*, *different*. HMT, 98.

פירוד *difference*, SA, 6.

הפריט *specify*. SI, 32.

מפורסמת see ה"א המודיעה והמ׳.

מפורסם *expressed*. HN, 6b. See שם.

פירוש *exegesis*. One should deviate from a literal rendering of the Bible for the sake of a philosophical interpretation, provided it does no violence to the language (HN, 4). Our author here seems to defend *ta'wil*, calling it דרך הישר. See PT. See גלגל המפריש and אופן המפרש.

פרוֹש *plane*, *surface*. HMT, 8. פרוש ישר *even plane*, *smooth surface*. HMT, 8.

פרושים *abstemious*, *saintly*. Such men disdain wordly matters and follow Ben ʿAzai, who assets: "Let the world be perpetuated through others." (HN, 37).

פירוש *elimination*, *removal*. MM, 6.

נפרש *different*. SI, 19. MM, 51.

מפורש *definite*, with the definite article. MM, 68.

מפריש see *'ofan mafrish*.

פשוט *simple*, *elementary*. HN, 1b. Minerals are the simplest beings on earth because they are mutable in form and are not endowed with the power of growth. Hence their matter is different from that of the firmament, which is not mutable. See SI, 39 for explanation of our word.

פשוט בלתי מתחלק *simple*, *indivisible*. HMT, XI.

פשוטה (1) *common or ordinary year*, as distinguished from a leap year or an embolismic year. The literal meaning of the term is, according to A., *nude*. SI, 39.

(2) *commonness* (of the year). Opposed to כבושה (q.v.). SI, 113. See צורה פשוטה.

פשיטת הנשמה *disengagement of the soul* to which wisdom is the key HN, 5b.

מופשט *separate*, *different* (or perhaps *simple*). See HN, 1b.

פשע see חטא.

פתוחה *open*, *receptive*, as matter is receptive for form. HN, 3. See *ṣurah*.

פתילות *irregularity* of the apogee's being in line not with the geocentric point but with another point on the diameter. It occurs only at the sixth or third part of the month. SA, 22. This applies to the moon, but other planets have similar irregularities. See SA, 32, 34. See also *ḥilluf* and *tiqqun*. פ׳ גובה ושפל irregularities of the *line of apsides* in an epicycle, beginning with perigee and apogee of the deferent and ending with one of the two nodes when it clings to the plane of the zodiac. SA, 34. פ׳ שני מרחקים אמצעיים irregularities of mean distances, beginning with one of the nodes and ending with the line of apsides when the epicycle reaches the maximum of inclination from the deferent. SA, 34.

נפתל *irregular*. The epicyclical line of apsides inclines east or west from the cause of the epicyclical center because it is governed in its revolution not by its own center, the center of the deferent, or of the earth, but by a point on a straight line with the earth's center and as distant from that center as the latter is distant from that of the deferent. It is also called גובה בינוני or mean apogee. SA, 21, 32.

צ

צד *viewpoint*. MM, 9; SA, 1.

צדקה see *zekut*.

(צוק) מוצקת ,מוצק *pyramid*, *cone*, *conic*. HMT, 96, 100. See ,מרובע מצבה, עגולה.

מוצקות חצובות, מ׳ קצוצות *frusta*. HMT, 104.

מצוקה *conicity*; *tapering*, gradual diminution of thickness in an elongated solid. HMT, 80.

תצוקה = מצוקה (q.v.). HMT, 104, 116, 117.

מצוק *narrow*, (as opposed to *raḥab*). HN, 4b.

מוצק הצל *umbra of an eclipse*, which is conically shaped. SA, 23.

צורה (1) *form* (HN, 2; HMT, XI), that is, the actuality or ἐνέργεια of matter or *hyle*, which is potentiality or δύναμις. It is the essence of a thing, the λόγος τῆς οὐσίας, or that which gives being to a thing and its essential attributes. Philosophers, A. informs us, start their inquiries with the form of man because he is the culminating point of all creation, endowed with something no other creature has—rationality, which is his form just as locomotion is the form, the distinguishing essence, of animals, and growth that of plants (HN, 1b). All material, including heavenly bodies, may be subsumed under the term body or *guf* (q.v.), which may be defined as something that is tridimensional. This definition points to a synthesis of form (tridimensionality) and *hyle* ("something"); the former is existible though not perceptible *per se* while the latter needs form for its very existence as it is *per se* mere potentiality. Form, like the *hyle*, falls into two classes: (1) the simple or the closed and sealed form (צורה סתומה וחתומה, HN, 2; צ׳ פשוטה, *ibid.*, 4), which never combines with the *hyle*, and (2) the hollow and open form (צורה חלולה ופתוחה, *ibid.* 2), which may be joined to the *hyle*. Form and *hyle*—one as a reality and the other as a potentiality—were hidden with God or Pure Thought (once מקום but twice מחשבה טהורה, q.v.) until the time, before which there was no time (see *zeman*), when Pure Thought "stengthened" the sealed form to clothe itself in its light, which no *hyle* can touch, and to produced the forms of angels and seraphim and "souls" (see *nefesh*) and all other forms of the upper world. The expression "Pure Thought" reminds one strongly of the Plotinic νοῦς and of the Philonic Logos, the mediator between God and the world, the operative reason in which are comprehended what Philo called ἰδέαι, δυνάμεις, or λόγοι, which are identical with the Greek "Daemons" and the Jewish angels. Comp. also *Kuzari*, IV, 25 (ed. Zifrinowitsch, 245): והקדים רוח אלהים והוא רוח הקודש ממנה נבראים המלאכים הרוחניים ובה מתחברות הנפשות הרוחניות. Concerning *ruaḥ hakadosh*, see Barzillai (comm. on *Book of Creation*), 185. Moreover the first immaterial form produced by Pure Thought, the generating Light, seems to correspond to the Neoplatonic World-Soul, the product of the suprasensible νοῦς, containing in itself a plurality of eternal ideas, which it seeks to project upon the sensible world, and generating the λόγοι σπερματικοί, which are the forms of all things. The light emanated upon the hollow and open form thereby causing it to be coupled first and inseparably with the pure *hyle*, giving rise to the sky; and after, with the "dregs and lees" of the *hyle*, producing all bodies, immutable and stationary, like the four elements and the plants (HN, 2, 2b). The form is what the Torah calls *bohu* (q.v.) and also *mayim* (q.v.), while the simple, closed, and sealed form, actualizing all things and surrounding all heavens, is called *'or* (q.v.), which was created on the first day (*ibid.*, 3, 3b).

So far we have three different forms: (1) the sealed form, which is the light created on the first day, (2) the open form inseparably combined with matter, constituting the firmament created on the second day, (3) and the open form separably combined with matter, composing the creations of the third day, some of which (e.g., minerals) change their form but cannot extend it, while others (e.g., plants) do possess this power of extension. It should be observed that the author is not quite consistent, for here he thinks of *ṣurah* as physical or external form only, which grows with the growing flower, but not of the internal or metaphysical form, which is unaffected by growth, which is in fact, as stated above, growth itself. After immovable matter came into being, a second emanation took place and the light of the self-existing form spread over the firmament, moving from point to point, causing the form that has been joined to the *hyle* to change its place, thus giving rise to the immutable but moving planets; and the light spread further until it reached mutable matter and produced moving animal beings (*ibid.*, 4b).

And here we come back to our starting-point, to man. We have seen that form falls into three classes; namely the self-existing form, the inseparable form such as that of the heavenly bodies, and the separable form, moving from matter to matter but having no independent existence. To complete the classification, reason demands a form that is separable and can exist independently after it leaves its matter; and that indeed is the form of man or his soul (*ibid.*, 5), which is immortal except in the case of the ignorant and the wicked (*ibid.*, 5b). Our author's attempt—which he takes as a duty, see *perush*—to harmonize the Biblical account of creation with Neoplatonic cosmogony current in his day, is interesting and novel. Yet, one is inclined to ask, how can *bohu* mean form when the closed and sealed form that is the form of forms is identified with *'or*, which was created on the first day and hence came after *bohu*? Moreover, what does it mean that the first pure, forever immaterial form was *created*, when, as stated at the beginning, it had reality even when it was in the bosom of Pure Thought?

(2) *geometrical figure*. HMT, 6.

(3) *horoscope*. MM, 120.

צורה פנימית *the inner form* (as distinguished from external form or physical appearance), or that which constitutes the nature or the essence of a thing. HN, 41. See *temunah*.

צורת הדוב *the Bear* (a constellation). MM, 112.

צורה חיונית *vital form*, the complex of one's life-forces. MM, 64.

צורות משתנות *flexed signs*. MM, 145. See *mazzalot*.

צייר *to form*. MM, 64. **מציירים** *draw*, *paint*. MM, 63. See *koaḥ meṣayyer*. **מצטיירת** *is formed*. MM, 7.

ציור *reason*, *proof*. HN, 38. Cf. Ar. **תצוֻּר**.

צלילות *sound*. MM, 42.

הצלים *to form, to shape.* MM, 54.
צלמניות *formal, physical, external.* MM, 55.
צלצלות *sound.* MM, 42.
צלע see מרבה.
צמידות *attachment, constancy.* HN, 20.
צומח v. *mazzal ṣomeah.*
(צרף) מצטרף *formed out of a verbal root, verbal form.* HN, 19b.

ק

קבלה (1) *tradition, transmission.* HMT, 11, 18; SI, 27, 35. MM, 14. See טעמים מקובלים.
(2) *post-Mosaic Scriptures.* MM, 83. מספר דניאל ורואים שהקץ מפורש בו יותר משאר ספרי ק׳. This usage, though talmudic, is very rare in post-talmudic literature. Comp. P.T. Ginzberg's note.

הקבלה *the moon's facing the sun in an eclipse.* SA, 25. הק׳ אמתית the moment when the moon's true place (see *maqom amitti*) is 180° from the sun's true place, so that the two luminaries are at the antidopal poles of the zodiacal diameter. This happens at half-months. SA, 25.

מקבילות *parallel.* HMT, 50, 111. SA, 2, 22, 25.

קיבוע *the "fixation" of the New Moon* or *a holiday*, whether it should be on the day of the *molad* or postponed. See *Yad, qiddush ha-ḥodesh,* V, 1, where it is called קביעות. The days suitable for the fixation of *Tishri* are בגה״ז, which are also called ארבעה שערים or "four gates," which help in determining whether the year is regular, defective, or full and on what day of the week Passover will fall. SI, 63. See *sha'ar.*

קבץ *to add.* HMT, 81. נקבץ (1) *he added, composed.* HMT, XI, 56, 63, 64.
(2) *multiplication-product.* HMT, 98. התקבץ *be added.* HMT, XI.

נקדם *preceding.* HMT, 33; HN, 23b; MM, 8.

מקבילה *parallel.* SA, 25.

קדמון (1) *uncreated, eternal.* MM, 10.
(2) *former sage*, that is, of the Talmud. MM, 19.

קדימה *priority*; (1) ק׳ בזמן (2) קדימת הטבע (3) ק׳ הסדר (4) ק׳ המעלה (5) ק׳ עלילה or ק׳ גררא MM, 8, 9. For the Aristotelian origin of this classification, see Guttmann, introd., XV. See also *Ruaḥ Ḥen*, ch. 8. See also *Metaph.*, VII, IX, 8, and Dieterici, *Alfarabi*, 1892, p. 134.

מוקדם *placed before its logical place.* והכתוב הוא מ׳ ומאוחר (HN, 16). "The verse is a violation of logical order." Comp. Talm. אין מ׳ ומאוחר בתורה where the middle two words mean an *observance* of logical —

or chronological—order. See also MM, 9. מתקדם *placed before its logical place*. HN, 23b. שעייני הכתובים האלה מתקדמים ומתאחרים. See מתאחר, מאוחר.

קו האמצעי *meridian*. SI, 7.

קו האורך *equator*. SI, 7. See אורך.

קו המישור *equator*. SI, 19.

קו המקיף *circumference*. HMT, 34.

קו הסובב *circumference*. HMT, 62.

קו עקום *curve, arc*. HMT, 65.

קו מעוקם *curve, arc*. HMT, 81.

קו השוה *equator*. SI, 6.

קום see מקום.

הקים *create, form*. MM, 8.

הקמה *creation, formation*. MM, 8.

קיום *creation*. MM, 28.

נתקיים (1) *came into being*. HN, 4b אחר שנ׳ הגוף במקומו.
(2) *to be unchanging*. *Ibid*., 5b, 6.

מקיים *give' existence to, realize*. HN, 3. המכסה את התהו והמ׳ אותו. MM, 8.

קיימא (1) *existence*. HN, 2b.
(2) *permanence*. HN, 5b.

קול see משמע הקול.

קוטב *celestial pole*. SI, 9; MM, 113.

קטומה, ק׳ הראש *a trapezoid* (a quadrilateral that has two and only two of its sides parallel). HMT, 53. See ק׳ מצבה and חצי ק׳.

קטומת הראש חלופה *a trapezoid with unequal legs*. HMT, 54.

קטומה מתמוטטת *a trapezoid one leg of which forms an obtuse angle with its base*. HMT, 57.

קטומת ראש שוה *an isosceles trapezoid*. HMT, 54.

(קטע) מקוטע *a figure bounded by two straight lines and by one curve*. HMT, 94.

קוטר *diameter*. HMT, 9.

קוטר הצל *diameter of eclipse*: at lunar apogee, 77′ of lunar epicycle; at perigee, 92′. SA, 24.

קל *the first conjugation*. As opposed to כבד (q.v.). HN, 19b.

קנה *acquire, obtain*. SA, 23.

קנין (1) *acquisition*. MM. 5.
(2) *creation* MM, 29.

קץ *Messianic era*. See MM, 1, 5. See *ge'ullah*.

קצוב MM 29. Read חצוב.

קצב, קוצב, קצבה *rate, amount, measure, magnitude.* SA, 2, 5.

קצב מנין *definite amount.* HMT, 2.

קצוצות *frusta.* HMT, 80, 104.

קצר *defective, imperfect.* HN, 36. See PT.

מקצר *failing, having only partial success.* HN, 9.

קרוב *approximation, inaccuracy.* HMT, 3, 5, 62; SA, 20.

קרן *angle.* HMT, 4.

קורות *accidents, qualities.* MM, 8.

מקרה *accident, quality.* MM, 7.

קשת *arc.* HMT, 65. See *galgal.* In SI, 15, it means declination or the distance of a point—here the zenith—from the celestial equator.

קשת חצי היום *astronomic meridian* or the hour circle passing through the zenith. SI, 9; SA, 35.

קשת נמיכות *obliquity of ecliptic*, the intercepted arc between the ecliptic and the celestial equator. According to Ptolemy, it is 23°51′, and according to Arabian astronomers—23°35′. SA, 5.

קשת שלישית *trine aspect* or a separation of 120°. A good aspect. See *mabbat.* MM, 134.

קשת רביעית *square aspect* or a separation of 90°. An evil aspect. See *mabbat.* MM, 129.

קשת שתות *sextile aspect*, that is, a separation of 60° between two planets. A good aspect. See *mabbat.* MM, 129.

קשת מראה *arc of visibility*, that is, the arc from which a Sign is visible. MM, 149.

ר

נראה v. *amitti.*

מראות *aspects.* MM, 153. See *mabbat, qeshet.*

ראשים *elements: matter, form, and non-being.* MM, 5.

רבוי *plurality.* HMT, 1.

רבוי וגדול *growth, capacity to grow.* HN, 1b.

מרבה הצלעות,—עים *polygon.* HMT, 121.

רבוע (1) *area.* HMT, 23. רבוע המרובע ואם תרצה אמור תשבורת המרובע. See also 101.

(2) *volume.* HMT, 101. רבוע מוצקן.

(3) *multiplication.* HMT, 13.

רבוע (*rabuʿa*) *square.* HMT, 23.

מרובע (1) *quadrilateral.* HMT, 3, 23.

(2) *square*, that is, the product of a number multiplied by itself. HMT, 13.

מרובע ארוך *rectangle.* מ׳ דומה למעוין rhomboid. מ׳ מעויין *rhombus.* מ׳ מושש לעגול *a circumscribed equilateral.* מ׳ נכוחי *parallelogram.* מ׳ נפתל *irregular quadrilateral.* מ׳ נצב *rectangle.* מרובע רבוע *square* (a figure having four equal sides and four right angles). HMT, 121. מ׳ שוה *square.* HMT, 25.

רביעה *quadrature*, *quarter-month.* SA, 20.

רביעית v. *mabbaṭ*, *qeshet.*

רברבנות v. *'olamot.*

רגע *minute*, 1/60 of a degree of a circle. SI, 16.

רגעי רגעים, רגעים שניים *seconds*, each one being 1/60 of a minute. *ibid.*

רהט, רהטון *minute, or 1/6(of a degree.* SA, 5.

רוח חיים see *nefesh.*

נרוחת see *zawit.*

רוחניים *spiritual.* MM, 55.

רומים, רומי רומים. רום גבוה, ר׳ גבה, ר׳ רומים *exaltation*, or the highest height. Each planet has a region of 90° in the zodiacal belt wherein it is at the very height of its influence. Thus the Sun, from Aries 20° to Cancer 19°, is at the height of its lowness (גובה שפילה); from Cancer 20° to Libra 19°, it is at its lowest lowness (שפל שפילה); from Libra 20° to Capricornus 19°, it is at its low height; and from Capricornus 20° to Aries 19°, it is at its very height. MM, 10–12, 144. See also ברייתא דמזלות, 14. In Aries 19°, the Sun is in *exaltation* and has the most influence.

רום *apogee.* SA, 22.

רוחב, מרחב *latitude*, the distance of a point from the ecliptic. SA, 8, 26. It is measured on a line from the zodiacal pole over the given star to the zodiacal belt. SA, 33. נרחב *in latitude.* SA, 36. מתרחב *moves away from* the ecliptic. SA, 11, 36.

רוחב, ר׳ הארץ *latitude.* SI, 7, 15. So called because the inhabited part from north to south is shorter than that extending from east to west. SI, 14. See ישוב.

הרחבת לשון *loose speech, inexactness.* See HN, 3 (as opposed to על האמת והעיקר), 20b (as opposed to על משמע הפעולה). See HMT, 101; SI, 22, 33. MM, 16. Ḥarizi also uses this expression in his translation of the *Guide* for the Ar. אתסאע פי אלקול, while Tibbon uses הרחבה במאמר, for which see PT.

רחוק מ... *inapplicable to, incongruous with.* HN, 9b.

נרחק *keeping aloof.* HN, 18.

מרחק see גובה גדול.

מרחקים *dimensions.* HMT, 98. MM, 113.

מרחקים אמצעיים *points midway between the nodes.* SA, 34.

מרחק קצה *extreme distance.* SA, 30.

מריץ *accelerates* (as opposed to ממתין). MM, 117.

מרכבה *complexity, compositeness.* HN, 1b. But read perhaps הרכבה. See however *Gabirol*, ed. Davidson, p. 176, note 54.

מתרכבות *compounded.* HMT, 68.

מרכז *center.* HN, 24; HMT, 9. See *ofan.*

מרכז הקפה *epicyclical center*, which is at apogee at conjunction and at half months, thus making two revolutions around the deferent in one month. SA, 18, 30.

רע (1) *sin* or *evil of the heart*, evil thoughts and intentions, as opposed to *resha*ʿ, which refers to deeds and speech. HN, 33b.

(2) *physical evil* or *suffering*. Our author discusses the origin of evil in HN, 30–33. Is God the cause of our suffering? It might be said, we are told, that evil is only apparent—and this is the view of the Karaite Joseph al-Basir who lived in the beginning of the eleventh century—but some thinkers find it hard to adopt such an attitude. Others say that pleasure is sent by God unconditionally and pain conditionally, contingent upon the refusal of the sinful to repent, to which A. objects because pleasure is also conditional upon the enduring of the righteous in their righteousness. Still others maintain that evil is only negative, the absence of good. God merely withdraws His pleasure and pain naturally ensues as darkness comes when light goes out. This Plotinian view, which Abraham ibn Daud (*Emunah Ramah*, ed. Weil, 93) and Maimonides (*Moreh*, III, 10) accepted, did not appeal to our author, perhaps because of his general sombre and ascetic temperament—just as the sombreness of Schopenhauer led that philosopher to take a contrary position that pleasure is negative, the absence of pain. It is really too easy and theoretic a way of cutting the Gordian knot. A. maintains that God is the origin of both good and evil, that although in the world to come God exercises loving-kindness and charity, in this world He reigns with *justice*. However, the suffering of the righte-

ous, as in the case of Job, is in the nature of a test and a trial and is followed by a double measure of reward.

רקיע *sky* (what Maimonides and later writers would call *galgal*). There are eight skies, one lower than the other, the highest all-embracing sky being called רקיע ראשון. SI, 16. See PT, s.v. *galgal.*

רקיעים *spheres.* Some philosophers think they are nine in number, others ten, but astronomers know only of eight spheres. SA, 11. See *'ofan.* Maimonides (see PT) speaks of nine, while Gabirol in his *Keter Malekut* sings of ten spheres.

רקיע שמיני *eighth sphere*, highest, westward moving, and diurnal. SA, 8.

רקיע הסובל *the deferent of the epicycle*, that is, a circle upon the circumference of which another circle or epicycle moves, carrying the body of a planet. SI, 19.

רשום *definite, clearly defined.* SI, 22.

רושם *impresses.* נרשם *impressed.* MM, 41.

רשע see נפש, רע.

ש

שביע *one seventh.* HMT, 63, 64. שביעית *one seventh.* HMT, 61.

משובעות *heptagons.* HMT, 76.

שברים (1) *something worthless.* SI, 81.
(2) *Segments.* HMT, 64.
(3) *fractions.* SI, 37. SA, 4.

שבר *minute, 1/60 of a degree.* "And the wise men of Ishmael call it *sheber.*" שבר שני *second, 1/60 of a minute.* SA, 5.

שובר *refutes, answers an objection.* HN, 31; SI, 54; MM, 74. נשברים. MM, 3.

שבר *to survey, to find the area.* HMT, 59 המשבר שני המשולשים ההם ומצרף תשברתם. See next word.

תשבורת (1) *geometry.* Guttmann—see HMT, XIII, note 3—connects this word, which appears in the title of HMT, with Ar. شبر meaning "measured by the span." This is strange, for the author himself connects it with تكسير See HMT, 23 תשבורת המרובע כאשר אומרים במדינת הארץ בל״ע תכסיר. Thus also ibn Tibbon in *Perush Millot Zarot*; ת׳ שם לחכמת המדות חדשוהו אשר לפנינו ונראה שקראום כן בעבור שבלשון ערבי קוראים חלקי המדות שברים from which it is evident that he too connects it with كسر See PT, s.v. *tishboret.*

(2) *area*. See quotation under *tishboret* (1). See also HMT, 66, 67, et al. and SA, 38.

(3) *volume* (solid contents). HMT, 99 תהיה מונה את משיחתו במנין הגובה ויעלה בידך תשבורת המצבה. The word *tishboret* therefore in the title of HMT, probably has the added meaning of solid geometry. See *meshiḥah*.

שביתה *cessation*. HN, 27b.

משוגע *Mohammed*. Concerning him A. says ותחלת טעותו היתה בחדש אב משנת י״ב למחזור רל״א והוא ד׳ שפ״ב. SI, 100. This corresponds to the year of the *hejra*, but I do not know what particular event he referred to as having occurred in the month of Ab. Mohammed's arrival at Kufa according to the Jewish tradition took place on the Day of Atonement. See also MM, 96, 97.

תשובה *repentance*. As to the kinds of "men of penitence" see *adam*. Repentance that vouchsafes life in this world and atonement in the next, must consist of three things: cessation from sin, cessation from thinking and speaking about sin, and the fear of God as a motive for the change of heart (HN, 27b). A premature death, however, is averted by a change of action even without that motive, which gives it a religious and moral character (*ibid.*, 28).

השיב *to translate*. SI, 39.

שוה *uniform* מדת חודש הלבנה הש׳ SI, 57. See גלגל, מהלך.

שור See *galgal*.

שטוח *plane*. SA, 2. See *zawit*.

שטח *plane*, *surface*. HMT, 8.

שים *regard*. HN, 6b. See PT.

שכלל *constitute*, *distinguish*. HMT, XI. The Tibbons would say מעמיד (q.v. See also PT), Ḥarizi מתקן.

שכונים *neighboring*, *adjacent*. SI, 27.

שכינות *resting*, as applied to God, it is to be taken negatively only, that is, the absence of motion and change. HN, 9b. MM, 31.

השליך *subtract*, *take away*. SI, 45.

שלשיים *seconds*. HMT, 70. A second is 1/60 of a minute, which is 1/60 of a circumferential degree, which is one of the 88 parts into which a circumference is divided.

שלישיי *1/60 of a second* (in angular magnitude). SA, 5.

משולש *triangle*. HMT, 6, 10. מ׳ מתחלף הצלעות *a triangle having no equal sides*. HMT, 10. מ׳ שוה *equilateral triangle*. HMT, 38. מ׳ שווה הצלעות

equilateral triangle. HMT 38. מ׳ שוה השוקים *isosceles triangle.* HMT, 10.

משולש הצל *umbra of an eclipse,* which is in the form of a triangle. SA, 23.

שמות *nouns.* HN, 3; MM, 42. שם לוי *a relative term.* HN, 9b.

שם מיודע, ש׳ מ׳ ומפורסם *noun with definite article.* MM, 29, 90. See *lashon.*

שם מנוכר *indefinite noun.* MM, 28.

ש׳ נדבקים (also דבוקים) בתיבות *hendiadys.* HN, 9, 9b.

משומן *octagon.* HMT, 121.

משמע, משמעת *means.* HN, 9b. See also *ibid.*, 10b, 27. In the Talmud, it is used as a noun.

משמע הלשון (1) *etymology.* HN, 3.
(2) *linguistic sense* (in distinction from ethical or religious significance). HN, 19b.

למשמע הקול *superficially.* HN, 31.

שמש *planet.* MM, 10, 12, 23.

שנה *a year* or a complete revolution of the sun around the zodiac. A year is either *peshutah,* common, or *me'uberet,* embolismic. The common year consists of 354 days distributed in 6 full months and 6 defective months if regular (*keseder,* q.v.), 355 days if perfect (*shelemah'* q.v.), in which case both Ḥeshwan and Kislew are full, and 353 days if defective (*ḥaserah*), in which case both Ḥeshwan and Kislew are defective. The embolismic year consists of 384 days if regular, 385 days if perfect, and 383 days if defective (SI, 58). The exact length of a lunar year is 354 days and 8 876/1080 hours if common and 383 days and 21 589/1080 hours if embolismic (SI, 46). The arrangement of defective, regular, and perfect years is designed to regulate the occurrence of the New Moons and festivals so as not to lead to a violation of the Sabbath or any other commandment (SI, 58), and to observe the traditional formula: לא בד״ו פסח לא גה״ז עצרת לא אד״ו ר״ה ולא אג״ו יוה״כ (SI, 59). A defective year will be either preceded or followed by a perfect year, though there may be two consecutive *perfect* years, for the reason that defectiveness is due only to one thing, to a lunar acceleration, while perfection may be due either to lunar retardation or to need for making up a defection (SI, 57). As to the length of the solar year (*shenat ḥammah*), there are three views; the first view measures the year by the return of the sun *to the same star* and therefore arrives at a conclusion that it is more than 365 days and 6 hours, but this is based on the erroneous idea that the fixed stars do not move, whereas in point of fact they do move at the rate of 1½ degree per 100 years. The second view is that taught in astronomic classrooms, that it takes just 365 days and 6 hours, but this is inexact though sufficient pedagogically. The third is that of Hipparchus and Ptolemy that the year should be measured from the moment the sun enters a certain zodiacal constellation—whether an equinoctial or a solstitial point—to its return, so that the length of the solar year is not affected by the motion of the fixed stars and is found to consist of 365 days, 5 993.60/1080 hours (SI, 76–79). The difference between these two last views will affect the measurement of the *tequfah* (q.v.).

שנה פרסית *Persian year, or 365 full days.* SA, 31. In SA, 19: ש׳ מצרית.

שניים *minutes.* HMT, 70. SA, 5. See PT, where it means "seconds."

ששי *mabbat.*

שעות ישרות *equinoctial hours* at each of which the sun moves over 15° by day as well as at night. שעה עקולה *uneven hours*, that is, 1/12 of the time from sunrise to sunset or the reverse. On parallels of latitude where days and nights are not equal a day-hour would be longer or shorter than a night-hour. ש׳ שוות *uniform hours*, each one being 1/24 of a day and a night together, so that a long day may have more than 12 hours but the day-hour equals the night-hour, that is, 15°. SA, 6.

שער *one of the four days* called "four gates" on which New Year's day may fall (בגה״ז). See קיבוע. The גבול or limit of a given "gate" is a stretch of time, so that if the *molad* of Tishri falls in that limit, then we can find out, from a certain mnemonic sign, the day of the week on which Passover will fall, and the number of days in Ḥeshwan and Kislew. Thus, if the limit of the first gate (i.e., Monday) is from Saturday noon to the end of 20 490/1080 hours of Sunday and if the *molad* of Tishri is within this limit, then the corresponding mnemonic sign is בח״ה, which means that the year is *ḥaser* or defective (i.e., Ḥeshwan and Kislew will have 29 days each), and the first day of Passover will be on Thursday. SI, 64, 71.

שיעור *magnitude, quantity.* HN, 1b; HMT, 12; MM, 69. See *ḥokmat ha-sheʿur.*

משער *measure.* SA, 30.

משפט see *zekut.*

שפל, ש׳ רום, ש׳ גובה הרום *perigee*. SA, 11, 12.

משקל *grammatical form*. HN, 19b.

שרש (1) *root of a verb*. SI, 38; MM, 41.
(2) *principle, basis*. SI, 92.

שרשים *elements* (as form and *hyle*). HN, 2. See also *ibid*., 1: שרשי הנמצאות, and *ibid*., 1b. שורשי יצירתו.

משושה, משושת,—תות *hexagon*. HMT, 76, 78, 99.

שיתוף, שתוף *homonymity* or identity of word with diversity of meaning. HN, 3b. 6b. MM, 62. שותפות *homonymity*. SI, 34. משותף *homonymous*. HN, 3b משתתף עם *having in common with*. HN, 11, 26b.

שתות v. *qeshet*.

ת

תאומים see *galgal*.

תאריך *history*. MM, 138. Arabic. See *Yesod ʿOlam*, IV, 17.

תיבות See *shemot*; letter. תיבת הא׳ MM, 28. תיבת וו׳ MM, 92, 104, 106. See *shemot*.

תהו in the Biblical account of creation, corresponds to the Greek *hyle*, for it denotes something devoid of form, magnitude, and even existence. HN, 2b. Comp. *Kuzari*, V, 2. See, however, *bohu*. See also Naḥmanides on Gen., 1, 1, who states: "and this matter called *hyle* is called in the sacred language *tohu*," and quotes a Midrash, which seems to be the source for the identification of *tohu* with matter and *bohu* with form.
So also Baya on Gen., I, 2 and *ʿEṣ Ḥayyim*, קיצור אבי״ע ch. 10.

תהום identified by our author with *tohu*. HN, 3. ותהום מלשון תהו והמם נוספת בו. Comp. ibn Ezra on Gen., 1, 2, אמר הגאון תהו שהוא מתהום וזה לא יתכן כי מם תהום שרש.

תיכוני *internal*. MM, 63.

תוכן (1) *arrangement, order*. SA, 1.
(2) *size*. SA, 4. See PT.

תכונה *sphere*. SA, 4. תכונות *spheres*. SA, 2. See PT and Ginzberg's note. See *kun*.

תורה See *adam*.

תחית המתים *resurrection of the dead*, after redemption and only for Jews. Dates: either 5208 or 5228 A.M. See MM, 46, 71, 79, 87, 102. See *ge'ullah*.

לכתחלה (1) *prima facie, superficially*. HN, 30.
(2) *directly*. MM, 5, 15.

תולה *connects.* HN, 14. תלוי *depending for its existence on something else, accidental.* HN, 2b שהזמן תלוי.

התלות *dependence.* HN, 2.

תלי = תנין q.v. SA, 17.

נתלה *depending.* MM, 6.

תמור See *mur.*

תנין *Dragon,* intersection of two spheres, especially the celestial equator and the zodical belt cutting each other at Aries (called ראש ת׳) and at Libra (called זנב ת׳). The former intersection, the Dragon's Head, is the ascending node where a planet crosses the ecliptic into the North latitude, constituting the vernal equinox; while the latter, the Dragon's Tail, is the descending node or the point where it crosses southward, constituting the autumnal equinox. MM, 121. Also called תלי. As for the reason of the name, see *Sefer ha-Gedarim,* and פי׳ על ס״י לר״י ברצלוני p. 209.

תקופה *a season,* or one fourth of the tropical year, assumed to consist of 91 days and $7\frac{1}{2}$ hours. As a matter of fact, however, since the earth is not quite in the center of the solar orbit, the line dividing the zodiac into two equal parts will divide the solar orbit into two unequal parts. Hence when the sun moves in the summer from Cancer to Virgo, it moves more than 90°, although it does not appear so in the zodiac and therefore takes $92\frac{1}{2}$ days. Similarly, from Libra to Sagittarius in autumn, it moves less than 90°, although it does not appear on the zodiac and hence takes only 82 days. Again in winter, from Capricornus to Pisces, it actually moves less than 90° and takes 90 days and 6 hours, while in spring, from Aries to Gemini, it really moves more than 90° and so takes $92\frac{1}{2}$ days. Spring (קיץ) and summer are 189 days, while autumn and winter are 178 days and 12 hours. But you obtain equal parts when you divide the year into opposite seasons (SI, 80).

תקופת ר׳ אדא בר אהבה *Ada bar Ahabah's calendar,* the basis of which is the "scientific" view (see *shanah*) that the solar year is 365 days, 5 hours, 997 parts, and 48 minutes (SI, 81). A season then is 91 days, 7 hours, 519 parts, and 31 minutes. The "margin" (see *motar*) of the season is 2 days, 17 hours, 300 parts, and 31 minutes, and that of 4 seasons is 10 days, 21 hours, 121 parts, and 48 minutes. At the end of the Metonic cycle—see *maqazor*—no margin is left because the 19 annual margins are equivalent to, and counterbalanced by, the seven intercalary months according to the lunar calendar, so that the solar and lunar years coincide and the *tequfah* returns to its original time. The "Nisan season" at the end of any Metonic cycle is the same as the very first one that preceded the ecliptical conjunction or *molad* by 9 hours and 642 parts (SI, 88). It should be observed that this calendar preferred by A. is right in so far as the tropical year is concerned, that is, the interval between one vernal equinox and the next, which is indeed less than the sideral year, owing to the precession of the equinoxes. See next entry.

תקופת שמואל *Samuel's calendar*, based on the pedagogic view (see *shanah*) that the duration of the solar year is 365¼ days, so that in terms of week days the difference between one New Year's day and the next is 1¼ day. A *teḳufah* or season is 91 days and 7½ hours, the difference in week days between one season and the next being 7½ hours. The "margin" (see *motar*) of the solar year is 10 days, 21 204/1080 hours, so that at the end of the Metonic cycle there is still a margin of 1 485/1080 hours. Since the difference between one solar year and the next in terms of week days is 1¼ days, the vernal equinox falls only at sunset, midnight, sunrise, or noon, and the cycle is completed at the end of 28 years, when the "Nisan season" returns to its original time, namely at the first hour of the eve of Wednesday when the first "Nisan season" in the history of the world occurred, preceding the Nisan conjunction or *molad* by 7 days and 9 642/1080 parts (SI, 81–82). This calendar is not favored by A. nor by Maimonides in his *Yad*, *Qiddush ha-Ḥodesh*, X, 6. Nevertheless if we take not the tropical but the sidereal years, that is, the return of the sun to the same point in relation to the fixed stars, into consideration, then the basis of this calendar that the duration of the year is 365¼ days is only 6 minutes short.

תקון (1) *improvement*. Human behavior may be said to fall into three types of relationship; that between man and God, that between man and the members of his family, and that between man and man. Each type is either of thought, speech, or action. There are therefore nine forms of relationship requiring improvement, which may come through two ways, either through legislation and convention, or through revelation. In the first case there are as many types of improvement as there are forms of behavior—nine, while in the latter case another element is added, revelation, which, in so far as it demands our faith in it, gives a total of ten ways of improvement—or the Ten Commandments—governing all human relationships. HN, 36.

(2) *straightness*. HN, 3. ת׳ הבנין או עיותו.

(3) *perfection* (comp. Ar. تقانة), the Aristotelian entelechy, which is the final realization of that which was *in posse*, the last stage in the process of change from potentiality to actuality. See HN, 3, תיקון יצירתו "the entelechy of its nature." See *yeṣirah*. Comp. הצורה מתקנת דמות הנוצר (*ibid.*), "form perfects or actualizes matter." See *noṣar*. The word מתקנת may also be translated "constituting the essence of." In this sense, the Tibbons would use the word מעמיד (q.v. See also PT, where indeed Ḥarizi employs the word מתקן).

(4) *the "regulation"* of the year as to whether it should be common or embolismic, and in either case whether it should be defective, regular, or perfect. This depends on the *qibuʿa* (q.v.) or fixation of Tishri. SI, 62.

(5) *the correct location* of a star against the zodiac by drawing through that star a radius from the center of the earth. Thus, let *ABCD* be

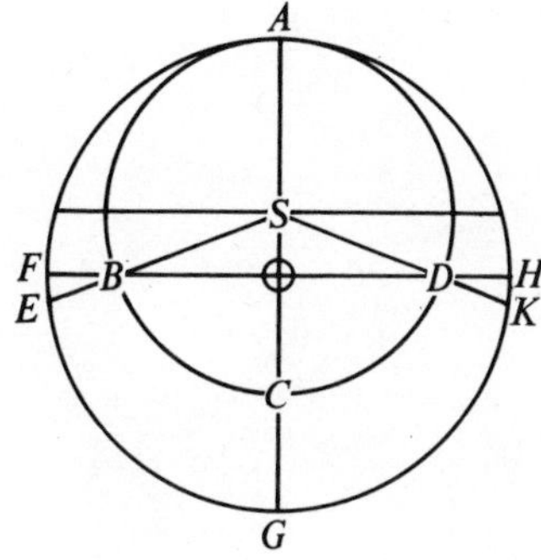

the solar eccentric circle, with *ASOC* as diameter, *S* is the center, *O* the center of the earth, *A* apogee, and *C* perigee. From *O* as the center of the earth, draw the circle *AFGH* representing the *ofan domeh* (q.d.), or the solar geocentric orbit. Now, in its eccentric circle, the sun moves at its mean velocity or 59°8′ per diem. The irregularity sets in because we look at the moving sun against the background of the geocentric belt *AFGH*. When the sun is at apogee there is no irregularity yet, because the two radii of the two circles are in the same direction. But let the sun be at point *B*. Then from *S* we see the sun at *E*, whereas from *O* which is the only view point for true velocity and position (v. *maqom* and *mahalak*), we find the sun at *F*, showing that the true place of the sun is not quite as far from apogee as it appears. We must therefore subtract (only on the east side of the solar geocentric orbit; on the west side we must add) the arc *FE* in order to arrive at the true solar position. This arc is measured by angle *ASB* minus angle *AOB*, which equals angle *SBO* or *FBE*, which is called the angle of correction (*zawit ha-tiqqun*). The line *SO*, or the distance between the two centers from which radii are drawn so as to form at their intersection the angle of correction, is called magnitude of correction or *erek ha-tiqqun*. In this way are the Ptolemaic irregularities (see *ḥilluf*) removed. SA, 13, 15, 18, 20, 21.

תקן (1) see *tiqqun* (3).

(2) *straighten out the difficulty*. HN, 31. מתוקן *precise, exact*. SI, X, 15, 21, 74. תקנה *perfection, precision* (as opposed to *qerub*). HMT, 117.

MORE ABOUT ABRAHAM BAR ḤIYYA'S PHILOSOPHICAL TERMINOLOGY

THIS sequel to my "Philosophical Terms and Ideas of Abraham bar Ḥiyya" is based mainly upon two sources that were not included among those of our author's five major works that constituted the basis of my study. These sources are: (1) an epistle to Yehudah b. Barzillai in defense of astrology, published by Z. Schwartz, in *Schwartz Festschrift*, pp. 23–36 (herein cited as Ig), and (2) fragments from an encyclopedic work known as *Yesode ha-Tebunah u-Migdal ha-Emunah*—to which Professor Alexander Marx has kindly referred me—published by Steinschneider in *Ha-Mazkir*, VII, and republished in his *Gesammelte Schriften*, I, 388–404 (herein cited as SS). Both writings, especially the encyclopedia, abound in new terms, in old terms invested with new meanings, and in new combinations of terms.

This study also contains some amplifications and corrections of my previous article, and an asterisk will indicate the term included herein for further discussion.

אבא אלטליצמאת (Ar. طليسمات translated by A. as בעלי התמונות) *talismanists.* When a certain planet enters a certain constellation or sign, the talismanists engrave the image of the sign, in corresponding metal,[1] which reenforces the influence of the planet if beneficial, and nullifies it if harmful. They know when the influence of any object waxes or wanes. They constitute the third class of idolatrous astrologers. Ig., 31. In the Bible they are called מכשפים Ig, 32. Comp. *Moreh*, III, 29, p. 42 וחלקו המוצאים והאקלמים לכוכבים. Also *ibid.*, p. 43. ואלו אשר הם נמצאים אצלנו יכללו רוב דעות הצאב״ה ומעשיהם... בנין היכלות ועשות הצורות מן המתכות והאבנים. Comp. ibn Ezra on Ex., II, 10; Maimonides, *Perush ha-Mishnayot* on Abodah Zarah, III; Shahrastani (Haarbrücker), p. 244; and Chwolson's *Sabier*, II, 199. Comp. צאחב אלטלסמאת referring to Apollonius in *Heb. Ueb.*, 845.

[1] Comp. *Shebile Emunah,* p. 37, where the seven metals are enumerated as corresponding to the seven planets.

אבו אסחק בן אזרקואלה or **אורקוילה** to whom is attributed a translation of Archimedes' (**ארישמידש, ארישמדש**) work on numbers from Arabic into Hebrew. SS, 392. But the passage according to Steinschneider is an interpolation.

אבלינוס *Apollonius*, author of **ס׳ הצורות האלוניות**. SS, 398.

אור *ray of light*. According to Steinschneider (SS, 402), A. divides the rays of light into rectilinear and broken (**א׳ נשבר**) the latter being either thrown straight back (**חוזרת אחורנית**) or penetrating **א׳ פשוט** from **פשט אל** to "invade"). The reflected ray is called **א׳ נזור**. We have a more clear-cut classification in Palqera's *Reshit Ḥokmah*, p. 44, where the rays or **שביבים** are divided into **ישרים** or rectilinear, **מתעקלים** or refracted, **מתהפכים** or thrown straight back as in a mirror, and **משתברים** or reflected. Rieti in his *Miqdash Me'at*, 15, speaks of **ישר נזור מתהפך ונשבר**.

אורקוילה v. **אבו אסחק**.

אוש v. **מעלה**.

איטימש v. **צד**.

אירן v. **משקל**.

אלהית v. **חכמה**.

אלוני *conic*. SS, 398. See **גלם**.

אמירה *expression*. Comp. *Kuzari*, II, 78, where it stands for Ar. **אלקול**. See HN, 2. **כי אין הזמן דבר שיש לו ממש ואינו כ״א אמירה (בכ״י אמידת) מעמדת הנמצאות ואם אין שם נמצאות אין שם אמירה שהזמן תלוי**. Comp. ibn Adret's *Responsa* (Venice, 1545), Resp. 9: **לא דברו בו אלא באמידת (בהוצ׳ ווין, תקע״ב ובשבילי אמונה לאלדבי 195: באמירת) המשכת העניין... ולפי שאין אמידה (בשבילי אמונה: אמירה) ידועה אצלנו רק בהצטרף אל הזמן**.

אנושית v. **חכמה**.

אצחאב אלאסחאר v. **אצ׳ אלחיל**.

אצחאב אלחיל (also called **אצ׳ אלאסחאר**, translated by A. as **בעלי הצדדין** and **מצדדים** q.v.) *a class of magicians* who at the proper time gather herbs, seeds, and fruits, and know the potencies of all their gleanings. They store them until necessity arises; and then they mix those herbs and fruits for which the time is suitable, so as to strengthen certain forces and weaken others. Both the gathering and the mixing are accompanied by the muttering of some unholy and diabolical incantations. These sorcerers constitute the fourth sect of *idolatrous* astrologers (see **כלדי**). The corresponding biblical term is **חרטומים** Ig, 32.

אקלידס v. **שורשים**.

ארישמדש v. אבו אסחק.

ארתמאטיקה *arithmetic*. SS, 391. See *ḥokmah*. In an interpolated passage in SS, 392, we have ארטימיטיקא and אריטמיתיקא.

אלאתבאע "*followers*" of idolatrous lawgivers (ואצעי אלוצאיא, Heb. נמשכים) making images and offering sacrifices to the stars. They belong to the first class of *idolatrous* astrologers, and in the Bible are called כשדים. Ig, 31, 32. See כלדיים.

אתימש v. צד.

מבואר *clear*, *obvious*. SS, 392. But Steinschneider thinks the passage an interpolation.

בינה *physics*. SS, 403. So also Anatoli, in his *Malmad ha-Talmidim*, p. 128b. See also references in Steinschneider's *Jewish Literature*, p. 351 and *Heb. Ueb*., p. 3, where the term is applied to mathematics. See *ḥokmah*.

בן רשד The three lines in SA, II, where this name strangely occurs, are missing in the three manuscripts in the possession of the Jewish Theological Seminary of America.

בעל דעת v. דעתן.

בעלי הצדדין v. צד.

בעלי התמונות v. אבא אלטליצמאת.

ביצני *oval*. SS, 397.

בריח v. ראשי ב׳.

גובר *ruling*, being the lord of the ascendant, as is the planet within the sign of the zodiac situated on the eastern horizon at any particular moment (e.g., birth). Ig, 25.

גבורה *physics*. SS, 403. See *ḥokmah*.

גדודי עולם *material bodies*. SS, 391, 394. Comp. ג׳ מעלה.

גדולים *magnitudes*. SS, 396. Ḥarizi uses this term in the *Moreh* for Tibbon's coined בעל שיעור, for which see פירוש מהמלות זרות. See PI.

גזרה *planetary forecast* or *influence*, Ig, 30.

גיאומטריא SS, 391.

גלגל המזלות v. כוכבי שבת.

גולם אלוני *conic body* (acorn-shaped). SS, 397.

גלמי המצבות *cylinders*. SS, 397. גלמי החרוטות *cones*. Also גולם חרוט SS, 397.

גלומה v. זוית.

גס v. מחקר.

נדבק ב... *based on*, *in harmony with*. Ig, 31.

דבר v. *ḥokmah.*

מדבר (corrupted, according to Steinschneider, foɪ דבר) v. *ḥokmah.*

דימומוס (an unknown name). SS, 399.

דמיון *image* (used for magical purposes). Ig, 31, 33.

דעת *conscience*, or *ethical judgment*; called by Aristotle φρόνησις. See *ḥokmah* and quotation s.v. דעתן. See Rosin, *Ethik des Maimonides*, p. 32, who notes that the term דעות in Maimonides' הלכות דעות is used in an ethical sense, so that the title means laws concerning character.

דעתן *conscientious* or *ethical person*. SS, 403, ובדעת זו חכמה אנושית אשר היא יסוד שלישי כי דרך העולם לקרוא למי שהוא מכוון בכל דבריו וזריז בד״א ולתת תושיה ועצה לבני עמו הוא דעתן ובעל דעת.

דקדוק *subtlety*. SS, 403, מעלתם ודקדוק הענינים אשר היא חוקרת עליהם.

דרך v. ישוב.

דרכי חשבון v. חשבון.

הכרחי *necessary*. SS, 392. But according to Steinschneider the passage is an interpolation.

הנדסה v. *ḥokmah.*

ואצׄעי אלוצאיא *lawgivers* who institute star-worship and are the leaders of what A. calls נמשכים, or the first class of idolatrous astrologers. Hebrew: מיסדי הנימוסים. Ig, 31.

זווית גלומה (as opposed to ז׳ שטוחה) *solid angle*. SS, 401.

זווית ישרה (v. ז׳ שטוחה) *plane angle*. SS, 396.

נזור v. אור.

חושי הגוף SS, 403.

חזרת החלקים *reducing fractions*. SS, 395.

אלחיל v. אצחאב.

חכמה A. divides philosophy into four sciences: (1) חכמת המוסר וח׳ הדבר mathematics and logic, (2) ח׳ היצורית physics, (3) ח׳ האנושית וח׳ המדינית ethics, (4) ח׳ האלהית theology or metaphysics. SS, 384.[2] Sciences also fall more generally into ח׳ עמלנית (v. עמלני) and ח׳ שכליית or practical and theoretical, the former referring to ח׳ אנושית or ethics. SS, 403. This classification seems to follow closely that attributed to Aristotle, according to which all sciences fall into three general classes: (1) theo-

[2] Comp. Anatoli, in his *Malmad*, p. 142b, who takes the four principal streams, into which the river, going out from Eden, is divided, as referring to the well-known triplet למודיות וטבעיות ואלהיות and the to חכמה מדינית included in the commandments of the Torah.

retical, or θεωρητική, consisting of physics, mathematics, and metaphysics; (2) practical, or πρακτική, consisting of politics, economics, and ethics; (3) productive or ποιητική, or *ars mechanica* (see Wolfson in the *Hebrew Union College Jubilee Volume*). It has, however, this Platonistic trace that it groups mathematics with logic, thus showing that it regards the former as well as the latter as a preliminary study or a propaedeutic. Comp. Anatoli, in his *Malmud ha-Talmidim*, pp. 38, 128, who likewise includes under mathematics geometry, arithmetic, and logic, all of which disciplines train the mind for the study of physics or **בינה** (q.v.). Comp. ibn Ezra on Ex., 31, 3.

That our author assigned this role to the science of mathematics is evident also from the following passage in SS, 402: **ואעפ״י שהיא חכמה גדולה ומוסרת** (a play on **ח׳ המוסר?**) **את לבו ודעתו** [*i.e.* mathematics] **של אדם כלפי הבינה אין נאה להאביד כל ימיו בלמודה... אבל יספיק לו ממנה מקצתה כדי שינהיג בה את לבו להבין שאר החכמות שאחריה... שלמודה צורך וחובה ללמוד שאר החכמות... אבל יהיה מנהיג את לבו בלימודה אל לימוד שאר החכמות שאחריה**. See also SS. 403: **וחכמת המספר הוא היסוד הראשון המעיין בראש החכמות ותחלתן שהן מתקנות את הלב ומקבילות אותו כלפי בינה**; this will throw light on the following almost similar passage from Barzillai's commentary on **ס״י**. (quoting *Al-Muqqammas*), with which Wolfson (*Hebrew Union College Jubilee Volume*, 269) has some difficulty: **והמעלה האמצעית ח׳ המוסר והשכל המאמצת דעות בני אדם והמנהגת להם דרך הבינה** "and the middle stage is the science of mathematics and logic [comp. A.'s **ח׳ המוסר וח׳ הדבר**] which strengthens the opinions of men and guides them to understanding [or, perhaps here also, "to physics"]," that is, it is a disciplinary and auxiliary science. Palqera also in his *Mebaqqesh*, p. 126, writes about mathematics **כי תכליתן לחדש[3] המחשבה**. Similarly on p. 133, he refers to both mathematics and logic as **הצעות**. Anatoli, in his *Malmad*, p. 128, includes logic under mathematics in the following statement: **החכמות הלמודיות הכוללות חכמת השעור חכמת המספר חכמת הדבור שהן תחבולה לחדד השכל ולהשכיל ולדעת האמת בח׳ הטבע... וקרא לטבע בינה**.

The very term **ח׳ המוסר** indicates its part among the sciences. Like its Arabic equivalent ادب by which it is usually translated in the Bible, it means *morals* as well as *learning* or *discipline*; and hence, like the

[3] Read perhaps **לחדד**. Comp. Anatoli, in his *Malmad*, p. 128b, stating that the aim of mathematics is **לחדר השכל** where we should also read **לחדד**. See also *ibid.*, pp. 38, 165.

terms למודיות, שמוש, הרגל, טורח, تعليم, رياضى and μάθησις (see discussion of these terms by Wolfson, *Hebrew Union College Jubilee Volume*, pp. 268, 270, and in the *Hebrew Union College Annual*, III, 372), it denotes that "learning," mental discipline, propaedeutic (ראש החכמות ותחלתן SS, 403), that is known as mathematics. It is also called חכמת המספר and חכמה. Anatoli, in his *Malmad ha-Talmidim*, p. 128b, also applies *ḥokmah* to mathematics.[4] Comp. Zeller, *Plato*, p. 219: "By διάνοια or ἐπιστήμη, Plato means (as Brandis observes) exclusively mathematical sciences." Similarly סוד, which in medieval *piyyut* is sometimes parallel to למד (comp. מסוד חכמים ונבונים ומלמד דעת מבינים), would also mean mathematics; and hence Steinschneider in SS, 402 is inclined to correct חכם מוסני או סורי by חכם מוסרי או סודי. Perhaps the term may be explaned as a synonym of יסוד with which it is often associated (see SS, 394); so that it would denote either the *foundation* of all sciences (ראש החכמות ותחלתן) or the cosmic foundation and principle. For, according to the Pythagorean doctrine, which left a strong impression on the mathematics of that period, all numbers go back to one (μονάς), which is called the secret of creation (v. *ibid.*, האחד שהוא יסוד המספר והוא העקר והסוד לכל בריות העולם). Indeed, all numbers constitute the universal principle (comp. Palqera's *Ha-Mebaqqesh*, 108: החשבון מהתחלות הנמצאים). Perhaps, therefore, the Talmudic סוד העבור and סוד הלבנה should be taken to mean the mathematics of intercalation and the mathematics of the lunar calendar. However, like some of the previously mentioned terms, סוד seems to have acquired the general meaning of *ḥokmah* or science. See SS, 444.

Mathematics embraces the Pythagorean quadrivium, that is, (1) ח׳ המניין Ar. עלם אלעדד or arithmetic (which is תחלת כל החכמות because even the child's mind can grasp it. SS, 391); (2) ח׳ השעור Ar. הנדסה or geometry; (3) ח׳ הנגון Ar. עלם אלתאליף or music; (4) ח׳

[4] Ibn Ezra in Exod., 31, 3 defines *ḥokmah* as the forms contained in the rear of the brains; *tebunah* and *binah* as the intermediary form, between *da'at* and *ḥokmah*, located in the middle fissure of the brains; and *da'at* or perceptions—in the front fissures of the brains. He gives the Arabic for *da'at*—„אלתכיי״ל, for *tebunah* אלפכר״ה, and for *ḥokmah*—אלחכמ״ה. Comp. the Platonic idea that mathematics is the intermediary or connecting link between sensible thought or opinion or perception, all having for their object the phenomenon, and pure thought having for its object the Idea (Zeller, *Pre-Socratic Philosophy*, I, 204; *Plato* (1857), p. 216). This would make *binah* (*q.v.*) and *tebunah* stand for mathematics. See *Heb. Ueb.*, p. 3, for similar usages.

הכוכבים Ar. עלם אלנג׳ום, or astronomy;[5] (5) ח׳ המראה or optics, is a branch of geometry. This science has two parts: the physical and the mathematical, the former studying the *quality* of optics, or the nature and manner of vision, and the latter concerned with the *quantity* of optics, or the measure and distances of things seen. SS, 401. The process of vision may be explained in one of two ways: either as a light emanating from the eye toward a certain object or as a form of the object carried by the light of the air to the surface of the eye and to its ḥumors (*ibid.*). The first view is that of Pythagoras, Plato (who proposed the compromising theory of a synaugeia, or a meeting of the rays of sight from the eye with the rays of light from the object seen), Damianus, Galen (who substituted for sight-rays a sight-pneuma in the eye, which touches the air and so comes in contact with the body), and the Arabian Al-Kindi; and the second view is that of the old Atomists—especially Empedocles, Leucippus, and Democritus—Aristotle and the Arabian Al-Hazen (see Emil Wilde, *Geschichte der Optik*, I, 6–77; Bjornbo and Vogl, "Alkindi, Tideus, and Pseudo-Euklid," in *Abhandlungen zur Geschichte der Mathematischen Wissenschaften*, XXVI, 3, 47–49). Steinschneider's published fragment does not indicate whether A. takes sides on this question. It is true, he speaks of האור היוצא מן העין, but there he is, as Steinschneider observes, borrowing from Euclid; and "in the case of Euclid and other mathematical writers, references to rays emanating from the eye can scarcely be looked upon literally" (Ernst Mach, *Principles of Physical Optics*, Dutton, p. 8). Other medieval Jewish thinkers are more committed. Thus on the side of the first view we have Gabirol,[6] and on the other side we have Abraham ibn Ezra (who writes that the causes of eye-sight are the images reflected in the pure air),[7] Abraham ibn Daud,[8] Palqera,[9] and Gerson b. Solomon.[10]

5 See Ig, 29, where this science is made to include both astronomy and astrology.

6 See the poem "Keter Malekut" in *Gabirol*, ed. Davidson, line. 97 כהמשך האור היוצא מן העין and see also *ibid.*, p. 3.

7 Ecc., 1, 8: סבות ראות העין התמונות שהם מתדמות באויר הזך.

8 *Emunah Rammah* (ed. Weil), p. 28: ומתנאיו שיהיה בתכלית הבהירות כדי שיוטבעו בו הצורות הנראות.

9 In his *Mebaqqesh*, p. 115, he cites the first view under the name of Plato and refers to the חכמי הטבע who disproved it by pointing to the fact that the eye needs an air medium in order to see, and also by other evidences. In his *Sefer ha-Nefesh*, p. 6, he adopts the second view which he describes with some detail.

It should be noted that Saadia varied his stand on this subject. In his *Emunot we-Deʿot*, I, 3, 70, he says: "Similarly the air receives the light and transmits it to our eyes,"[11] which view is Aristotelian. But in VI, 7, 159, he says: "the light [i.e., of the fire] penetrates the substances of these lamps and the vision of the beholder penetrates to the light," which seems to follow Plato. See also Saadia's theory of a conjunction between the eye and the object, *supra*, pt. 1, ch. 2, under the sub-heading "Sensation."

A. states the following propositions, which lie at the foundation of the science of optics, and which, as Steinschneider notes, are taken from Euclid's optics. (1) Light emanates from the eye in rectilinear rays and moves toward an object. (2) Every ray has a corresponding point in the field of vision (נכח) so that there are as many points of vision (נכחיים) as there are rays of sight. (3) These rays emerge from the eye and diverge so as to form a cone, the apex of which is at the eye and the base at the object. (4) That which is reached by the luminous ray is seen; and that which is not reached by it is not seen. (5) Anything seen by the eye at a certain angle may reach a point where it is no longer seen. (6) Whatever is near the eye appears in one magnitude. (7) The greater the angle at the apex of vision, the larger the appearance of the object. Comparing these propositions with those of Euclid, we find that A.'s first proposition corresponds to Euclid's first; A.'s second may be inferred from Euclid's second and theorem 1; A.'s third corresponds to Euclid's second; A.'s fourth, to Euclid's third; A.'s fifth is an implication of Euclid's theorem 3;

10 In his *Shaʿar ha-Shamaim* (1875), pp. 53–54, he discusses the Plato-Galen view and its proofs and the Aristotle-Averroes rebuttal. The whole section is reproduced verbatim with some abridgement and transposition in Aldabi's *Shebile-Emunah*, pp. 72–73. On Aldabi's plagiarism, see *Heb. Ueb.*, p. 17.

11 וכל הקרוב אל העין יראה על שעור אחד. It may however correspond to the final proposition in the beginning of Euclid's *Optics* according to a variant reading given in *Euclidis Optica*, ed. Heiberg (Lipsiae, 1895), "Prolegomena," XXXV, "omnes visus equiveloces esse, qui secundum equales angulos deferuntur, non autem sunt equiveloces, qui secundum inequales lineas deferuntur." And in a variant of the proof of theorem I, we find (*ibid.*) "omnes visus transpositii secundum equales lineas sunt equiveloces." The meaning therefore of our proposition would be that all objects equidistant from the eye are seen with the same speed. The expression על שעור אחד may also mean *with the same perspicacity*, and in that case the proposition would correspond to Euclid's second theorem "Aequalium magnitudinum in distantia iacentium propius iacentia perspicacius videtur."

A.'s sixth is not clear;[11] A.'s seventh corresponds to Euclid's fourth. It should be observed that our author's emphasis on points of vision shows that he follows Euclid's belief, in opposition to Ptolemy and Alkindi, that the base of the cone of vision is not continuous but presents a number of lacunae, so that a small object such as a needle falling between two rays of sight will not be perceived. These lacunae grow in magnitude in proportion to the distance of the object from the eye because the divergence between the rays of the cone of vision becomes greater. (Bjornbo and Vogl, "Alkindi, Tideus, and Pseudo-Euklid," pp. 50–51). It may also be added that the Arabian Alhazen attacks Euclid's fourth, or A.'s seventh proposition, on the ground that it leaves out of consideration the supposed distance, as in the case of heavenly bodies that appear larger at or near the horizon owing to the fact that they appear at a greater distance, measured by the intervening terrestrial objects, while the angle of vision does not change (Wilde, *Geschichte der Optik*, I, 75).

Optics is also divided into חכמת המראה הישרה or catoptrics, that is, the study of light-reflection, and ח׳ המראה המעוקלת or dioptrics, that is, the study of light-refraction. SS, 402. See אור.

In general, geometrical works fall into two classes: those dealing with surfaces and those dealing with intrinsic qualities of bodies (e.g., the study of weights). SS, 398–99.

Other terms for physics ח׳ היצורית in SS are: ח׳ היצורים, בינה, גבורה (*q.v.*), and תבונה. The terms for ethics are ח׳ האנושית, ח׳ האנושית וח׳ המדינית,[12] and דעת (*q.v.*). This latter term corresponds to the Aristotelian φρόνησις, or practical wisdom, which designates that part of the *Politics* that deals with individual morality (cf. Zeller, *Aristotle*, I, 186; II, 107). Ethics is also designated by עושר. SS, 403.

As for metaphysics (ח׳ האלהית), A. also calls it ח׳ אלהות, ח׳ השכל, רוח אלהים ות״ת, and השכל for the reason that the objects of this study are entirely intellectual and hidden from our senses. SS, 403. The term ח׳ השכל may also signify that it is a study of Intelligences. Comp. ח״ה introd.: ח׳ האלהות והוא דעת האל יתʼ ודעת תורתו ושאר המושכלות כנפש וכשכל וכאישים הרוחניים. He also calls it רוח, because it necessitates the guidance of the Divine Spirit. Comp. Aristotle, *Metaphysics*,

12 Plato does not know the term Ethics, and uses the term Politics instead (Zeller, *Plato*, p. 166).

928b, 28: "the possession of it [i.e., metaphysics] might be justly regarded as beyond human power."

The four branches of science may be arranged, according to A., in two ways (מנהגים): (1) according to the order of study (סדר חיוב בלמוד), metaphysics coming first, because it is too important o be postponed, although it is the most difficult, and then, from the easy to the difficult, mathematics, physics, and ethics; (2) according to the ascending order in rank and in subject matter (מעלתם ודקדוק הענינים), mathematics, physics, ethics, and metaphysics. Our author regards mathematics lowest and least subtle because it deals with the superficies of things (על תכלית הנמצאות), while physics studies the essence of things (על הנמצאות ועקרם). Comp. Aristotle (*Metaphysics*, 1026a10, and see Wolfson, *Hebrew Union College Jubilee Volume*), who regards some mathematical branches as higher than physics. Metaphysics deals, as already stated, with the subtlest beings, which can be mentally grasped only with divine aid. Comp. Aristotle (*ibid.*, 982), who argues that metaphysics especially deserves the name σοφία because it deals with things "that are difficult and not easy for man to know." See also Zeller, *Aristotle*, I, 184. At any rate, we see that opening the course of study with metaphysics, although designated in *Kuzari*, V, 2, as "the way of the Karaites," was not monopolized by them. Hence, Steinschneider's and Kaufmann's proof that al-Mukammas was a Karaite on the ground that he enumerates metaphysics first, is weakened; aside from the fact that, as Wolfson (p. 287) points out, al-Mukammas refers to the order of rank.

חכמת אמת *true science*, as A. explains it, based on true evidence. Ig, 27, 28. See PT, *s.v.* ח׳ התורה על האמת and Ginzberg, a.l.

חכמת הכוכבים *general science of the stars*, embracing both astronomy and astrology. Ig, 29. See *ḥokmah.*

חכמת המספר *mathematics*. SS, 403.

חכמות פילוסופיות *philosophical sciences*, that is, sciences other than mathematics, which is only a propaedeutic. SS, 402. See hokmah.

חלוק v. חשבון.

חלקים *fractions*. See חזרה.

מחנות הלבנה See also Abudraham on daily morning prayers, p. 42: ר׳ כוכבי לכת וכ״ח מ׳ הל׳. Comp. Yehudah Mosconi's statement, published by Steinschneider, in his *Gesammelte Schriften*, I, 566. Mosconi is opposed to al-Kindi, who assumed 27 *mansiones lunae*. Each mansion is supposed to take up $13^1/_3$ מעלות or degrees of the ecliptic, which is divided into 360 degrees, and every sign of the zodiac occupies about $2\frac{1}{2}$ mansions. These lunar mansions have different meteorological effects. Comp. ibn Ezra, on Ecc. 3, 1: וי״א כי אלה הכ״ח עתים כנגד כ״ח צורות גלגל המזלות שהלבנה נראית בהן בכל חדש.

חסר a *deficient number*, which is greater than the sum of all its aliquot parts (exact divisors), viz. 14, which is greater than 1+2+7. SS, 393. See עודף מלא.

על המחקר הגס *at first thought*. Ig, 24. Elsewhere A. usus עיון גס, which expression occurs also in the *Moreh*. See PT.

חרוט *cone*. SS, 397. See PT. See also גלם.

חושב *mathematician*. SS, 402. חושבים למזלות, חושבי הכוכבים *astrologers*. Ig, 30.

חשבון מנין במנין v. *infra*.

דרכי החשבון *six arithmetical operations*: (1) חשבון מנין במנין multiplication, (2) חלוק מנין על מנין division, (3) קצב מנין ממנין ratio, (4) לפחות מנין ממנין subtraction, (5) תוספת חלק על חלק במנין, להשלים מנין addition, (6) להשיב מ׳ על מ׳ חזרת החלקים אחד על אחד, reduction of fractions. SS, 395.

חשבוני *mathematician* (so also Palqera's *Mebaqqesh*, ed. 1924, 104, 108), especially one versed in astrology. The Latin word *mathematicus* also means *astrologer*. Ig, 31.

טביעת עין *appearance*, *concrete shape*. Ig, 28. שח׳ הכוכבים נותנת להודיע מן הדבר העתיד להיות כללי ואינה יכולה להודיע את פרטי ואת טביעות עינו וגופו ממש... ואינו רואה טביעות עינו בארץ אבל רואה מינו וכללו.

טבלת הרובע *a quadrant*, that is, a quadrilateral instrument having a right angle, used for the construction of right angles. HMT, 108. The other name for this instrument כלי הרובע should not be confused with the *quadrans novus* or *quadrans judaicus* (Heb. רובע ישראל) invented in 1288 by Jacob b. Machir and designated in a Hebrew translation by כלי הרובע. (*Heb. Ueb.*, 612).

טולקוס v. כדור.

טליצמאות v. אבא.

יומטריה *geometry*. SS, 395.

מיסדי הנימוסים v. ואצֿעי אלוצֿאיא.

יסוד v. אוש.

יסודות The expression ארבע י׳ *four elements* is found in a poem or Sahlal Gaon (11th century) published by Davidson in *Heb. Union Col.*

Annual, III, 239. Incidentally, the line ועל כל ניב מקודמות רשומות on p. 240 means that "in every letter there are propositions inscribed." Ḥarizi uses the term מקודמת for Tibbon's הקדמה, for which see PT.

יסודי התבונה ומגדל האמונה the name of an encyclopedic work translated from Arabic into Hebrew by A. See SS, 399, 388–404. It is divided into two מאמרים or treatises: the first corresponds to יסודי התבונה or foundations (i.e., branches) of science (see *ḥokmah*), while the second is entitled מגדל האמונה or tower of faith, which is built upon those foundations. The first treatise is divided into יסודות and עמודים. SS, 389. Steinschneider thinks that HMT is a part of this encyclopedic work, but Guttmann, in his introduction to HMT, maintains that these are two independent works.

תוספת v. חשבון.

יצורית v. *ḥokmah*. For the derivation of the term, comp. יצור.

ישוב *position*. SS, 396. מדרך ישובם. Comp. על דרך ההנחה והישוב in PT, p. 33.

יושר (1) *regularity* of a planet, as opposed to נזירה (*q.v.*), or *recession*. Ig, 29.

(2) *beneficence*. See כוכבי יושר.

מיושר *a straight line*. SS, 396.

ישרה v. זוית.

כדור a book on "spheres in motion" (Ar. כתאב אלכרה̈ אלמתחרכה̈) by טולקוס or Autolykos (350 B.C.E.). *Heb. Ueb.*, 503. SS, 398.

הכידור והמצבה a book on the sphere and the cylinder by Archimedes. SS, 398.

כחות v. מזילי הכ׳.

כוכבים v. *ḥokmah*. כוכבי יושר *beneficent planets*. Ig, 31. כוכבי נזק *evil planets*. Ig, 24, 31. כוכבי שבת. Ibn Ezra (Deut., 7, 9) thinks that the *galgal ha-mazzalot* moves at the rate of one degree per seventy, and not per one hundred, years.

מכוון *correct*. SS, 403: שהוא מכוון בכל דבריו.

כלדי *a Chaldean*. The question of the permissibility of consulting a Chaldean is the theme of A.'s *Iggeret* or epistle to Yehudah b. Barzillai. Marx gives the gist of this *Iggeret* in his "Correspondence between the Rabbis of Southern France and Maimonides about Astrology," in the *Hebrew Union College Annual*, Vol. III. A more detailed account follows. It begins with the contention that astrological advice and warning should be volunteered as well as heeded, as is evidenced by the fact that Samuel assigned, on astrological grounds, favorable and unfavorable days for blood-letting. Ig, 24. It was on this principle that A. cautioned a friend against being married at such an inauspicious time as at the sixth hour on Friday,[13] and incurred the charge of violating the Talmudic principle: "one must not consult Chaldeans." But the truth is that to cast a horoscope is no more reprehensible than to prescribe a drug, as both carry no finality; for the stars exercise their power, not consciously nor voluntarily, but conditionally, subject to the divine command (Ig, 25). Moreover, it is not *heeding*, but *consulting*, the Chaldean that is prohibited, for we find that no less a man than R. Akiba heeded a Chaldean's warning. And this prohibition cannot be said to refer to astrology, for many Talmudic passages testify to its permissibility and to its having been an unchallenged practice (Ig, 26). Chaldeanism in so far as it resembles astrology must therefore be exonerated, for the latter is a *true science*. Yet Israel, being the aim of creation, cannot be regarded as subject to planetary influence (אין מזל לישראל), for prayer and repentance will automatically nullify an evil aspect (Ig, 27). Comp. Ptolemy's and Thomas Aquinas' assertion that the wise man rules the stars (Thorndike, *Hist. of Magic*, II, 614). As to other peoples, the aversion of a catastrophe necessitates a change in the very position of the planets that rule them. There is, however, this difference between astrology and the Chaldean art: the former makes general forecasts, while the latter goes into details (Ig, 28).

The general science of the stars embraces astronomy (in which some non-Jewish scholars are more proficient than the Jews) and astrology, the latter being pursued by Jews and Gentiles who differ only in so far as the former maintain that the planetary influence goes back to the will of God (Ig, 29). These two sciences are required of the Jew. The prohibition rests on those sciences that are based on idolatry. Such *idolatrous* astrologers fall into the following four categories: (1) star-worshippers, called מיסדי נמוסים (q.v.) or נמשכים (q.v.). (2) those that call down the planetary powers, called מזילי הכחות (q.v.).

[13] The calculations of our author become clear by remembering the principle explained by Rashi on *Erubin*, 56a, that the first hours of the seven days of the week are ruled by the seven planets חל״ם כצנ״ש respectively and that the order of succession of these planets is כל״ש צמח״ן. See ibn Ezra on Gen., 1, 31.

(3) talismanists, or בעלי התמונות (q.v.). (4) artificers, called בעלי הצדדין (q.v.) Ig, 31–32.

Other forms of magic, which the Bible mostly calls קסמים and which may not be designated as חכמה but as מלאכה וערמה, include arrow-throwing, crystal-gazing, liver inspection, as well as declaring that a certain day in the week is good or bad for a certain thing — this is based on observation (נסיון) and not on astrology, for the position of the planets does not give the same indication for a given day in *every* week—and making forecasts on the basis of black circles around the moon, redness near the sun, a raven's croak at night, a cock's crow at night-fall, or a cat's mewing and jumping. All these may be studied but not practiced nor consulted. Ig, 33, 34.

It is these magic practices and the above four categories of idolatrous astrology that the Talmudists had in mind when they prohibited the consulting of Chaldeans.

While the term כלדיים denotes the Babylonian people and all classes of magicians, the term כשדים denotes only the royal family of Nebuchadnezzar, who belonged to the class known as מזילי הכחות (q.v.), or those that bring down the planetary powers. So that the words כלדי and כשדי have the mutual relation of general and particular terms (Ig, 35). By the way, this may explain the Maimonidean expression כשדיים וכלדיים with which Munk, M. Friedlander, and Marx find difficulty (See Marx, "Correspondence between the Rabbis of Southern France and Maimonides about Astrology," p. 320, note 16.).[14]

כלי הרובע v. טבלת הרובע.

כריתות (v. כדוריות or some similar term, according to Steinschneider) a book on spheres by תאודוסיוס ומיליאוס, that is, by Theodosius whose work is known in Arabic as כתאב אלאכר or פי אלכרה֞, and by Menelaus, the Arabic title of whose work is כתאב אלאשכאל אלאכריה֞ or כתאב אלאכר. SS, 398. *Heb. Ueb.*, 515, 541.

כשדי r. כלדי.

ליחות *humors of the eye.* SS, 401. The text erroneously has לוחות.

מדות טובות *virtues.* A. gives us four virtues, manifested in the acquisition of four sciences: metaphysics, mathematics, physics, and ethics;

[14] Incidentally, it may be mentioned that the whole passage, in the letter of the Rabbis of Southern France to Maimonides on p. 348, from וכן אמרו לעולם to והאריך רפ״ז, seems to be taken almost verbatim from ibn Ezra on Ex., 2 (where the phrase המעמד הקוצב proves by collation to be a corruption from המ׳ הקצר).

or, psychologically speaking: divine spirit, wisdom, understanding, and knowledge (see *ḥokmah*). SS, 402. For other classifications of virtues, comp. the Aristotelian five virtues: reason, an immediate cognition of presuppositions of all knowledge; knowledge, a mediate and inferential way of attaining to necessary truths; wisdom, "the union of reason and knowledge in the cognition of the highest and worthiest objects;" insight (φρόνησις), our author's *da'at*, q.v., or conduct; and art (*Ethics*, VI, ch. 3–7; Zeller, *Aristotle*, II, 179). See also *The Eight Chapters of Maimonides*, ch. 2, where four purely dianoetic virtues (מעלות שכליות) are enumerated, viz. ...מהן החכמה ומהן השכל אשר ממנו השכל העיוני... וממנו שכל נקנה... ומהן זכות התבונה וטוב ההבנה, and *Olam Qatan*, p. 38, ענוה, תוחלת, צדק, מדע which "four virtues," according to S. Horovitz in his introduction, note 27, are Platonic.

מדינית v. *ḥokmah*.

מוסר v. *ḥokmah*. מוסרי (which Steinschneider reads for מוסני) *mathematician*. SS, 402.

מוסתנזל ביאלקוי v. מזילי הכחות.

מושיקא *music*. SS, 391.

מיליאוס v. כריתות.

מלא *a perfect number*, which is equal to the sum of all its aliquot parts (exact divisors), viz. $6=1+2+3$. SS, 393. See חסר, עודף.

ממלא *fulfills, actualizes the potentiality of*. SS, 403. Harizi uses this term for Maimonides' מכמל; while ibn Tibbon uses משלים (constitutes the essence of), for which see PT.

מנין v. *ḥokmah*.

מנטיק v. *ḥokmah*.

נמשכים v. אלאתבאע.

ממשלת הכוכבים *planetary influence*. Ig, 24.

משקל וחכמת משא a book on weights by אירן or Heron. SS, 399.

נג׳ום v. *ḥokmah*.

נגון v. *ḥokmah*.

מנהג *behavior, conduct*. SS, 403. Hence תורות מנהגיות (Ar. שראיע סיאסיה) as opposed to ת׳ שכליות in *Kuzari*, II, 48; III, 11. See also *ḥokmah*.

מנהיג *pursuing, studying*. Ig, 35.

נודני for נוראני, see *Heb. Ueb.*, 347.

מוסתנזל ביאלקוי v. מזילי הכחות.

מזילי הכחות (Ar. מוסתנזל ביאלקוי) *those who know the proper time to sacrifice* to a certain planet so as to draw down its power, which is to do their bidding and to answer their questions. They constitute the second class of idolatrous astrologers. Ig, 31. The corresponding Biblical term is **אשפים**. Ig, 32. A. here admits the Arabic root نزل into Hebrew. See *infra.* In *Moreh*, III, 29, and in *Kuzari*, I, 79, this art is called **הורדת הרוחניות**, Ar. **אסתנזאל אלרוחאניאת**.

הזיל *to draw down.* Ig, 31. See *supra.*

נזור (r. *nizzur*) *recession.* Ig, 29. See **נזירה**.

נכחי a point, in a field of vision, that is touched by a ray of sight. See **חכמת המראה** s.v. *ḥokmah.*

נמוסים (2) *revealed legislation, cult.* See **מיסדי נמוסים**. See also Wolfson, *Heb. Union Col. Annual*, III, 374.

נופל על *applied to.* SS, 394. Comp. Ar. **יקע עלי**. See PT.

מצבה *cylinder.* SS, 397.

סודי (which Steinschneider reads for **סורי**) *mathematician.* SS, 402. See, *ḥokmah.*

סוראנים *Chaldeans.* Ig, 35. See **כלדי**.

עגול v. **ציר ע׳**.

עד״ד v. *ḥokmah.*

עדות *planetary forecast.* Ig, 30, 31.

עודף *an abundant number*, the sum of the aliquot parts (exact divisors) of which exceeds the number itself. Thus 12 is an abundant number, for the sum of its aliquot parts (1+2+3+4+6) is 16. SS, 392. See **חסר, מלא**.

מעיינים במזלות *astrologers.* Ig, 32.

מעלה *degree*, or power of ten, articulate number. There are four such powers, that is, ones, tens, hundreds, and thousands. Comp. *Mebaqqesh*, p. 107, where these powers are called **מדרגות**. Ibn Ezra, in his **יסוד מספר** "principle or science of number" (v. 310), speaks of *five* **מעלות**. See SS, 465. A. gives the Arabic term **אוש** (أسّ) and its Hebrew equivalent **יסוד** SS, 394.

על״ם v. *ḥokmah.*

עמדה *duration* HN, 2. cf. **עומד*** (2), PT, p. 95, and Wolfson in *The Jewish Quarterly Review*, X, 8.

עמלנית *practical*, as opposed to **שכליית** or theoretical science. See *ḥokmah.* This term is clearly influenced by the Ar. الصنائع العملية, as opposed to الصنائع علمية, a division used by the Ikhwan al-Ṣafa (see Wolfson, *Hebrew Union College Jubilee Volume*, 1925, p. 265).

ענין v. תורף.

עקומים (which Steinschneider reads for עמוקים) *solids having inclined surfaces*, for example, conic sections. SS, 398. עקמומי SS, 396, *crooked*, according to Steinschneider; but more correctly, *convex*, as opposed to קבוב q.v.

עקר *principle*, *essence*. SS, 403.

ערך *astrological influence*. Ig, 31.

עושר *ethics*. SS, 403. See *ḥokmah*.

מתעשתין (b. h.) *contrive*, *find a way*. HMT, 80.

נעתק The word is also found in the sense of *translated* in ibn Ezra on Ex. 2, 10, and is also quoted in Talmudic Dictionaries; yet ibn Tibbon in his *Perush meha-Millot Zarot* claims to have coined the *nifal* of this verb.

פחות v. חשבון.

פילוסופיות v. *ḥokmat philosofiot*.

פנות החכמה *corners*, or *four branches*, *of knowledge*. SS, 389. See חכמה and PT.

פסיקה *decree*. Ig, 24.

נפרד *odd*. Such hours are lucky. Ig, 25.

מתפרד *simple*, *uncompounded*. SS, 396.

פשוט, פושט *rectilinear*, *penetrating*. SS, 402. See אור.

פתח *introduction*. SS, 394, 395.

צד *contrivance*. It is sometimes parallel to תחבולה. Thus see HMT, 101. אנו מבקשים צד לדעת את הקו הזה התיכוני HMT, 103 אתה צריך אל צד המעשה אשר הראיתיך בתשבורת הקרקע התלוי בראש ההר... אתה צריך בכלם HMT, 104 אתה אל צד המעשה והתחבולות אשר עשית בקרקע התלוי בהר צריך אל הצד והתחבולות אשר הראיתיך בתשבורת הקרקע התלויה בראש ההר או לצד שהוא דומה לו. In *Millot Higgayon*, ch. 3, our term has the kindred sense of *manner* or *modality*. See also PT. We also have the verb צדד meaning *to contrive* or *to find* a way. Comp. HMT, 79, 104, 108 והמבינים דרך האומנות הזאת צדדו להקל על עצמם... ומצדד להוציא עליה את העמוד כך. In HMT, 80, the term מתעשתין is used in this sense. Hence the title ספרי הצדדין in SS, 399, may mean *books on contrivances* or *mechanics* (see *Heb. Ueb.*, p. 230: אלמכאניקי והי אלחיל, which subject may be indeed regarded as a division of geometry. Thus, Palqera writes in his *Reshit Ḥokmah*, p. 48 תחבולות התשבורת והם רבות מהם מלאכת ראשית הבנין. Contrivance and magic are related concepts. Hence, in Ig, 32, the term צדדין denotes a form of magic, consisting of gathering and mixing herbs, practiced by the members of the fourth class of idolatrous astrology, known in Arabic as אצחאב אלחיל (q.v.) and in Hebrew as בעלי הצדדין and מצדדים. Similarly, the word תחבולה, which as we have seen is synonymous and associated with צד, also has the two meanings of the Ar. חיל, that is, magic and mechanics. Thus in *Moreh*, I, 73 for כתאב אלחיל we have ספר התחבולות *a book on mechanics*, while in *Kuzari*, I, 61, we read בצלמיהם ואליליהם ותחבולותם for the Ar. באותנהם וטלאמסהם וחילהם and in I, 84 לא מכשפים ולא מתחבולה for the Ar. מן סחר או חילה, where the term means magic.

צד המעשה *contrivance*. See quotation s.v. צד.

מצדדים v. צד.

צורה *essence* צורת המנין וגדריו. SS, 394.

צורות אלוניות *conic sections*, a book by אבלינוס or Apollonius. SS, 398.

מצוייר *conceived, represented to the mind*. SS, 403. Ibn Tibbon in his *Glossary of Strange Terms* claims to have created this term.

ציר העגול *center*. SS, 396.

צלע (b.h.) *side of a geometrical figure*. SS, 397. It is common in *Mishnat ha-Middot*.

קבוב *cube*. SS, 396. This is how Steinschneider takes it. Perhaps it is better to render it by *concavity*, in which sense the term is used in the *Moreh*. See PT. Our author uses עקב for cube. Comp. קעב for the Ar. כעב in *Heb. Ueb.*, 566, and SS, 450. The opposite of קבוב is עקמומי, which should be taken in the sense of *convex*.

מקביל *leads, directs*. SS, 403. Ar. اقبل.

התקבץ *to be formed* (an angle). SS, 401.

קו״י v. מוסתנזל ביאלקוי.

מקיימת (= משכללת) *constitutes* (the essence). SS, 391.

קצב v. חשבון.

מראה v. *ḥokmah*.

ראשי בריח *diametrical poles*. SS, 397.

רובע v. טבלת הר׳.

מרובע There are 18 different quadrilateral figures. SS, 396.

מרגיש ל... *taking into consideration* (parallel to חושש q.v.). HMT, 114. Comp. also *Kuzari*, IV, 25 ושהמלאכים יותר חוששים לה ומרגישים for the Ar. אשׁד אנפעאלא להא.

רכוב *combination*. SS, 394.

שבת v. כוכבי ש׳.

להשיב על *reduce numbers*. SS, 395. See חשבון.

שכל v. *ḥokmah.*

שכלית v. *ḥokmah.*

משתכל *reflected, imaged.* See Ig, 29 ומשתכל כח מהם בארץ. Perhaps, from the Ar. root شكل and تشكل *to assume a shape.* For our author's Arabisms, see for example, מזילי הכחות. The context does not very well permit it to be regarded as a variant of מסתכל. Comp. מתדמות *reflected, imaged,* in quotation s.v. *ḥokmah.*

השלים v. חשבון

שימוש *negotiation, intercourse, conduct.* SS, 403.

שיעור See *ḥokmah.*

שרשים *Elements,* by אקלידס or Euclid. SS, 398. Comp. ארבעה ש׳ in ibn Ezra, on Ecc., 5, 2.

תאודוסים v. כריתות.

תאליף v. *ḥokmah.*

תבונה *science.* See יסודי הת׳. Particularly, physics, which is higher than mathematics or חכמה. Also called בינה q.v. SS, 403.

תכלית *limiting surface, superficies.* See SS, 403 ח׳ המוסר שהיא חוקרת עליהם על תכלית הנמצאות. See the word in various quotations in my *Space in Jewish Medieval Philosophy,* pp. 67, 69.

תכנית Aristotelian *form, essence.* SS, 391.

תמונות v. בעלי הת׳.

תמימות *perfection.* SS, 403. Comp. תמות and שלמות in PT.

התנה על *mentioned.* SS, 389. A Hebraized form of the Talmudical Aramaic אתני. It may mean, however, *expected, excluded* (from the Ar. استثنى). The term is used in this sense in the *Moreh.* See התנות ב... in PT.

תורף *form.* Ig, 33. התרפים הם ממשמע תורף הדבר אשר הוא ענינו ודמותו. Comp. for the term ענין the expression in HMT, 104: צורת הראש ממין צורת התושבת ומענינה. In the *Moreh,* the term, as I attempted to show in PT, has the meaning of *text,* and refers to a direct quotation. Gerson b. Solomon in his *Shaʿar ha-Shamaim* (1875, pp. 81, 82) also used *toref* after a direct quotation beginning with וז״ל. It is not clear whether our author took the term to mean *text* or *context.* On the other hand, Abraham, the son of Maimonides, evidently uses it in the sense of *gist* or *content.* See his *Milḥamot ha-Shem* (Hanover, 1867), p. 20, ומהנה אתחיל להשיב על תורף דברי אלה האנשים החטאים בנפשותם ולא אדבר בנוסח דבריהם שאפילו תורף דבריהם אינו כדאי להשיב עליו... אלא מפני מעשה שהיה. Comp. astrological explanation of תרפים

in ibn Ezra on Gen., 31, 19. Comp. also Y. Giṭṭin, III, 44c, כתב תרפו בטופס where the term has a similar meaning of *form*, that is, the blank part of a document to be filled out.

INDEX OF NAMES AND IDEAS

INDEX OF HEBREW TERMS

(Apart for Abraham bar Ḥiyya's Alphabetical List)

INDEX OF ARABIC TERMS